Reading Literature

Roger Gower and Margaret Pearson

Longman

Longman Group UK Limited,
Longman House, Burnt Mill, Harlow,
Essex CM20 2JE, England
and Associated Companies throughout the world.

© Longman Group Limited 1986

First published 1986.
This impression 1987.

ISBN 0-582-74501-2

BRITISH LIBRARY CATALOGUING IN PUBLICATION DATA
Gower, Roger
    Reading literature.
    1. English language—Text-books for foreign
    speakers   2. Reading—Examinations, questions, etc.
    I. Title
    428.4'076   PE1128
    ISBN 0-582-74501-2

Produced by Longman Group (FE) Ltd
Printed in Hong Kong

ACKNOWLEDGEMENTS

We are grateful to the following for permission to reproduce
copyright material:

Text
Edward Arnold (Publishers) Ltd. for an extract from the essay
'Anonymity: an inquiry' in *Two Cheers for Democracy* by E. M.
Forster (Penguin, 1951); Associated Book Publishers (UK) Ltd. for
extracts from *A Taste of Honey* by Shelagh Delaney (Methuen
London, 1959) and *Old Times* by Harold Pinter (Methuen London,
1971); Faber and Faber Ltd. for the poems 'Marina' in *Collected
Poems 1909–1962* by T. S. Eliot (1936), 'The Thought Fox' from *The
Hawk in the Rain* by Ted Hughes (1957), 'Full Moon and Little
Frieda' from *Wodwo* by Ted Hughes (1967), 'Homage to the
Government' from *High Windows* by Philip Larkin; Faber and Faber
Ltd. and the author's agents for an extract from the poem 'As I
walked out one evening' from *Collected Poems* by W. H. Auden;
Fulcrum Press Ltd for two poems by Lorine Niedecher from 'In
Exchange for Haiku' in *Collected Poems* (1970); the Executors of the
Earnest Hemingway Estate and Charles Scribner's Sons for the
story 'A Day's Wait' from *The First Forty-Nine Stories* and *Winner
Take Nothing* (US title – Copyright 1933 Charles Scribner's Sons;
copyright renewed © 1961 Mary Hemingway; the author, David
Holbrook for his poem 'Ecce Homo' from *Selected Poems* (Anvil
Press, 1980); the author, Brian Lee for an extract from 'London,
England – An Essay in Imitation' in *Haltwhistle Quarterly* No. 5
(Spring 1977); New Directions Publishing Corporation for the
poem 'A Negro Woman' by William Carlos Williams from *Pictures
from Benghal* Copyright © 1955 by William Carlos Williams;
Routledge & Kegan Paul for an extract from *A London Childhood* by
John Holloway (1966); the William Saroyan Foundation and the
author's agents for a shortened version of the story 'The Great
Leapfrog Contest' from *Best Stories of William Saroyan* Copyright ©
1968 by the William Saroyan Foundation; the author's agents for an
abridged extract from *The Loneliness of the Long Distance Runner* by
Alan Sillitoe Copyright © Alan Sillitoe 1959.

Pictures
Ardea Photographics for page 40 (top right); Rousseau, Henri, The
Waterfall, 1910, oil on canvas, 45½" × 59", Helen Birch Bartlett
Collection, 1926. 262 © The Art Institute of Chicago, All Rights
Reserved, page 197 (bottom); Barnabys Picture Library for pages 40
(bottom right) (Andrew Besley), 70 (top left), 219 (middle) (Mervyn
Rees) and 265 (right); BBC Enterprises for page 44 (left); BBC
Hulton Picture Library for pages 47 (left), 111, 174, 187 (left) and
187 (right); Camera Press Limited for pages 8 (top left) (Elizabeth
Vago), 8 (top right) (Jon Blau), 51 (top right) (Cecil Beaton), 219
(right) (Colin Davey) and 225 (bottom left); J. Allan Cash Photo
Library for pages 3 (middle left and bottom), 146 (right), 179 (right)
(Allen Denny), 219 (left), 225 (top left) and 265 (left); Bruce
Coleman Limited for pages 18 (Hans Reinhard) and 225 (right);
Donald Cooper (a RSC Production, 1971) for page 81; Dominic
Photography for pages 21 (bottom right) and 44 (right); Fay
Godwin for page 99 (top); Hammer Film Productions Limited for
page 40 (bottom left); Robert Harding Picture Library for page 14;
Camilla Jessel for page 3 (top right) and 8 (top middle); Van Gogh,
Mountain Landscape, 1890, Otterlo, Kröller-Müller Museum for
page 197 (middle left); Nicholas Judd for page 3 (top middle and
right); London Weekend Television Limited for page 70 (bottom
right); Longman Photo Unit for page 47 (right); Mary Evans Picture
Library for page 70 (top right) and 189 (right); Metro Goldwyn
Mayer for page 52 (bottom right); Mondadori-Flammarion for page
56; John Murray Limited for page 160 (bottom); Museum of Art,
Rhode Island School of Design for page 202 (left); Constable, The
Haywain, reproduced by courtesy of the Trustees, The National
Gallery for page 197 (top); The National Portrait Gallery for page 99
(bottom), National Portrait Gallery/Weidenfeld Archive for page
159 (bottom middle); Newstead Abbey, Nottingham Museum/
Weidenfeld and Nicolson Archives for pages 159 (top right and
bottom right), 160 (top), 161, Newstead Abbey, Nottingham
Museum for page 159 (bottom left); Paris, Musée d'Orsay for page
202 (right); Pictorial Press Limited for page 51 (top middle);
Picturepoint Limited for pages 8 (bottom), 51 (bottom left) and 179
(left); By kind permission of the daughter of Arthur Rackman for
page 29; Betty Rawlings for page 3 (top left) and 146 (left);
'Reproduced by Gracious permission of her Majesty the Queen' for
page 159 (top left); Royal Shakespeare Company (photo by Donald
Cooper) for page 246 (bottom); Shakespeare Birthplace Trust
(photo by Angus Mcbean) for page 246 (top); Ronald Sheridan's
Photo Library for page 51 (top left); The Trianon Press for page 13;
Copyright by Universal Pictures, a Division of Universal City
Studios, Inc., Courtesy of MCA Publishing Rights, a Division of
MCA Inc., for page 40 (top left); Victoria and Albert Museum for
page 21 (left).

Cover photograph by The Image Bank.

We have been unable to trace the copyright holders of the pictures
on pages 21 (top right) and 189 (left), and would be grateful for any
information that would enable us to do so.

Contents

General introduction to the teacher

Acknowledgements

We are very grateful for the help we received from Clive Wilmer for his comments on the early units, the students of the Bell School, Cambridge for trying out the exercises and the many Italian teachers of English who gave their lively encouragement.

We also wish to express our gratitude to Ruth Dendy for her invaluable secretarial assistance.

R G and M P

General introduction to the teacher

Reading Literature provides students with an introduction to the reading of British and American literature. It concentrates on helping them actually read what are sometimes difficult texts, while at the same time giving them some help with literary history, biography, differences in genre, technical literary terminology and literary criticism.

Since the primary focus is on reading, the book may be used either by students of literature or by students wishing to improve their English language skills. For either type of class it may be selected as a main course book. The literature teacher, however, may choose it to accompany an anthology or an encyclopaedic survey of some kind whereas the language teacher may choose it to accompany an English language course book.

How the book is organised

The book consists of ten Units. Each Unit centres around a particular focus of attention that a class of students might give a text (e.g. *Comprehension, Style,* etc). No Unit has any one exclusive focus. The Units are sequenced according to how the focuses of attention might be related

e.g. *Unit 1* The focus is on building up the students' interest (the first main activity a teacher might carry out with a group *before* they read a text).

Unit 2 The focus is on helping the students understand the content of what they read (the first activity a teacher might carry out with a group *after* they have read the text).

Unit 3 The focus is on getting the students to talk about how they react to what they have read.

However, this is a possible sequence only, and should not be interpreted too rigidly.

Students' language level

If all the work is to be done in English then the assumption is that the students' language level is intermediate to upper-intermediate, although parts of the book can very profitably be used with lower-intermediate students and other parts of it work very well with advanced classes. If, however, your students' speaking and writing skills are weak, much of the discussion and essay work may be done – if you prefer – in the students' own language. This would enable the book to be used consistently with students whose English is lower-intermediate.

The level of the book is not determined by how difficult the texts are but by such criteria as

- how *long* they are (the texts are usually shorter if they are difficult, longer if they are easy)
- the amount of language assistance given to students (quite a lot with difficult texts)
- the limited expectations of the exercises (i.e. if the text is difficult students won't be expected to understand everything the first time they read it).

The book aims to ease the student in gently.

Original texts	Texts have sometimes been 'abridged' but they have never been re-written to make them simpler. Care has been taken with 'abridged' versions (indicated by dots between sections where abridgement has taken place) not to change the meaning of the whole. Many texts are 'difficult' both in terms of the language used and the ideas expressed, but even in classes where language skills are weak, work on the texts can be very rewarding provided that it is done gently and with care, giving as much assistance as possible. Notice that on occasions several extracts have been taken from a single work to give a greater sense of the whole.
General guidance	First, if possible try to encourage students to read in their own time some of the whole works from which extracts are taken as well as other works by the same writers, even if they are translations in their own language. Try to get them to enjoy their reading instead of seeing it as a chore. You might even be able to find 'parallel' works by different writers – perhaps writers they are familiar with from their own country.
	Secondly, students are generally better able to read difficult texts if they work in a co-operative atmosphere and if you help build up their motivation and confidence. What's more, extra student involvement *in* the classes will increase both interest and willingness to work *outside* the classroom. It should also increase memory and enjoyment of the texts. Try to promote such an atmosphere. Many of the exercises are designed to help you.
	Please note that there are frequent instructions to 'Discuss in pairs'. This is because 'pair work' can also help build up a good atmosphere of co-operation in the classroom as well as stimulate discussion and awareness. If you prefer that the work is done in groups instead of pairs, then group work will usually have the same positive effect but it might take longer.
	However, if 'pair work' or 'group work' are unsuitable for your class, then all the work *can* be done by the students working on their own – even at home – or, alternatively, if you prefer, by the teacher working with the whole class together.
	You will notice that the activities in the book are designed to encourage students to discover things for themselves as they read. However, explicit guidance is given from time to time and a teacher may elicit and guide answers where necessary.
How to use the book	You may start at the beginning and work through. There is progress from one Unit to another. Some themes are linked and some of the later exercises are more successful if students have done the earlier ones. There is also occasional reference back to previous Units. However, it is possible, with careful planning, to dip into the book and move out of sequence.
	One important thing: it is essential that you do not use any exercises which are not suitable for your class. If your students do not need an exercise, or they have too little time to complete it, then don't use it. If an exercise is too easy or too difficult for your group then again, don't use it. It is also essential that you provide any additional material you think the class needs (for example, the literature teacher may feel that he or she needs to give more background information).

If you are a language teacher using the book to help improve the students' English language skills, then you will have to integrate work with your classes' language learning aims. The primary focus for such a class using this book as a main book, however, would probably be something like 'developing reading skills' although the book can very well be used in a vocabulary development class or a grammar exploration class. (The texts offer a marvellous source of language and many of the exercises focus on it explicitly.) Unit 10 is more obviously focused on language and language skills.

Let's look at some of the specific exercises you will find in the book:

Anticipation work

This is vital because

– it helps get the students into the right frame of mind for reading a difficult text

– it helps build up confidence (vital if they are to read texts which, in terms of their language level, are 'too difficult' for them).

– it helps motivate them to read text in the classroom.

Some exercises (e.g. 1.2.2) encourage the students to relate personally to the 'theme' of the text, perhaps through discussion. Others (e.g. 1.2.1) are language-based. Language exercises can provide an interesting and worthwhile warm-up, even for the literature class.

Be careful not to make students feel inferior when confronting a difficult text. (Also in 1.1.1 don't give the questionnaire if you know that some students have not read anything and might be ashamed of the fact.)

Language exercises

Language exercises usually focus on either grammar (e.g. 1.3.5) or vocabulary (e.g. 1.3.1). Sometimes they are intended to come before the students encounter a text (e.g. 1.3.1) in which case they come under the heading *Language Work*, sometimes afterwards (1.3.5), in which case they come under the heading *Language*. However, there is no reason why the 'before' exercises could not, if desired, be done *after* the reading. Literature teachers – as distinct from language teachers – may prefer to keep such work to a minimum.

Note: While the pre-reading language exercises have a link with the text it is usually too time-consuming and demoralising for students if you try to teach in advance all the words which will be new to them. They can better learn the words from the context or after they have read the text.

If you wish to *extend* the language work there are some ideas in Unit 10 and some guidance in 10.3. There is no reason why work in the rest of the book should not be expanded in a similar way.

Listening to/reading the text

It is usually better if the students can first listen to the text without having to read it because

– it helps them get a sense of the whole (the speaker's voice can help with this)

– it discourages them from getting too concerned with the bits they don't understand (it's therefore important not to stop during the reading). However, you will have to assure the students that at this stage they're not *expected* to understand everything. Either encourage students to relax and get the general idea of what they are going to hear, or give them in advance a very simple task (e.g. a few simple questions which either focus on the gist of the whole or on some prominent details).

Read the text aloud yourself or play the tape (texts read on tape are indicated by [🔲] in the margin). Then either let the students read the text silently at their own speed or read it silently the same time as they listen to it. The aim of this second encounter will be to encourage the students towards greater understanding. After that, it is preferable if students help each other to understand the difficult parts but of course they can, at your discretion, get assistance from the glossary, a dictionary, or you.

In general, it is usually better to let students read/listen as often as they like so that they feel comfortable with the text. Naturally it all depends on how much time you've got available. On most occasions, it is advisable not to get the students to read the texts aloud. It can be rather defeating for the student doing the reading and rather time-wasting for the others.

Improving understanding

The aim of all the comprehension exercises is to *assist* understanding rather than *test* it. Most of the exercises, then, can more beneficially be given to the students either *before they read the text* (e.g. 1.14.4) to help direct and focus the students' attention, or *after a first encounter with the text* but while they are working on it in detail (e.g. 1.7.2).

If students are not allowed access to the text when doing comprehension exercises you are in effect really checking up on their ability to have understood and remembered what they have read. This is likely to make the whole task of reading difficult texts much more difficult. It is essential that you give as much help as possible with understanding (e.g. help the students to understand your questions by directing their attention to where in the text the answers can be found).

If possible, work out what kind of understanding the exercise aims at (e.g. Does it focus on the gist of a passage? Does it encourage the students to focus on detail? Does it encourage a surface or 'in-depth' understanding?) You will probably need different types of exercises to help with different kinds of understanding.

As a general rule, don't expect a full, profound understanding after the students' first encounter! If necessary, work towards understanding gradually.

Glossaries

Glossaries are provided to help students with the less common (e.g. archaic and 'poetic') words. However, it's better if you can slowly get the students to be less dependent on glossaries by encouraging them to guess unknown words from the context in which they appear. If you are only expecting the students to get the general idea of a text or to simply enjoy it, discourage reference to the glossary altogether.

There are more 'active' glossaries in the *Language Sections* (e.g. 1.2.6). These are particularly of interest to those students who wish to improve their vocabulary. They encourage the students to explore (or try to guess) the meaning of the words in context.

Be careful: too much vocabulary work can hinder efficient reading, so unless your primary aim is vocabulary development, do it with care and restraint. Feel free *not* to use the *vocabulary* exercises in the book.

Notes

For reasons of space the Notes on the writers are usually short. Classes which need more background/biographical information can be referred to an encyclopaedia, or something like the Pelican Guide to English literature (ed. Ford, Penguin 1984). (See e.g. 6.3.1 – 6.3.10 for ways of bringing background and biography to life in the classroom.)

Discussion

Exercises labelled 'discussion' are usually designed to encourage the students to relate personally to the theme of the text. However, most of the language and comprehension exercises can be discussed by the students sitting in pairs or groups co-operating on the answers. Be careful, though: discussion can take a long time in the classroom if students have a lot to say. Try to estimate how long each discussion will take and allow enough time for it.

Reading without assistance

Whilst poems or passages in this section link in – usually loosely – with some thematic aspect of what has gone before or what is to come, they are meant simply for the students' enjoyment. No formal work is intended to be attached to them.

Follow-up work

There are some suggestions in the book for this. In the Units containing more difficult texts, written work has mainly been omitted since you may find it more beneficial to get the students to do the text-related exercises at home in their own time. If you do set written work, why not get the students to read each others' work? In that case you may not feel it necessary to correct all the language mistakes. To prepare for composition work you might like to

– have a discussion on the subject in advance (in groups?)
– help the students to make notes
– give ideas as to what content might be included
– discuss an outline of the structure of the composition.

UNIT 1

Getting ready

1.1 Finding out about you

**1.1.1
What have you read?**

i In your own language

NOVELS:_____

PLAYS:_____

POEMS:_____

SHORT STORIES:_____

BIOGRAPHIES/AUTOBIOGRAPHIES:_____

ii In English

NOVELS:_____

PLAYS:_____

POEMS:_____

SHORT STORIES:_____

BIOGRAPHIES/AUTOBIOGRAPHIES:_____

Write the names of at least two. If none, write none.
Use a separate piece of paper.

1.1.2
What do you like best?

i Give a mark 0–5 next to the following literary forms (0 = I don't like them. 5 = I like them very much).

Novels　　　　　　＿＿＿＿＿＿＿＿
Poems　　　　　　＿＿＿＿＿＿＿＿
Short stories　　　＿＿＿＿＿＿＿＿
Biographies　　　 ＿＿＿＿＿＿＿＿
Autobiographies　＿＿＿＿＿＿＿＿
Plays　　　　　　 ＿＿＿＿＿＿＿＿
Essays　　　　　　＿＿＿＿＿＿＿＿

ii Give a mark 0–5 next to the titles you have written in 1.1.1.

1.1.3
What do you think?

i Tick (✓) those statements you agree with.

> Poetry is the highest form of human expression.
>
> I only like to read English literature when the language is simplified.
>
> Poetry is silly.
>
> I like novels because they have a story.
>
> Plays are interesting to watch but not so interesting to read.
>
> Novels are too long when you don't understand the language very well.
>
> I don't like to offer opinions about literature in case I'm wrong.
>
> It's not easy to talk about English literature in English.
>
> I like someone to translate any words I don't understand.

ii Re-write those statements you don't agree with; make them closer to your views. Add others which express your opinion about literature and reading literature in English.

iii Discuss your answers in pairs.

1.2 Beginnings

1.2.1
Language work

In pairs, complete the following:

Childhood　　is the time of life when one is a *child*.
Infancy　　　is the time of life when one is an ＿＿＿＿＿＿＿＿＿＿
Adolescence　is the time of life when one is an ＿＿＿＿＿＿＿＿＿＿

What is the approximate difference in ages between the three categories? What other English words/phrases do you know which describe the different stages of one's life?

1.2.2
Anticipation

i When and where were you born? (Give date, day or week, exact time, place.)
What is your earliest memory?
What have you been told about your early days?

Tell each other in pairs.

ii Look at the following pictures. Choose at least one that reminds you of an early experience and, in pairs, tell each other about the experience.

1.2.3 Listen to the following passage:

 Out of the darkness of my infancy there comes only one flash of memory. I am seated alone, in my baby-chair, at a dinner-table set for several people. Somebody brings in a leg of mutton, puts it down close to me, and goes out. I am again alone, gazing at two low windows, wide open upon a garden. Suddenly, noiselessly, a large, 5 long animal (obviously a greyhound) appears at one window-sill, slips into the room, seizes the leg of mutton and slips out again. When this happened I could not yet talk. The accomplishment of speech came to me very late, doubtless because I never heard young voices. Many years later, when I mentioned this recollection, there was a shout of 10 laughter and surprise: 'That, then, was what became of the mutton! It was not you, who, as your Uncle A. pretended, ate it up, in the twinkling of an eye, bone and all!'

GLOSSARY
mutton (l.3): meat of a mature sheep
greyhound (l.6): dog used for racing
in the twinkling of an eye (l.12–13): very quickly

1.2.4
Improving understanding

Notice the person speaking is the first person narrator in an autobiography. Read and/or listen to the passage as often as you like. In pairs, help each other to understand what it is about. Try to guess unknown words from the context and answer the following questions:

What event did the child witness?
What did the child say at the time?
Did the family know the truth of what happened at the time?
What was the joke?

1.2.5
Language

Say whether in context each of the words in the left-hand column is a noun, verb, adverb or idiomatic expression. Match the words with the definitions.

flash	probably
gazing	horizontal piece at the base of a window
noiselessly	memory
window sill	takes hold of quickly
seizes	happened to
accomplishment	looking long and fixedly
doubtless	successful achievement
recollection	sudden rush
became of	silently

Underline all the verbs in the passage and where possible write the names of the tenses next to each (e.g. past simple).
Say what time each tense refers to (past, present or future).
Do you notice anything unusual?

1.2.6
Discussion

Tell each other any incidents you can remember in your life which are similar to the one in the passage.

1.2.7
Notes

The previous extract is from Father and Son *by Edmund Gosse (1849–1928). It is part of an autobiography written 'as a document, as a record of educational and religious conditions which have passed away and will never return'. It is also 'a study of the development of moral and educational ideas during the progress of infancy'.*

1.3 Building up interest

1.3.1
Language work

Two uses of the verb 'smell' are

to notice a pleasant/unpleasant odour (transitive verb)
to give out a pleasant/unpleasant odour (intransitive verb)

Write two sentences to illustrate the difference. (See 2.5.1.ii for a definition of transitive/intransitive).

1.3.2
Anticipation

i Write down your earliest memory of something you remember having a pleasant or unpleasant smell.
How old were you?

ii Ask someone in the class about his/her memory.

iii Which smells do you like most?

1.3.3

Listen to the following passage. Help each other to understand as much as possible.

GLOSSARY
sainfoin (l.1): herb given as feed to cattle
chaff (l.1): cattle feed after it is cut
plastery (l.7): like plaster (the white powder which, when mixed with water, is put on the surface of walls)
meal (l.10): powdered grain

The very first thing I remember is the smell of sainfoin chaff. You went up the stone passage that led from the kitchen to the shop, and the smell of sainfoin got stronger all the way. Mother had fixed a wooden gate in the doorway to prevent Joe and myself (Joe was my elder brother) from getting into the shop. I can still remember standing there clutching the bars, and the smell of sainfoin mixed up with the damp plastery smell that belonged to the passage. It wasn't till years later that I somehow managed to crash the gate and get into the shop when nobody was there. A mouse that had been having a go at one of the meal-bins suddenly plopped out and ran between my feet. It was quite white with meal. This must have happened when I was about six.

5

10

1.3.4
Improving understanding

Notice the speaker is the first person narrator; this time in a novel. Read the passage again and try in pairs to answer the following questions:

Where do you think his parents worked?
Why couldn't the brothers get out of the other end of the passage?
What two smells does the writer remember?
Why was the mouse white?

Find a word or phrase in the passage that means:

holding firmly   trying to break into (with some success)

a little wet   fell out suddenly

In the passage, 'smell' is a noun. Does it mean the 'perception' or the 'giving out' of an odour? Does it have a pleasant or an unpleasant association for the writer?

Discuss the difference between the words 'elder' and 'older'. What does 'elder' tell you about Joe and his brother?

The previous extract is from Coming up for Air *(1934) by George Orwell (1903–1950), the author of* Nineteen Eighty Four *and* Animal Farm. *As well as being a novelist Orwell was a journalist and satirist.* Coming up for Air *is a novel about a man who gets very nostalgic about his past and eventually makes a journey back to the most important place of his childhood. He is totally disillusioned.*

1.4 Into a harder passage

i Find out how many people in the class were born on a Friday.

ii Find out how many were born near midnight.

iii Find out if any were born at midnight on a Friday.

The following passage refers to the birth of the narrator.
Listen.
In pairs help each other to understand as much as possible.

Whether I shall turn out to be the hero of my own life, or whether that station will be held by anybody else, these pages must show. To begin my life with the beginning of my life, I record that I was born (as I have been informed and believe) on a Friday, at twelve o'clock at night. It was remarked that the clock began to strike, and I began to cry, simultaneously.

In consideration of the day and hour of my birth, it was declared by the nurse, and by some sage women in the neighbourhood who had taken a lively interest in me several months before there was any possibility of our becoming personally acquainted, first, that I was destined to be unlucky in life; and secondly, that I was privileged to see ghosts and spirits; both these gifts inevitably attaching, as they believed, to all unlucky infants of either gender, born towards the small hours on a Friday night.

I need say nothing here, on the first head, because nothing can show better than my history whether that prediction was verified or falsified by the result. On the second branch of the question, I will only remark, that unless I ran through that part of my inheritance while I was still a baby, I have not come into it yet. But I do not at all complain of having been kept out of this property; and if anybody else should be in the present enjoyment of it, he is heartily welcome to keep it.

GLOSSARY
station (l.2): position
gender (l.13): sex (male or female)
heartily (l.21): in all sincerity; thoroughly

1.4.3
Improving understanding/tone

  i Re-read as often as you like. Try to answer the following questions:

    What were the nurse's two predictions about someone born in the middle of a Friday night?

    Do we know if the nurse was correct?

  ii How do you know from the passage that it is from a novel and not a conventional autobiography? (Look at the first sentence.)

  iii Can you describe the narrator's attitude to himself?

  iv Do you find any of the passage funny? If so, which parts? (Give reasons.)

1.4.4
Language

Find a word or phrase in the passage that means:

    at the same time

    wise

    prophecy

    turned out to be correct

What do the words 'inheritance' and 'property' suggest?
Here 'property' could mean 'characteristic'. In what way could it be a *pun* (i.e. a play on words)?

The passive voice consists of the verb 'be' + past participle (e.g. he was given ...). Circle all examples of the passive voice in the passage. Underline those examples of the verb 'be' + adjective (e.g. I was happy). For each example of the passive voice say whether it is possible to change it to the active voice (not 'he was given', but 'gave it to him') and, if so, say what difference it would make to the meaning.

1.4.5
Notes

The last extract is the opening of the novel David Copperfield *(1849–50) by Charles Dickens (1812–1870). Dickens worked as a clerk in a solicitor's office, a reporter in the Law Courts and a parliamentary reporter. In all he wrote fifteen novels, primarily set in an urban, industrial world. As a man he was reputed to be full of charm, enthusiasm and exuberance.* David Copperfield *has some autobiographical elements but is essentially a novel about the growth of a young man from childhood to maturity.*

1.5 Introduction to literary forms

1.5.1

  i The main literary forms are listed in 1.1.2. In pairs, agree on at least three characteristics of each literary form (e.g. POETRY: 1. A poem often has a rhythmic pattern).

  ii Each frequently overlaps with the others. So a play may be poetic and a novel semi-autobiographical.

    Make a list of the forms and draw lines between them to show which overlap with which, e.g. DRAMA

               POETRY

Discuss.

1.6 Follow-up work

i Look at the following pictures:

ii *Either:* Write the story of the first few days of your life. Use your imagination. Begin something like:

'I was born ———————————— It was ————————————

My mother ———————————————————————————————

Or: Write the story of one or two early memories. Begin something like:

'I remember ———————————— I was ————————————

(Maximum 300 words)

1.7 Making comparisons

1.7.1 *Like the passage from* David Copperfield *the following is also the beginning of a novel where a first-person narrator tells you about himself.*
Listen.
In pairs, help each other to understand as much as possible.

If you really want to hear about it, the first thing you'll probably want to know is where I was born, and what my lousy childhood was like, and how my parents were occupied and all before they had me, and all that David Copperfield kind of crap, but I don't feel like going into it. In the first place, that stuff bores me, and in the second place, my parents would have about two haemorrhages apiece if I told anything pretty personal about them. They're quite touchy about anything like that, especially my father. They're nice and all – I'm not saying that – but they're also touchy as hell. Besides, I'm not going to tell you my whole goddam autobiography or anything. I'll just tell you about this madman stuff that happened to me around last Christmas before I got pretty run-down and had to come out here and take it easy. I mean that's all I told D.B. about, and he's my brother and all. He's in Hollywood. That isn't too far from this crumby place, and he comes over and visits me practically every weekend. He's going to drive me home when I go home next month maybe. He just got a Jaguar. One of those little English jobs that can do around two hundred miles an hour. It cost him damn near four thousand bucks. He's got a lot of dough now. He didn't use it. He used to be just a regular writer, when he was home. He wrote this terrific book of short stories, The Secret Goldfish, in case you never heard of him. The best one in it was 'The Secret Goldfish'. It was about this little kid that wouldn't let anybody look at his goldfish because he'd bought it with his own money. It killed me. Now he's out in Hollywood, D.B., being a prostitute. If there's one thing I hate, it's the movies. Don't even mention them to me.

5

10

15

20

25

GLOSSARY
lousy (l.2): awful (colloquial – usually American)
crap (l.4): rubbish (colloquial – usually American)
apiece (l.6): each
touchy (l.7): easily angered
goddam (l.10): damned (colloquial – usually American)
run-down (l.12): exhausted and weak
crumby (l.14): worthless (colloquial)
Jaguar (l.16): an expensive English car
bucks (l.18): dollars (colloquial American)
dough (l.19): money (colloquial American)
killed me (l.24): made me laugh a lot

**1.7.2
Improving
understanding**

Try to build up a picture of the narrator. Answer the following questions first:

About how old is he?
Is he in good health at the moment?
What does he tell you about his parents?
Where does his brother live?
What is the brother's job?

i The passage is written in a very informal style, close to the rhythms of contemporary speech. Underline some words and phrases to illustrate this. For example:

Noun phrases (e.g. my lousy childhood)
Exaggerations (e.g. my parents would have about two haemorrhages apiece)
Slang expressions (e.g. this madman stuff)

ii There are also many words and patterns of speech that are American rather than British. Some are given in the glossary. Can you give others?

iii Is this a novel or an autobiography? Give reasons.
How would you describe a person who begins his book: 'If you really want to hear about it, ...'?

iv The writer is conscious of how *David Copperfield* began. In what way is he trying to be different? (Indicate any similarities.)

Would you like this young man if you met him? Give reasons.

Try to substitute 'whether' for 'if' in the first sentence. Is it grammatically possible? (How does *David Copperfield* begin?)

The title of the previous story is Catcher in the Rye *by J. D. Salinger. Salinger was born in 1919 in New York City.* Catcher in the Rye *is an episodic novel about a young man – Holden Caulfield – and his adolescent view of the world. It was written in 1951.*

Try to get hold of a copy of *Catcher in the Rye* and continue reading it. Discuss it with others in the class.

1.8 Beyond the apparent meaning

Many writers use the newly-born to suggest innocence and the beginnings of life – themes full of meaning for all of us.

Tick (✓) which of these words come to mind when you think of the early days of life (look up in a dictionary any you don't know). Add others.

innocence	joy	hunger	thirst
singing	misery	struggle	sorrow
noise	smiles	tears	tiredness
pleasure	despair	need	sleep

1.8.2   **i** Listen:

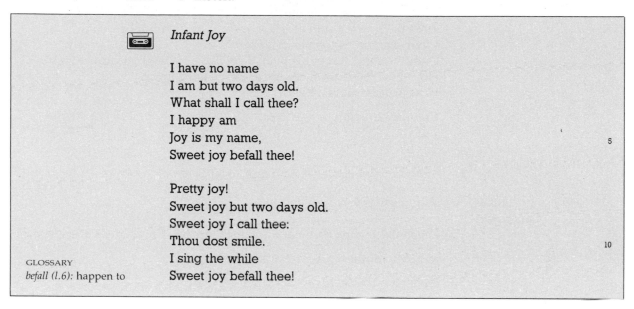

Infant Joy

I have no name
I am but two days old.
What shall I call thee?
I happy am
Joy is my name,   5
Sweet joy befall thee!

Pretty joy!
Sweet joy but two days old.
Sweet joy I call thee:
Thou dost smile.   10
I sing the while
Sweet joy befall thee!

GLOSSARY
befall (l.6): happen to

ii Improving understanding

Who do you think is speaking each line?
Who is smiling? What is the other person doing?
How old is the child?
Do we know the child's name?
Can you describe the different feelings expressed in this short poem?
How realistic is the dialogue?

Compare in pairs.

1.8.3   **i** Listen:

GLOSSARY
groaned (l.1): made
a sound expressing pain
wept (l.1): shed tears
piping (l.3): high pitched
and piercing
fiend (l.4): devil
striving (l.6): fighting
swaddling (l.6): strips of
cloth wrapped around a
baby
bound (l.7): tightly
wrapped
sulk (l.8): show bad
humour in silence

Infant Sorrow

My mother groaned! my father wept.
Into the dangerous world I leapt:
Helpless, naked, piping loud:
Like a fiend hid in a cloud.

Struggling in my fathers hands: 5
Striving against my swaddling bands:
Bound and weary I thought best
To sulk upon my mothers breast.

ii Improving understanding

Who is speaking to whom?
Does the poem sound as if it is spoken by an adult or a child?
What event does the poem refer to?
Does the child accept his fate? If so, how, willingly or unwillingly?
How does the child show his or her real feelings?
How realistic is the poem?

Compare in pairs.

1.8.4
Language

For both poems (*Infant Joy* and *Infant Sorrow*):

i Listen to the tape and mark the main stresses the reader's voice makes

(e.g. My móther gróaned! my fáther wépt)

ii Underline the words which rhyme.

1.8.5
Tone

i Tick any of the following words you think describe the 'voice' of the second poem (look up any you don't know in a dictionary). Add others.

childish	adult
resigned	cynical
sorrowful	world-weary
dismissive	resentful
child-like	angry

ii Compare with the first poem.

1.8.6
Symbolic meaning

The first poem above (1.8.2) comes from the Songs of Innocence *(1789) and the second (1.8.3) from the* Songs of Experience *(1794).*

i What do the following lines suggest beyond the apparent dramatic meaning:

'Sweet joy befall thee' (Could the writer be speaking to us?)
'like a fiend hid in a cloud' (Is there a suggestion of Christian symbolism?)

ii What else do the poems suggest to you?

Discuss in pairs.

iii Look at the etchings the poet did for these poems. Do they add anything to the meaning?

1.8.7 Compare the two poems under the following headings. Write two or three
Follow-up work sentences for each.

   i The narrator of the poems.

   ii The structure of the poems.

   iii What each poem is 'about' and suggests.

1.8.8 *William Blake (1757-1827) was a poet and engraver who lived and worked in London. His*
Notes *best known poem is probably* The Tyger *although his main poetic output lay in the*
Prophetic Books *begun in 1797. The later part of his life was spent in poverty.*

1.9 Focus on anticipation

If you have a strong desire to read something and you are full of curiosity, you are likely to find greater pleasure in what you read. You will also be more inclined to try to make greater sense of it. Many of the exercises in this book are designed to arouse your interest in what you are going to read before you read it.

1.10 Reading without assistance

1.10.1 Does this picture remind you of a story you know? If not, invent one.

Tell each other in pairs. Give as many details as you can.

Once upon a time there was a sweet little maiden who was loved by
all who knew her, but she was especially dear to her grandmother,
who did not know how to make enough of the child. Once she gave
her a little red velvet cloak. It was so becoming and she liked it so
much that she would never wear anything else, and so she got the   5
name of Red Riding Hood.

One day her mother said to her, 'Come here, Red Riding Hood! Take
this cake and bottle of wine to grandmother. She is weak and ill, and
they will do her good.

Her grandmother lived away in the wood, a good half hour from the   10
village. When she got to the wood she met a wolf, but Red Riding
Hood did not know what a wicked animal he was, so she was not a
bit afraid of him.

'Good morning, Red Riding Hood,' he said. 'Good morning, wolf,' she
answered. 'Whither away so early, Red Riding Hood?' 'To   15
grandmother's.' 'What have you got in your basket?' 'Cake and wine.
We baked yesterday, so I'm taking a cake to grandmother. She wants
something to make her well.' 'Where does your grandmother live,
Red Riding Hood?' 'A good quarter of an hour farther into the wood.
Her house stands under three big oak trees, near a hedge of nut trees   20
which you must know,' said Red Riding Hood.

The wolf thought, 'This tender little creature will be a plump morsel!
She will be nicer than the old woman. I must be cunning and snap
them both up.'

He walked along with Red Riding Hood for a while. Then he said,   25
'Look at the pretty flowers, Red Riding Hood. Why don't you look
about you? I don't believe you even hear the birds sing. You are just
as solemn as if you were going to school. Everything else is so gay
out here in the woods.'

Red Riding Hood raised her eyes, and when she saw the sunlight   30
dancing through the trees, and all the bright flowers, she thought, 'I'm
sure grandmother would be pleased if I took her a bunch of fresh
flowers. It is still quite early. I shall have plenty of time to pick them.'

So she left the path and wandered off among the trees to pick the
flowers. Each time she picked one, she always saw another prettier   35
one farther on. So she went deeper and deeper into the forest.

In the meantime the wolf went straight off to the grandmother's cottage and knocked at the door. 'Who is there?' 'Red Riding Hood, bringing you a cake and some wine. Open the door!' 'Lift the latch,' called out the old woman. 'I am too weak to get up.' The wolf lifted the latch and the door sprang open. He went straight in and up to the bed without saying a word, and ate up the poor old woman. Then he put on her nightdress and nightcap, got into bed and drew the curtains.

Red Riding Hood ran about picking flowers till she could carry no more, and then she remembered her grandmother again. She was astonished when she got to the house to find the door open, and when she entered the room everything seemed so strange. She felt quite frightened but she did not know why. 'Generally I like coming to see grandmother so much,' she thought. 'Good morning, grandmother,' she cried. But she received no answer. Then she went up to the bed and drew the curtain back. There lay her grandmother, but she had drawn her cap down over her face and she looked very odd. 'Oh grandmother, what big ears you have,' she said. 'The better to hear you with, my dear.' 'Grandmother, what big eyes you have.' 'The better to see you with, my dear.' 'What big hands you have, grandmother.' 'The better to catch hold of you with, my dear.' 'But grandmother, what big teeth you have.' 'The better to eat you with, my dear.' Hardly had the wolf said this than he made a spring out of bed and swallowed poor little Red Riding Hood.

1.10.3 'Red Riding Hood' is a well-known European fairytale. In pairs, tell each other any other fairytale you know.

1.11 Reading with interest

1.11.1 Anticipation

Have you ever written

	Yes	No
a poem in your language?		
in English?		
a novel in your language?		
in English?		
a short story in your language?		
in English?		
a play in your language?		
in English?		
your autobiography?		

Have you ever kept a diary?

Tell each other in pairs.

1.11.2 In the following poem, the poet, Ted Hughes, suggests that the moment of creative inspiration is like a fox coming out of a forest. However the stanzas have been jumbled up.

   i Read them quickly as often as you like.

   ii Work with a partner. Write numbers next to each stanza to show their correct order. The first one has been done for you. Discuss reasons for your decision.

   iii Help each other to understand what the whole poem is about. Try to guess any unknown words from the context.

The Thought Fox

Sets neat prints into the snow
Between trees, and warily a lame
Shadow lags by stump and in hollow
Of a body that is bold to come

Through the window I see no star;   5
Something more near
Though deeper within darkness
Is entering the loneliness:

Across clearings, an eye,
A widening deepening greenness,   10
Brilliantly, concentratedly,
Coming about its own business

I imagine this midnight moment's forest;   **1**
Something else is alive
Beside the clock's loneliness   15
And this blank page where my fingers move.

Till, with a sudden sharp stink of fox
It enters the dark hole of the head.
The window is starless still; the clock ticks,
The page is printed.   20

Cold, delicately as the dark snow,
A fox's nose touches twig, leaf;
Two eyes serve a movement, that now
And again now, and now, and now

GLOSSARY
warily (l.2): carefully, on guard
lame (l.2): weak
lags (l.3): moves slowly
stump (l.3): lower part of tree trunk left in ground after the rest has been cut
hollow (l.3): shallow depression in the ground
bold (l.4): brave
clearings (l.9): land cleared in forest
blank (l.16): empty
stink (l.17): strong smell
twig (l.22): small shoot from branch of tree

1.11.3   i   Read over the poem again – the right order is in the Key at the back of the book.

ii **Improving understanding**
Describe the 'story' of the poem. What is the narrator doing? Where is he? Where does the action take place?
Does the following picture adequately suggest the fox he 'sees'?

iii **Style**
The description in the poem is both realistic and unrealistic. Underline phrases that seem to be part of a realistic description and circle phrases that suggest something other than a realistic description.

Why do you think the poet repeats the word 'now'?
Which stanza has the longest words? What effect does this have on the way you read it? Why do you think the poet has done this?
Why do you think the poet starts the last stanza with the word 'till'?

iv **Poetic form**
Which words at the end of lines are rhymes or near-rhymes?
Is the rhythm in all the lines regular? (Try to beat it out.)
Does it suggest the movement of the fox? If so, where?

v **Language**
Say what tense each of the verbs is in.
What tense is used several times? What effect does it have?

vi **Reactions**
What feelings do you have as you read the fifth stanza (after it has been re-arranged)?
What feelings do you have as you read the last stanza?

1.11.4   Find one of the following:
Extension
i   another poem by Ted Hughes

ii   a poem in your language about a fox

iii   a folk tale about a fox

Share with other people in your class.

1.11.5
Notes
Ted Hughes was born in 1930 in Yorkshire, and educated at Cambridge. He has written several volumes of verse, including some for children. The Thought Fox *is from the collection of poems entitled* The Hawk in the Rain.

1.11.6 **i Discussion**
Read what Hughes has said about the poem:

> 'This poem does not have anything you could easily call a meaning. It is about a fox, obviously enough, but a fox that is both a fox and not a fox. What sort of a fox is it that can step right into my head where presumably it still sits … smiling to itself when the dogs bark? It is both a fox and a spirit. It is a real fox; as I read the poem I see it move, I see it setting its prints, I see its shadow going over the irregular surface of the snow. The words show me all this, bringing it nearer and nearer. It is very real to me. The words have made a body for it and given it somewhere to walk.'

ii In pairs, discuss:
How far do you agree?
Does the poem succeed in suggesting the moment of inspiration? How would *you* describe that moment?
Do you like the poem?

1.12 Openings

1.12.1 How do you begin to decide what kind of book will give you enjoyment? Do you look at the first page – or even at the first sentence – and feel you know what sort of story lies ahead? Or do you think you have to work a bit harder than this and let the pages unfold as the author takes you further into his confidence?

Here are a few opening sentences.
Match the sentence with the descriptions below (e.g. 8 b).

1 The naked man who lay splayed out on his face beside the swimming pool might have been dead.

2 It was a bright cold day in April, and the clocks were striking thirteen.

3 It is a truth universally acknowledged, that a single man in possession of a good fortune, must be in want of a wife.

4 Two households, both alike in dignity,
In fair Verona, where we lay our scene,
From ancient grudge break to new mutiny,
Where civil blood makes civil hands unclean.

5 Last night I dreamt I went to Manderley again.

6 Hale knew they meant to murder him before he had been in Brighton three hours.

7 There was a woman who was beautiful, who started with all the advantages, yet she had no luck.

8 In the beginning was the Word, and the Word was with God, and the Word was God.

9   56 Green Street, Oct. 1844

My Dear Lady Carlisle,

From your ancient goodness to me, I am sure you will be glad to receive a bulletin from myself, informing you that I am making good progress; in fact, I am in a regular train of promotion from gruel, vermicelli, and sago, I was promoted to panada, from thence to minced meat, and (such is the effect of good conduct) I was elevated to a mutton-chop.

10 When Mr Bilbow Baggins of Bag End announced that he would shortly be celebrating his eleventy-first birthday with a party of special magnificence, there was much talk and excitement in Hobbiton.

a A romantic novel.
b The Gospel of St. John in the King James Bible.
c A letter from an eighteenth-century parson.
d A thriller.
e A fictional story about the future.
f A sixteenth-century drama.
g A modern adventure story for children.
h A nineteenth-century ironic story of love and marriage.
i A murder mystery.
j A modern fairy tale.

Give reasons for your choice.

1.13 Longer openings

Discuss in pairs what the following sets of words mean. What do they have in common? How are they different? Look them up in a dictionary if necessary.

1 ghost, ghoul, spectre, phantom, spirit, demon, fiend, werewolf.

2 witch, oracle, prophet, fortune-teller, clairvoyant.

Divide each set into two: those words which usually provoke a negative reaction (e.g. werewolf) and those which usually provoke a positive reaction (e.g. fortune-teller).

1.13.2
Anticipation

i Tick which of the following are true for you:

I believe in: ghosts
 UFOs (unidentified flying objects)
 telepathy

I have had experience of: poltergeists
 table-turning
 unexplained happenings

Compare and discuss in pairs.
Tell each other your experiences.

ii Describe what a witch is and does.
iii Are there any witches in your country?

1.13.3 Shakespeare presented witches on the stage in *Macbeth*.
Look at the following representations of them:

Compare their clothes and attitudes. What do you think the producer/artist
saw them as?

1.13.4 Listen and help each other to understand as much as possible. If you can, perform the extract in groups.

MACBETH

Act One

Scene I. An open place.
Thunder and lightning. Enter THREE WITCHES.

1 WITCH

When shall we three meet again,

In thunder, lightning or in rain?

2 WITCH

When the hurlyburly's done,

When the battle's lost and won.

3 WITCH

That will be ere the set of sun. 5

1 WITCH

Where the place?

2 WITCH

Upon the heath.

3 WITCH

There to meet with Macbeth.

1 WITCH

I come, Graymalkin!

ALL

Paddock calls. – Anon! – 10

Fair is foul, and foul is fair:

Hover through the fog and filthy air.

GLOSSARY
hurlyburly (l.3): noisy, energetic chaos of battle
ere (l.5): before
heath (l.7): large open area usually with sandy soil and very little vegetation
Graymalkin and Paddock (l.9–10): names of a cat and a toad. These animals were the 'familiars' of witches – that is, creatures often associated with them, whose bodies they sometimes inhabited.
Anon (l.10): at once

---

i **Improving understanding**
What are the witches discussing?
What do they agree?
What do you understand by the phrase 'Fair is foul and foul is fair'?

ii **Poetic form**
Underline the words which rhyme.
What is the difference in rhythm between lines 1–5, 6–9, 10–12?
What rhythm do lines 1–4 and 11 and 12 have in common?

iii **Style and tone**
a) Write down some words which suggest an atmosphere of darkness and evil.
b) Shakespeare often uses the first scene of a play to set the tone for what is to follow. Write a few sentences about the atmosphere of this scene to see if you can indicate what effect it has. (Comment on the setting, the characters and the language they use.)

iv Notes

William Shakespeare (1564–1616) was born in Stratford upon Avon. He married Ann Hathaway when he was 18. His plays include Romeo and Juliet, Hamlet *and* Macbeth. *Most of them fall into the following categories: history plays, comedies and tragedies. When* Macbeth *was written (1605–6), witchcraft was a subject of great interest, James I the new King of Great Britain having written a book on the subject in 1597.*

1.14 A whole story

In this Unit, apart from the poems, you have read *extracts*.
The following exercises, however, relate to a whole story.

1.14.1
Language work

In pairs:

i Check that you know what the following words mean (look up any you don't know in a dictionary):

ill	shake
shiver	fever
temperature	headache
tired	sick

ii Say whether each is a noun, adjective, or verb. Some fit into more than one category. Change the adjectives into nouns.

iii Write sentences to show the difference in use between:

shiver/shake
ill/sick
fever/temperature

1.14.2
Anticipation

In pairs, tell each other about:

i a time you had 'flu (influenza). Give an account of the symptoms. How were you cured?

ii a time you were seriously ill. How were you cured?

1.14.3 The following story is called *A Day's Wait* by Ernest Hemingway. Can you make guesses as to what it might be about?

1.14.4 When you read, try to find answers to these questions in the passage that follows:

Who is 'he' at the beginning of the story?
How old is he?
What seems to be wrong with him?
How is the narrator involved in the story?
How did the narrator know 'Schatz' was ill?
Was the doctor worried? (Give a reason.)
What did he prescribe?

Read:

> He came into the room to shut the windows while we were still in bed
> and I saw he looked ill. He was shivering, his face was white, and he
> walked slowly as though it ached to move.
> 'What's the matter, Schatz?'
> 'I've got a headache.' 5
> 'You better go back to bed.'
> 'No, I'm all right.'
> 'You go to bed. I'll see you when I'm dressed.'
> But when I came downstairs he was dressed, sitting by the fire,
> looking a very sick and miserable boy of nine years. When I put my 10
> hand on his forehead I knew he had a fever.
> 'You go up to bed,' I said, 'you're sick.'
> 'I'm all right,' he said.
> When the doctor came he took the boy's temperature.
> 'What is it?' I asked him. 15
> 'One hundred and two.'
> Downstairs, the doctor left three different medicines in different
> coloured capsules with instructions for giving them. One was to bring
> down the fever, another a purgative, the third to overcome an acid
> condition, he explained. The germs of influenza can only exist in an 20
> acid condition, he explained. He seemed to know all about influenza
> and said there was nothing to worry about if the fever did not go
> above one hundred and four degrees. This was a light epidemic of flu
> and there was no danger if you avoided pneumonia. Back in the room
> I wrote the boy's temperature down and made a note of the time to 25
> give the various capsules.

Discuss the answers in pairs. Help each other to understand any words
you don't know.

1.14.5 Try to find answers to these questions in the passage that follows:

Does the narrator read the whole book aloud?
What was he waiting for?
Does he find the boy's behaviour normal? (Give reasons.)
What is the relationship between the writer and the boy?

Read on:

> 'Do you want me to read to you?'
> 'All right. If you want to,' said the boy. His face was very white and
> there were dark areas under his eyes. He lay still in the bed and
> seemed very detached from what was going on. I read aloud from
> Howard Pyle's *Book of Pirates*; but I could see he was not following 5
> what I was reading.
> 'How do you feel, Schatz?' I asked him.

'Just the same, so far,' he said.

I sat at the foot of the bed and read to myself while I waited for it to be time to give another capsule. It would have been natural for him to go to sleep, but when I looked up he was looking at the foot of the bed, looking very strangely.

'Why don't you try to go to sleep? I'll wake you up for the medicine.'

'I'd rather stay awake.'

After a while he said to me, 'You don't have to stay in here with me, Papa, if it bothers you.'

'It doesn't bother me.'

'No, I mean you don't have to stay if it's going to bother you.'

I thought perhaps he was a little lightheaded and after giving him the prescribed capsules at eleven o'clock I went out for a while.

Discuss the answers in pairs.

1.14.6 The next extract is more descriptive. The English is quite difficult. Remember, the narrator goes out for a walk.
Read on:

GLOSSARY
sleet (l.1): partly melted snow
brush (l.3): thick growth of small trees and bushes
setter (l.4): type of gun-dog
creek (American use) (l.5): small stream
slipped (l.6): lost balance
slithered (l.6): moved very unsteadily
slide (l.7): move smoothly
flushed (l.8): drove from hiding place
covey (l.8): group
quail (l.8): small game birds
lit in (l.10): descended into
scattered (l.10): went in various directions
mounds (l.11): piles
poised unsteadily (l.13): insecurely balanced
springy brush (l.13): small bushes that jumped back when you stood on them

It was a bright, cold day, the ground covered with a sleet that had frozen so that it seemed as if all the bare trees, the bushes, the cut brush and all the grass and the bare ground had been varnished with ice. I took the young Irish setter for a little walk up the road and along a frozen creek, but it was difficult to stand or walk on the glassy surface and the red dog slipped and slithered and I fell twice, hard, once dropping my gun and having it slide away over the ice.

We flushed a covey of quail under a high bank with overhanging brush and I killed two as they went out of sight over the top of the bank. Some of the covey lit in trees, but most of them scattered into brush piles and it was necessary to jump on the ice-coated mounds of brush several times before they would flush. Coming out while you were poised unsteadily on the icy, springy brush they made difficult shooting and I killed two, missed five, and started back pleased to have found a covey close to the house and happy there were so many left to find on another day.

Answer the following questions in pairs:

Paragraph 1
What time of the year was it?·
How do you know?
What was the narrator carrying?
Why wasn't it easy to walk?

Paragraph 2
How many birds did the narrator kill?
Why was it difficult to kill more?
Why did he feel happy at the end of
    the walk?

1.14.7 Try to find answers to these questions in the passage that follows:

Why didn't the boy let people into his room?
Had he got better?
Why do you think the narrator didn't tell the boy the correct temperature?
What did the narrator give him?
Why did he stop reading to the boy?
Did the boy think he was going to die?
Do you think he is going to die?

At the house they said the boy had refused to let anyone come into
the room.
'You can't come in,' he said. 'You mustn't get what I have.'
I went up to him and found him in exactly the position I had left him,
white-faced, but with the tops of his cheeks flushed by the fever,   5
staring still, as he had stared, at the foot of the bed.
I took his temperature.
'What is it?'
'Something like a hundred,' I said. It was one hundred and two and
four-tenths.   10
'It was a hundred and two,' he said.
'Who said so?'
'The doctor.'
'Your temperature is all right,' I said. 'It's nothing to worry about.'
'I don't worry,' he said, 'but I can't keep from thinking.'   15
'Don't think,' I said. 'Just take it easy.'
'I'm taking it easy,' he said, and looked straight ahead. He was
evidently holding tight on to himself about something.
'Take this with water.'
'Do you think it will do any good?'   20
'Of course it will.'
I sat down and opened the *Pirate* book and commenced to read, but I
could see he was not following, so I stopped.
'About what time do you think I'm going to die?' he asked.
'What?'   25
'About how long will it be before I die?'
'You aren't going to die. What's the matter with you?'

Discuss your answers in pairs.

1.14.8   Try to find answers to these questions in the passage that follows:

How high was the boy's temperature?
Who told the boy what it was?
In what way was the boy confused?
Why did the narrator talk about miles and kilometres?
In your own words, what were the boy's feelings after the explanation?
Can you account for them? Why did he cry easily the next day?

'Oh, yes, I am. I heard him say a hundred and two.'
'People don't die with a fever of one hundred and two. That's a silly
way to talk.'
'I know they do. At school in France the boys told me you can't live
with forty-four degrees. I've got a hundred and two.'   5
He had been waiting to die all day, ever since nine o'clock in the
morning.
'You poor Schatz,' I said. 'Poor old Schatz. It's like miles and
kilometres. You aren't going to die. That's a different thermometer.
On that thermometer thirty-seven is normal. On this kind it's ninety-   10
eight.'
'Absolutely,' I said. 'It's like miles and kilometres. You know, like how
many kilometres we make when we do seventy miles in the car?'
'Oh,' he said.
But his gaze at the foot of the bed relaxed slowly. The hold over   15
himself relaxed too, finally, and the next day it was very slack and he
cried very easily at little things that were of no importance.

GLOSSARY
gaze (l.15): fixed look

Discuss the answers in pairs.

Further questions
How many kilometres are there in a mile?
What does the word 'But' tell you in the last paragraph?

1.14.9   **i** Section 1.14.4: Find the words describing illness explored in 1.14.1. Is
Language   their meaning the same as you had discussed?

    ii Section 1.14.6:
        – Underline words that describe the landscape
        – Circle words that describe the weather
        – Write adjective, noun or verb next to each
        – What verb tense is mainly used in this section? Why?
        – Are the sentences shorter or longer in this section than the rest of the
          story? Why?
        – Check in a dictionary that you understand the difference in meaning
          between

            slip   slither   slide

iii The phrase 'a covey of quail' is used. What are the collective nouns to describe the following:

a _____ of cows
a _____ of sheep
a _____ of wolves
a _____ of bees

iv 'Sleet' is a word used to mean partly melted falling snow. What are the following:

small pellets of ice falling from clouds: h_____

watery melting snow on the ground: sl_____

1.14.10
Discussion

i Discuss the differences between the passage in 1.14.6 and the rest of the story.
ii What does it tell you? What effect does it have on the story?
iii What did you think of the man going shooting while the boy was sick?
iv Did you enjoy the story? (Give reasons.)
v Do you approve of blood sports? What sort of person usually enjoys them?

1.14.11
Follow-up work

Either: In pairs, tell each other about a walk you have taken – if you have! – in similar weather.
Or: Write about a death or a serious illness based on your own experience.

1.14.12
Notes

The author of the story, Ernest Hemingway, was born in 1899 in Illinois, U.S.A. He was a keen skier, fisherman and hunter and enjoyed bullfighting. His novels include For Whom the Bell Tolls, A Farewell to Arms *and* The Old Man and the Sea. *They reflect his hedonistic, 'masculine' nature as well as his fascination with war. In 1961 he killed himself with a shotgun.*

1.15 Background

1.15.1

Look back over the Unit. Find out more about one writer you liked. Make notes under the following:

1 Education
2 Marriage/children (if any)
3 Where lived/living

4 Main achievements
5 Main historical events and social changes in lifetime.

Share your findings with the rest of your class. Enter them on a 'biography card' under the author's name. Why not try to keep a card index of authors throughout the course?

1.16 Conclusion

1.16.1

i Which passages/poems etc. in the Unit did you like and which didn't you like? (Give reasons.)

ii Which did you think was the best written? (Give reasons.)

UNIT 2

What it's about

2.1 On the surface

2.1.1 Anticipation

Look at this picture:

Discuss in pairs:

i   Imagine waking up in a strange land where you were very big and
    everyone else was very small. Make a list of words (or write two
    sentences about each) which describe:

    – what you might feel towards the small people (e.g. pity)
    – what they might feel towards you (e.g. horror)

ii How do you think the man in the picture got there?
    What do you think the situation is?

2.1.2 **i** Read the following passage:

I lay down on the grass, which was very short and soft, where I slept
sounder than ever I remember to have done in my life, and, as I
reckoned, above nine hours; for when I awaked it was just daylight. I
attempted to rise, but was not able to stir: for as I happened to lie on
my back, I found my arms and legs were strongly fastened on each   5
side to the ground; my hair, which was long and thick, tied down in
the same manner. I like-wise felt several slender ligatures across my
body, from my armpits to my thighs. I could only look upwards, the
sun began to grow hot, and the light offended mine eyes. I heard a
confused noise about me, but, in the posture I lay, could see nothing   10
except the sky. In a little time I felt something alive moving on my left
leg, which advancing gently forward over my breast, came almost up
to my chin; when bending my eyes downwards as much as I could, I
perceived it to be a human creature not six inches high, with a bow
and arrow in his hands, and a quiver at his back. In the meantime, I   15
felt at least forty more of the same kind (as I conjectured) following
the first. I was in the utmost astonishment, and roared so loud, that
they all ran back in a fright; and some of them, as I was afterwards
told, were hurt with the falls they got by leaping from my sides upon
the ground.   20

GLOSSARY
ligatures (l.7): things used
    for tying up
quiver (l.15): case for
    arrows
utmost (l.17): most
    extreme

Help each other to understand as much as possible.

ii Improving understanding

Write T (true) F (false) DK (don't know) next to the following
sentences. Re-write the false sentences to make them true.

The extract is from an autobiography.
It is narrated in the first person singular.
It is mainly written in the past simple tense.

The narrator slept very badly.
He woke up at dawn.
He couldn't get up.
It was a cold day.
He found it difficult to see who was standing on him.
Only one person was able to stand on him.
He frightened them all when he shouted.

Compare in pairs.

2.1.3 **i** The story is about a man called Gulliver, who is shipwrecked in the
land of Lilliput.

You are going to read another extract which almost follows on from the
previous one. Find out:

How Gulliver was attacked
What it felt like
What his plan was

I heard one of them cry aloud, *Tolgo phonac*, when in an instant I felt above an hundred arrows discharged on my left hand, which pricked me like so many needles; and besides, they shot another flight into the air, as we do bombs in Europe, whereof many I suppose fell on my body (though I felt them not), and some on my face, which I immediately covered with my left hand. When this shower of arrows was over, I fell a-groaning with grief and pain, and then striving again to get loose, they discharged another volley larger than the first, and some of them attempted with spears to stick me in the sides; but, by good luck, I had on me a buff jerkin, which they could not pierce. I thought it the most prudent method to lie still, and my design was to continue so till night, when my left hand being already loose, I could easily free myself: and as for the inhabitants, I had reason to believe I might be a match for the greatest armies they could bring against me, if they were all of the same size with him that I saw. But Fortune disposed otherwise of me.

5

10

15

GLOSSARY
Tolgo phonac (l.1): (some Lilliputian language!)
whereof (l.4): of which
volley (l.8): succession of shots fired at the same time
buff jerkin (l.10): leather jacket without sleeves

In pairs, help each other to understand the passage. Discuss answers to the questions. What do you think will happen next?

ii Language
Say whether each of the words in the left-hand column in context is a verb, adjective or noun. Match them with the definitions on the right:

groaning	struggling
grief	cautious
striving	penetrate
pierce	making a sound expressing pain
prudent	dealt with
disposed (of)	deep sadness

2.1.4   i Read another extract from a bit further on in the book:

The Hurgo (for so they call a great lord, as I afterwards learnt) understood me very well. He descended from the stage, and commanded that several ladders should be applied to my sides, on which above an hundred of the inhabitants mounted, and walked towards my mouth, laden with baskets full of meat, which had been provided and sent thither by the King's orders, upon the first intelligence he received of me. I observed there was the flesh of several animals, but could not distinguish them by the taste. There were shoulders, legs, and loins, shaped like those of mutton, and very well dressed, but smaller than the wings of a lark. I ate them by two or three at a mouthful, and took three loaves at a time, about the bigness of musket bullets.

5

10

GLOSSARY
stage (l.2): raised platform
laden with (l.5): carrying with difficulty
thither (l.6): to that place
musket (l.12): long-barrelled shoulder gun carried by foot soldiers (16th–18th century)

31

ii What do you think has happened between extracts?

iii Underline words/phrases which show what they gave him to eat.

2.1.5   **i** Read the next extract:

I had three hundred cooks to dress my victuals, in little convenient huts built about my house, where they and their families lived, and prepared me two dishes apiece. I took up twenty waiters in my hand, and placed them on the table; an hundred more attended below on the ground, some with dishes of meat, and some with barrels of wine 5 and other liquors, slung on their shoulders, all which the waiters above drew up as I wanted, in a very ingenious manner, by certain cords, as we draw the bucket up a well in Europe. A dish of their meat was a good mouthful, and a barrel of their liquor a reasonable draught. Their mutton yields to ours, but their beef is excellent. I have 10 had a sirloin so large, that I have been forced to make three bits of it; but this is rare. My servants were astonished to see me eat it bones and all, as in our country we do the leg of a lark. Their geese and turkeys I usually ate at a mouthful; and, I must confess, they far exceed ours. 15

GLOSSARY
victuals (l.1): food
apiece (l.3): each

---

ii Language

Find a word/phrase in the passage which means the following:

thrown carelessly   is inferior

very clever   are better than

iii Improving understanding

From the extracts so far, build up a picture of the inhabitants of Lilliput under the following headings:

SIZE:_____

NAME FOR THE MOST IMPORTANT LILLIPUTIAN HE MET:_____

ATTITUDE TO GULLIVER:_____

LANGUAGE:_____

WEAPONS USED:_____

FOOD:_____

WAY OF LIFE:_____

MISCELLANEOUS:_____

Use a separate piece of paper.

iv Discussion

Discuss in pairs how you would feel and what you would do in Gulliver's situation.

2.1.6   *The previous extracts are from the* Voyage to Lilliput, *the first book in* Gulliver's Travels
Notes   *(written 1721-5, published 1726) by Jonathan Swift (1667-1745). Swift was born in Dublin of English parentage. He wrote both political propaganda and satire.*

2.1.7
Style

In this part of the book, Swift sounds like a plain man telling a plain tale. He is imitating the style of contemporary travel books. And yet what he is describing is not ordinary at all. It is extraordinary. By putting ordinary people in extraordinary situations, Swift is able to satirise human attitudes and behaviour, as you will see in the next section.

2.2 Beneath the surface

2.2.1
Anticipation

This following extract from Gulliver's Travels *comes from the next book* A Voyage to Brobdingnag.

i Look at the picture.

Gulliver is in Brobdingnag. What is the difference between the land of Lilliput and the land of Brobdingnag? Who do you think the large hand might belong to? What is Gulliver, the small man, doing?

ii Imagine waking up in a strange land where you were very small and everyone else was very big. Make a list of words (or write two sentences about each) which describe:
– what you might feel towards the big people
– what they might feel towards you.

What would your life be like?

iii What do you think Gulliver's life is like now in comparison to his life in Lilliput?

33

2.2.2   **i**   Read the following extract:

It now began to be known and talked of in the neighbourhood that
my master had found a strange animal in the field, about the bigness
of a *splacknuck*, but exactly shaped in every part like a human
creature; which it likewise imitated in all its actions; seemed to speak
in a little language of its own, had already learned several words of   5
theirs, went erect upon two legs, was tame and gentle, would come
when it was called, do whatever it was bid, had the finest limbs in the
world, and a complexion fairer than a nobleman's daughter of three
years old. Another farmer who lived hard by, and was a particular
friend of my master, came on a visit on purpose to enquire into the   10
truth of this story. I was immediately produced, and placed upon a
table, where I walked as I was commanded, drew my hanger, put it
up again, made my reverence to my master's guest, asked him in his
own language how he did, and told him he was welcome, just as my
little nurse had instructed me. This man, who was old and dim-   15
sighted, put on his spectacles to behold me better, at which I could
not forbear laughing very heartily, for his eyes appeared like the full
moon shining into a chamber at two windows. Our people, who
discovered the cause of my mirth, bore me company in laughing, at
which the old fellow was fool enough to be angry and out of   20
countenance.

GLOSSARY
splacknuck (l.3): (some
   Brobdingnagian
   language!)
hanger (l.12): sword
made my reverence (l.13):
   bowed
forbear (l.17): cease
out of countenance (l.20–21):
   disconcerted

In pairs, re-tell Gulliver's situation in your own words.

ii   Improving understanding
Not everything is explicit. We learn a lot about the attitude of the
inhabitants of Brobdingnag to Gulliver from the following phrases:

my master
shaped in every part like a human creature
a little language of its own
do whatever it was bid
I was immediately produced
I was commanded
made my reverence
my little nurse had instructed me

Say what they suggest.
What effect does the 'passive voice' have? (e.g. 'I was produced'
instead of 'they produced me')

How has life changed for Gulliver? Is the passage written with such
good humour as the passages about Lilliput? (Give reasons, if
possible.)

2.2.3   **i**   Read another extract:

My master, pursuant to the advice of his friend, carried me in a box the next market-day to the neighbouring town, and took along with him his little daughter, my nurse, upon a pillion behind him. The box was close on every side, with a little door for me to go in and out, and a few gimlet holes to let in air. The girl had been so careful to put the quilt of her baby's bed into it, for me to lie down on. However, I was terribly shaken and discomposed in this journey, though it were but of half an hour. For the horse went about forty feet at every step, and trotted so high, that the agitation was equal to the rising and falling of a ship in a great storm, but much more frequent: our journey was somewhat further than from London to St. Albans.

ii   Improving understanding

Answer the following questions:

How did Gulliver feel?

Why was he 'shaken and discomposed'?

What is the girl's attitude to him? How do you know?

Where do you think they are taking him and why?

iii   Language

What do you think the following mean in context:

quilt   trotted

iv   Discussion

Imagine what it would be like to be kept in a box and taken on a journey. Describe your feelings in pairs. What would you do in Gulliver's situation?

2.2.4   **i**   Read another extract:

I was placed upon a table in the largest room of the inn, which might be near three hundred foot square. My little nurse stood on a low stool close to the table, to take care of me, and direct what I should do. My master, to avoid a crowd, would suffer only thirty people at a time to see me. I walked about on the table as the girl commanded: she asked me questions, as far as she knew my understanding of the language reached, and I answered them as loud as I could. I turned about several times to the company, paid my humble respects, said they were welcome, and used some other speeches I had been taught. I took up a thimble filled with liquor, which Glumdalclitch had given me for a cup, and drank their health. I drew out my hanger, and flourished with it after the manner of fencers in England. My nurse gave me part of a straw, which I exercised as a pike, having learned the art in my youth. I was that day shown to twelve sets of company, and as often forced to go over again the same fopperies, till I was half dead with weariness and vexation.

ii Improving understanding

What were they doing to him?

Why do you think they were doing it?

iii Beneath the surface

Obviously, Gulliver's feelings are revealed in phrases such as 'weariness and vexation' but otherwise Swift is not very explicit about them. He hopes that the facts themselves will arouse our human feelings.

Which words describe your attitude about the treatment Gulliver receives? Look up any you don't know in a dictionary.

Tick those you feel suitable/appropriate. Add your own words.

angry	indifferent	shocked
upset	concerned	indignant
hurt	amused	

iv Discussion

What aspects of human behaviour is Swift satirising in this episode? Can you think of an example of similar behaviour either from your own experience or in recent history? (e.g. with an unusual foreigner, a strange animal or a child prodigy). How do you think we would treat Martians if they landed on Earth?!

2.2.5
Extension
Get hold of a copy of *Gulliver's Travels*. Read the two parts, the *Voyage to Lilliput* and the *Voyage to Brobdingnag* and discuss them with your class.

2.2.6
Background
Either:

Look in an encyclopaedia for help and write out a 'biography card' for Swift to include:

MAJOR LITERARY WORKS (AND DATES):

RELIGION:

POLITICS:

OTHER POINTS OF INTEREST:

Or:

Here are some things that happened in Swift's lifetime:

i Tick those which:

– interest you

– you think are important when considering the year *Gulliver's Travels* was written

1707 An Act of Union made Scotland and England one country (Great Britain).

1714 The death of Queen Anne, thus ending the reign of the Stuarts. The Georgian period began under George I of Hanover who could hardly speak English.

1719   *Robinson Crusoe* published. Readers were becoming interested in non-European cultures.
Traders had begun to travel to distant lands and brought back potatoes, sugar, spices, tea and coffee.

1721   The Treaty of Nystadt between Russia and Sweden marked the end of Swedish dominance in Northern Europe and the rise of Russia.

1715-1774 The reign of Louis XV in France.

ii   Discuss in pairs.

2.3   Guesses and predictions

Sometimes the title of a play or a novel or a poem will give an indication of what it is about. It may also help you decide whether or not it will interest you.

2.3.1   Look at the following titles:

Bleak House

White Fang

The Love Song of J. Alfred Prufrock

Look Back in Anger

In Memoriam

The Pilgrim's Progress

Much Ado about Nothing

Pride and Prejudice

(Look up any other words you don't know in a dictionary.)

i   Which titles interest you?

ii   Say whether you think each is
– a play
– a poem
– a novel
Is it possible to tell?

iii   What do you think they might be about? (Of course, if you *know* you will have a distinct advantage!)

iv   Now try to match the titles with these descriptions:

1   A long poem by Tennyson celebrating his dead friend.
2   A play by the contemporary playwright, John Osborne, about a man who, in condemning the times in which he lives, looks back at the past.

3 Dickens' dark novel about decay and corruption at the heart of English society.
4 A religious allegory about a man journeying towards salvation, written by Bunyan.
5 The story of a wild animal, one quarter dog, three quarters wolf, eventually tamed by Man – by the writer Jack London.
6 A novel by Jane Austen in which the manners and morals of early 19th century society are explored with humour and a delicate irony.
7 A poem by T. S. Eliot about a middle-aged man, remembering his romantic dreams, expressing his disillusionment with the modern world.
8 An early Shakespearian comedy whose complicated plots are finally resolved in a happy ending.

Discuss in pairs.

v **Extension**
Get hold of a copy of one of these books and see if it interests you.

2.4 Focus on understanding

Things you have probably found difficult in this book:

– the words (the exercises encourage you to ask each other for help, to make guesses by making use of the context, to look in your dictionaries, to ask your teacher; very difficult, unusual or out-of-date words can be found in the glossaries).
– the grammar (you may have problems with structures which are used differently in everyday, contemporary English).
– the thoughts and feelings expressed.

Many of these most native speakers find difficult too!
Many of the exercises are meant to do some of the following:

– guide you towards the general idea of the poem or passage
– help you extract important detail from it
– help you distinguish what is important from what is not so important
– direct you towards a fuller understanding of what is beneath the surface

The first time you read a difficult poem or passage you can probably only

either: get the general idea (and miss the detail!)

or: pick out some detail (and miss the general idea!)

The exercises take this into account. On subsequent re-readings, though, you will be encouraged to try to get beneath the surface. What is the writer really expressing?

With whole books, don't get discouraged! Try to understand as much as you can. Read and re-read what interests you.

2.5 Working with vocabulary

i The following words all have associations with fear. In pairs, agree on their meanings. Write out any you don't know and either a) ask another student what they mean, b) ask the teacher, c) look the word up in a dictionary.

blood	terror	threaten
faintness	horrible	ghastly
sickness	torment	pallor
clammy	weapon	beat
cruel	shriek	apprehensive
gruesome	victim	panic

ii Put the words into the following columns (some may go in more than one column)

NOUNS	VERBS	ADJECTIVES

Write in related class words for some of them.

	NOUN	VERB	ADJECTIVES
e.g.	terror	terrify	terrified
		terrorise	terrifying
			terrorised

Write Tr (transitive) or Int (intransitive) next to the verbs. (A transitive verb has to be followed by a direct object e.g. he terrified the town. 'The town' is a direct object in this sentence so 'terrify' is transitive. If in any doubt, consult your dictionary.)

iii Try to match the words for parts of the body in the left-hand column with the verbal expression relating to fear on the right (the first one has been done for you). They are more literary than colloquial expressions.

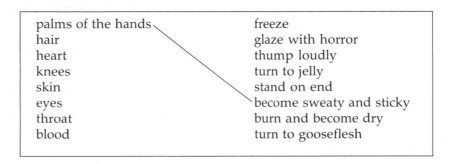

palms of the hands	freeze
hair	glaze with horror
heart	thump loudly
knees	turn to jelly
skin	stand on end
eyes	become sweaty and sticky
throat	burn and become dry
blood	turn to gooseflesh

What expressions in your language describe the physical sensation of fear?

2.5.2 Look at the following photographs:

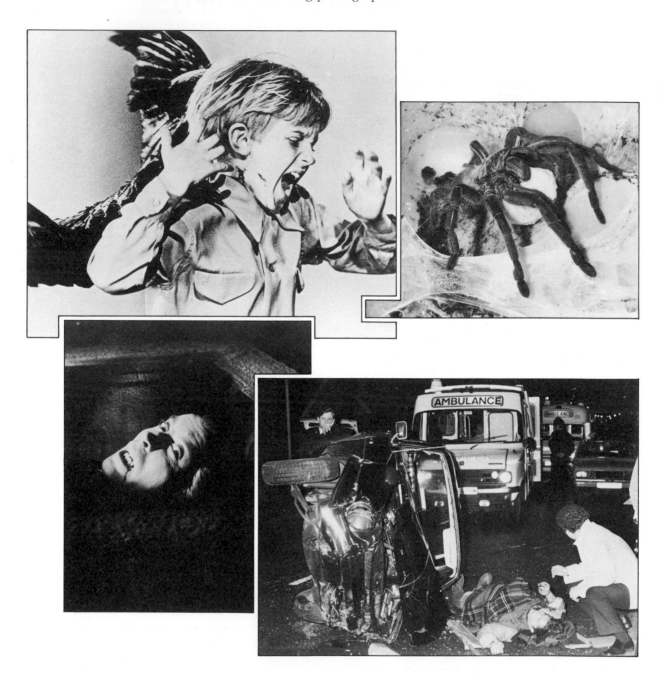

Discuss in pairs:

   i   how many of these situations arouse sensations of fear?

   ii   what kind of situations frighten you?

   iii   what stories/films have frightened you?

   iv   is the sensation always fear or are there mixed emotions?

2.5.3   **i** Listen to the following extracts from *Hamlet* (first printed 1603). Horatio, Hamlet's friend, tells Hamlet that two soldiers on watch at the castle saw the spirit of Hamlet's dead father appear to them:

a)

GLOSSARY
truncheon (l.3): straight stick carried as a sign of power

'Thrice he walked
By their oppressed and fear-surprised eyes
Within his truncheon's length, whilst they, distilled
Almost to jelly with the act of fear,
Stand dumb and speak not to him.'   5

b) A little later, the ghost appears to Hamlet and speaks to him:

GLOSSARY
doomed (l.2): destined
fast (l.3): suffer torment
days of nature (l.4): lifetime
But that (l.5): If it were not for the fact that
unfold (l.7): tell
harrow (l.8): cause distress to
thy (l.8): your
start from their spheres (l.9): jump out of their sockets
locks (l.10): strands of hair
quills (l.12): spines
fretful porpentine (l.12): bad-tempered porcupine

'I am thy father's spirit,
Doomed for a certain term to walk the night,
And for the day confined to fast in fires,
Till the foul crimes done in my days of nature
Are burnt and purged away. But that I am forbid   5
To tell the secrets of my prison house,
I could a tale unfold, whose lightest word
Would harrow up thy soul, freeze thy young blood,
Make thy two eyes like stars start from their spheres,
Thy knotted and combined locks to part,   10
And each particular hair to stand on end
Like quills upon the fretful porpentine.'

ii   Improving understanding
In pairs help each other to understand the passages.
Tick which of the following you think are true:

Passage a)
The ghost has walked three times
'Their' refers to the two soldiers
The ghost was very far away
The soldiers were very frightened
They spoke to the ghost

Passage b)
The ghost only appears during the day
He is compelled to appear
He spends the nights in agony
He is made to suffer for his sins
He is not allowed to tell about his life after death
He is in purgatory
Hearing about purgatory would terrify Hamlet

iii **Language**

Which phrases suggest sensations related to fear?

What expressions and ideas might arouse feelings of apprehension and excitement in the audience?

2.5.4   i   Read this following more complex extract from *Macbeth*

Here Macbeth is alone before he goes to murder King Duncan, who is asleep in bed, the guest of Macbeth and Lady Macbeth. He is speaking to himself (this is known as a soliloquy) – and the audience!

GLOSSARY

sensible to feeling (l.5–6): able to be touched

thou marshall'st me the way (l.11): you guide me in the direction

dudgeon (l.15): wooden handle

gouts (l.15): large drops

o'er the one half world (l.18): over that 'half-world' where it is night

curtained (l.20): (in Shakespeare's time beds had curtains drawn round them for privacy)

Pale Hecate's offerings (l.21): offerings to the goddess of witchcraft

sure (l.22): safe

prate (l.24): talk idly

which now suits with it (l.26): which is now suitable for it

heat of deeds (l.27): deeds (acts) are 'hot' – mere words are 'cold'

knell (l.29): sound of a bell rung to announce a death

Is this a dagger which I see before me,
The handle toward my hand? (*He speaks to the dagger*) Come,
let me clutch thee:-
I have thee not, and yet I see thee still.
Art thou not, fatal vision, sensible   5
To feeling as to sight? or art thou but
A dagger of the mind, a false creation,
Proceeding from the heat-oppressed brain?
I see thee yet, in form as palpable
As this which now I draw.   10
Thou marshall'st me the way that I was going;
And such an instrument I was to use. –
Mine eyes are made the fools o' the other senses,
Or else worth all the rest: I see thee still;
And on thy blade and dudgeon gouts of blood,   15
Which was not so before. – There's no such thing.
It is the bloody business which informs
Thus to mine eyes. – Now o'er the one half world
Nature seems dead, and wicked dreams abuse
The curtained sleep: witchcraft celebrates   20
Pale Hecate's offerings; ...

... – Thou sure and firm-set earth,
Hear not my steps, which way they walk, for fear
Thy very stones prate of my where-about,
And take the present horror from the time,   25
Which now suits with it. Whiles I threat, he lives:
Words to the heat of deeds too cold breath gives.

(*A bell rings.*

I go, and it is done: the bell invites me.
Hear it not, Duncan; for it is a knell
That summons thee to heaven or to hell.   30

(*Exit

ii Improving understanding

Read the extract again. Help each other to understand as much as possible.

a) Say in which lines:

– Macbeth is addressing the dagger
– he is addressing nobody or nothing in particular
– he is addressing the earth

Are the distinctions clear?

b) Tick which of the following you think are true:

Macbeth can see a real dagger in front of him.
He can see it but cannot touch it.
He draws his own dagger but this does not seem
   as real to him as the one in front of him.
The dagger in front of him is leading him to Duncan
Suddenly he sees his own dagger is covered with blood
He thinks what he sees is caused by fear
He is frightened that his footsteps will give away
   his movement
He thinks that a feeling of horror is quite unsuited
   to the occasion
Throughout the speech he is trying to summon up the
   courage to commit murder
He thinks words are better than actions
He decides not to commit the murder.

iii Language

Which phrases suggest Macbeth's own feelings of fear?
Which phrases arouse fear in the audience?

iv Shakespeare's language

In Shakespeare's time the English used to have a singular pronoun for addressing friends, relatives or servants. The subject form was THOU; the object form was THEE; the possessive form was THINE. There was also a possessive adjective, THY.

The verb associated with the subject THOU ended in -st or -est.
For example:
thou goest, thou walkest (or *thou walk'st*), *thou dost* (pronounced 'dust')

The verbs 'to be' and 'to have' were irregular.
   thou art, thou hast

YOU was used for the plural (as it is today) or as the polite form of the singular. Look back over this extract from *Macbeth* and underline examples. What or who do they refer to?

2.5.5
Discussion Discuss in pairs:

    i What impression did the extracts from *Hamlet* and *Macbeth* make on you? Did you like them?

    ii Look at the following pictures:

Do they accurately convey the impression the passages made on you? How do you think the ghost and the dagger should be presented on stage?

2.5.6
Background Prepare a biography card for Shakespeare. Consult an encyclopaedia.

2.5.7
Extension *Either:* Learn by heart bits of the speeches and act them out in the classroom.

Or: Find out about the 'plots' of *Hamlet* and *Macbeth* and write them on a card to accompany the biography card for Shakespeare.

2.6 Making comparisons

2.6.1 Why do writers very often compare what they are describing with something else? For example:

> 'Shall I compare thee to a summer's day?
> Thou art more lovely and more temperate.'
>
> *(Shakespeare)*

Two main reasons:

i to help the reader see what is being described more clearly, more vividly and with more force.

ii to extend the range of meaning and suggestion

so:

> Day after day, day after day
> We stuck, nor breath, nor motion
> *As idle as a painted ship*
> *Upon a painted ocean.*
>
> *(Coleridge)*

What is being described here? The narrator's ship motionless on the sea, waiting for a wind to blow its sails.

What is it being compared to? A painting of a ship.

What the two have in common is *motionlessness*. However, a ship in a painting *never* moves. This gives the image of the narrator's ship, in a real sea unable to move, greater intensity. The comparison is an exaggeration of course – presumably wind will come sometime – but because we often exaggerate when our feelings are intense we are helped to feel the narrator's sense of frustration at being unable to move. The writer hasn't told us this explicitly; he creates the feeling in us. In this way the poem's range of meaning has been extended.

2.6.2
Techniques used for comparison

Similes
The words 'like' or 'as' are used. For example:

a)

> FOIBLE Your Ladyship has frowned a little too rashly indeed madam. There are some cracks discernible in the white varnish.
>
> LADY WISHFORT Let me see the glass – cracks sayest thou? Why – I look like an old peeled wall.
>
> *(Congreve)*

The face and the wall have cracks in common but as in many comparisons of this sort it is the *dis*similarity between them which intensifies the image and, in this case, makes it funny.

b)

> Golden lads and girls, all must
> As chimney sweepers, come to dust.
>
> *(Shakespeare)*

Here the dissimilarity between 'golden lads and girls' (clear, bright, colourful, innocent) and chimney sweepers (dirty, black, somehow degraded) also intensifies the image. What they have in common is that they both die. This is witty because the phrase 'come to dust' can mean both 'die' and when the chimney sweepers sweep the chimney 'reach the dust they are sweeping'.

ii **Metaphors**

The thing described *becomes* the thing it is compared to but the function is similar to that of the simile:

> The pink spider of a hand beats the guitar.
>
> *(Katherine Mansfield)*

Here instead of saying 'his pink hand is like a spider' she says the 'pink spider of a hand'. Again there is *similarity* in that the long fingers look like spiders' legs, but *dissimilarity* in the exaggeration: the fingers weren't really so thin! The range of meaning and suggestion has been extended in that since we guess the writer is repulsed by spiders we deduce she is also repulsed by the sight of the hand!

iii *Metaphors* and *similes* together form the main part of a writer's *imagery*. Some images are effective; some are not. Many are cliches (stereotyped expressions) and say nothing: e.g. he appeared as if by magic; he was as white as a ghost. They awaken nothing in us. Others are idiosyncratic and distract us from the very thing they set out to describe.

**2.6.3
Consolidation**

In pairs, discuss the following extracts.

Say:
– what the images are made up of.
– what effect they have.
– how the effect is achieved.
– how you would describe the images (e.g. vivid, effective, powerful, weak, horrible etc.).

i

GLOSSARY
skein: coil
railing: fence with metal bars

> Like a skein of loose silk blown against a wall
> She walks by the railing of a path in Kensington Gardens.
>
> *(Ezra Pound)*

ii

> The sand is settling into the sea like powder into the curls of a stale wig.
>
> *(Lawrence Durrell)*

iii

> Now does he feel
> His secret murders sticking on his hands.
>
> *(Shakespeare)*

iv

> The winter evening settles down
> with smell of steaks in passageways
> Six o'clock
> The burnt-out ends of smoky days.
>
> *(T. S. Eliot)*

2.7 Looking at the more difficult words

2.7.1
Anticipation

i Look at these two pictures:

Discuss the following questions:

What is the difference in attitude between the two teachers?

What is the difference in how the children are expected to learn?

Which classroom situation do you think is better?

ii Tick which of the following you agree with:

I think a teacher must be: authoritative
patient
talkative
happy
silent
kind
dictatorial

Add other words.

iii Discuss which of the following you agree with:
Schooldays are the best days of your life.
In education, you should only teach facts.
Teachers should develop their students' imaginations.
Learning is learning things by heart.
Fantasy can be dangerous in the modern world.
Children need a sense of wonder.

Change the words of any statement you don't agree with so that it expresses your opinion.

2.7.2 i Listen to the following and decide:
Who is talking to whom and where.
What the speaker's view of children is.
What his view of education is.

 'Now, what I want is, Facts. Teach these boys and girls nothing but Facts. Facts alone are wanted in life. Plant nothing else, and root out everything else. You can only form the minds of reasoning animals upon Facts: nothing else will ever be of any service to them. This is the principle on which I bring up my own children, and this is the principle on which I bring up these children. Stick to Facts, sir!'

ii What is the speaker trying to convey by the phrase 'root out'?

iii Discuss in pairs.

2.7.3
Vocabulary i Read the next extract quickly. There will probably be many words you don't know. At this stage, leave them; get only a rough idea of what the passage is about. Some of the words are missing. Don't try and fill them in yet. Simply write the word *adjective*, *noun* or *verb* above each space according to the meaning.

The scene was a plain, bare, (1) _____vault of a schoolroom, and the speaker's square forefinger emphasised his observations by underscoring every sentence with a line on the schoolmaster's sleeve. The emphasis was helped by the speaker's (2) _____wall of a forehead, which had his eyebrows for its base, while his eyes found commodious cellarage in two dark caves, over-shadowed by the wall. The emphasis was helped by the speaker's mouth, which was wide, thin, and (3) _____. The emphasis was helped by the speaker's voice, which was inflexible, dry, and (4) _____.The emphasis was helped by the speaker's hair, which bristled on the skirts of his bald head, a plantation of firs to keep the wind from its shining surface, all covered with knobs, like the (5) _____of a plum pie, as if the head had scarcely warehouse-room for the hard facts stored inside. The speaker's obstinate carriage, square coat, square legs, square shoulders – nay, his very neckcloth, trained to take him by the throat with an unaccommodating grasp, like a (6) _____fact, as it was – all helped the emphasis.

5

10

15

ii Listen to the whole extract. Write in the missing words in the spaces as you hear them. If you don't know the word guess the meaning and the spelling.
The answers are in the Key at the back of the book.

iii Check the meaning and spelling of the missing words in a dictionary.

iv Look at the meanings of the following words:

vault (l.1): underground room often used for burying people
emphasised (l.2): stressed
cellarage (l.6): cellar-like area
inflexible (l.9): rigid
skirts (l.11): borders
firs (l.11): coniferous trees
carriage (l.14): manner or movement
nay (l.15): no (or 'indeed')
grasp (l.16): firm hold

v In pairs, discuss any of the following words you don't know. Guess what they might mean in context. Look carefully at the context.

bare	commodious	plantation	warehouse-room
underscoring	overshadowed	shining	stored
sleeve	bristled	knobs	obstinate
forehead	bald	plum pie	unaccommodating

Look up in a dictionary any words you can't guess.

2.7.4
Improving
understanding

Read the whole passage again.
What do you think of the man described? Would you like him as your headmaster? Can you draw what you think he looks like? (Add as many details as you can.) Show each other your pictures. What does the word 'square' tell you about the man and his attitudes?

i   Write out phrases from the passage under the following headings:

SIMILES   METAPHORS

What are his eyes compared to?
What is his hair compared to?
What is his head compared to?

ii   What words are used to describe the schoolroom?

In what way do they relate to the description of the speaker?

iii   Put a box round the noun 'emphasis' and the verb 'emphasise' in the passage. How many sentences begin:

'The emphasis was helped ...'?
What effect does the repetition have?

The previous extracts are from *Hard Times* by Charles Dickens.

Write an essay giving your views on education, making reference to the beginning of *Hard Times*.

i   Read the following account to help you build up a 'biography card' for Dickens. Try to make your card lively and interesting, perhaps with pictures – not just the plain 'facts'!
Perhaps consult a reference book. First, discuss in pairs the headings you will use.

Charles Dickens was born near Portsmouth in 1812, the year Napoleon invaded Russia. He was the son of a clerk in a Navy Pay office. Schooling was fairly primitive for large sections of the community in those days, and Dickens himself never went to school regularly. In fact it wasn't until Victoria became Queen in 1837 that the Government began to build schools for working-class children. Even then, though, the best chance of education for the poor was to learn religion, morality and reading in a Church or Charity School. An alphabet book in those days began: A stands for Angel who praises the Lord, B stands for Bible that teaches God's will. In 1824 the family moved to London. Dickens worked for a time in a warehouse; his father was imprisoned for debt.

Throughout Britain manufacturing towns were springing up in the Midlands and the North of England – around the coal mines and the iron industry – and people moved in from the country to work in the factories. Much of the old village and family stability was destroyed and while there was wealth created through business there was also great poverty.

In Dickens' lifetime the middle-class and the business class grew in strength and there were many discoveries and inventions (e.g. 1832 – the electric telegraph, 1847 – chloroform used for the first time as an anaesthetic, 1859 – Darwin published the Origin of Species, although the scientific 'spirit of the times' probably culminated in the Great Exhibition in 1851, organised by Prince Albert to show British goods to visitors from all over the world.) It was the time, too, for the growth of public libraries, evening classes and museums.

Dickens worked with a solicitor and later became a Parliamentary journalist before he married Catherine Hogarth in 1836, the year his first book Sketches by Boz was published. Hard Times was a comparatively late book, not written until 1854. A portrait of a Lancashire mill town in the 1840s, the book shows how both education and industrialisation can damage the human spirit and its essential goodness.

Dickens was overall a hugely successful writer. He died in 1870 after a strenuous reading tour of the U.S.A. in 1867.

ii Why do you think the novel was called *Hard Times*?

iii Do you know what important European events – unconnected with Dickens – occurred in 1848 and 1854–6?

iv Write a paragraph about the state of education in your country in 1854. Compare it with education in your country now.

2.8 Making us feel what is meant

2.8.1
Anticipation

i What differences in use are there between the words:

fantasy   wonder (noun)?

Which word is the more likely to be used pejoratively?

ii Which of these – if any – suggest a sense of wonder? What feelings do they arouse in you?

iii What other things can you think of that suggest fantasy? What other things suggest a sense of wonder?

Discuss in pairs.

2.8.2 i Read the following:

> To me the word Galilee has a wonderful sound. The Lake of Galilee! I don't want to know where it is. I never want to go to Palestine. Galilee is one of those lovely, glamorous worlds, not places, that exist in the golden haze of a child's half-formed imagination. And in my man's imagination it is just the same. It has been left untouched . . . 5
>
> The moon, perhaps, has shrunken a little. One has been forced to learn, about orbits, eclipses, relative distances, dead worlds, craters of the moon, and so on . . .
>
> . . . willy-nilly, the intrusion of the mental process dims the brilliance, the magic of the first apperception. 10
>
> It is the same with all things. The sheer delight of a child's apperception is based on *wonder*, and deny it as we may, knowledge and wonder counteract one another. So that as knowledge increases wonder decreases . . . Anybody who looks at the moon and says, 'I know all about that poor orb', is, of course, bored by the moon. 15
>
> Now the great and fatal fruit of our civilisation, which is a civilisation based on knowledge, and hostile to experience, is boredom. All our wonderful education and learning is producing a grand sum-total of boredom. Modern people are inwardly thoroughly bored. Do as they may, they are bored. 20
>
> They are bored because they experience nothing. And they experience nothing because the wonder has gone out of them. And when the wonder has gone out of a man he is dead. He is henceforth only an insect.

GLOSSARY
haze (l.4): obscured perception
craters (l.7): bowl-shaped depressions
willy-nilly (l.9): whether we like it or not
apperception (l.10): conscious awareness
sheer (l.11): complete
henceforth (l.23): from this time on

ii This is an explicit statement of the writer's point of view (i.e. it is plainly and clearly expressed). Do you agree with it? Does he make us feel what he feels? If so, how does he do it? Do you think the word 'Galilee' creates in him a sense of wonder as he is writing? How does the writer's view contrast with the headmaster's in *Hard Times*?

iii **Notes**

The writer is D. H. Lawrence (1885-1930). He wrote several novels, many poems and short stories, travel books and essays. He was also a painter. His style as you can see from the previous extract from an essay called Hymns to a Man's Life *is very lively and direct and sounds as though someone is speaking rather than writing.*

2.8.3 **i** Lawrence also wrote a poem called *Last Lesson of the Afternoon* (which is abridged here). Read it and help each other to understand as much as possible.

> When will the bell ring, and end this weariness?
> How long have they tugged the leash, and strained apart,
> My pack of unruly hounds! I cannot start
> Them again on a quarry of knowledge they hate to hunt,
> I can haul them and urge them no more.   5
>
> ....
>
> I will not waste my soul and my strength for this.
> What do I care for all that they do amiss!
> What is the point of this teaching of mine, and of this
> Learning of theirs? It all goes down the same abyss.
> What does it matter to me, if they can write   10
> A description of a dog, or if they can't?
> What is the point? To us both, it is all my aunt!
> And yet I'm supposed to care, with all my might.
> I do not, and will not; they won't and they don't; and that's all!
> I shall keep my strength for myself; they can keep theirs as well.   15
> Why should we beat our heads against the wall
> Of each other? I shall sit and wait for the bell.

ii Improving understanding

What is the narrator's job? Who is he talking about? Tick those words which describe his attitude.

irritable	dismissive	exasperated
impatient	despairing	stubborn
passionate	bored	inflexible
contemplative	defiant	

iii Language

a) Match the words in the left-hand column with the definitions on the right.

pack	dogs used for hunting
amiss	pull with sharp, powerful movements
haul	strength
abyss	encourage
unruly	search for
might	wrong
tug	lead used to control a dog
urge	indisciplined
leash	pull with effort
quarry	very deep chasm
hounds	group

b) Find at least one metaphor in the poem.

iv **Discussion**
    Discuss in pairs.
    Either:
a) The poet sounds like a man talking.
    The poem was written in the heat of the moment.
    The poet's attitude is obvious and explicit.
    The poet makes us feel what he feels.
    I sympathise with him.
    Or:
b) What do you think your teacher thinks about you?
    Would you like to be a teacher?
    What is your favourite lesson of the week?
    Which is your least favourite?

v **Follow-up work**
   Write a short poem – or a paragraph – about either your feelings
   during lessons, or what you think are your teacher's feelings during
   lessons.

2.9 Suggesting what is meant

In the Lawrence essay (2.8.2) the writer's meaning is fairly explicit. He
says what he means to say and makes us feel what he's feeling. In
Gulliver's Travels and *Hard Times* the meaning is less explicit. Both Swift
and Dickens help us feel what they feel – and their intention is clear – but
they don't tell us exactly what their point of view is. Sometimes, modern
poets deliberately leave us uncertain. Using few words they encourage us
to make connexions – often ambiguous and contradictory – between a
whole range of meanings and experiences.

2.9.1 i Read the following poem as many times as you like:

GLOSSARY	
eaves (l.4): the edge of a roof that goes beyond the wall	If only my friend
	would return
trough (l.5): i) narrow channel: gutter	and remove the leaves
	from my eaves
ii) depression; low point	troughs 5

ii Discuss in pairs what it suggests to you. Have you ever felt similar
    emotions?

2.9.2
Interpretation

i Note the pun (i.e. the play on words) in the word 'troughs'. In context,
   the word could carry *both* of those meanings.
   One literal interpretation of the poem, ignoring the pun, might be:
   'I wish my friend would come back and take the leaves out of the
   gutter in the eaves.'

54

But what we don't know is: which friend? what sort of friend? return from where? why 'leaves'? Does she (the poet) really mean 'leaves' or does she mean something else? Is it really autumn? Why can't she do it herself? Why the word 'troughs' and not the more usual word 'gutter'?

ii Which of the following feelings do you think are suggested? (Note: they can only be suggestions; the poem is not explicit.)

I miss my friend
I am dependent on my friend
Depression
Something inside of me is all bottled up
I need to be released
I need to be cleansed
I simply want my friend back

2.9.3   i   Read another poem by the same poet:

I've been away from poetry
many months

and now I must rake leaves
with nothing blowing

between your house   5
and mine.

ii Discuss in pairs what it suggests to you. Do you agree that the real meaning is difficult to explain? Does it sound like someone speaking naturally? Do you like the poem?

iii **Interpretation**

Write down any questions that you would like to have answers to (e.g. who is 'I'?)

Write down words, phrases, sentences which express what you think the poem is about and what it suggests to you.
What is the poet's mood?

Exchange your ideas with others in the class.

Form groups and discuss.
Look in the Key in the back of the book for ideas *only* if you are stuck.

2.9.4
Notes   *The poet is Lorine Niedecker. She was born in Wisconsin, U.S.A., in 1903. Most of her poems are set in the river and rush country where she grew up. The first poem comes from a selection of poems entitled* In Exchange for Haiku. Haiku *is an epigrammatic Japanese verse form in 17 syllables. What similarities does the first poem have with* haiku?

2.9.5
Follow-up work   Can you write a similar poem – of any length – about one of your experiences?

UNIT 3

Feelings into words

3.1 Responding to narrative

3.1.1
Language work

i Look at the picture:

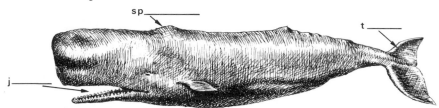

Name the parts. Complete the following: A w_____ is not a fish but a m_____.

ii Look at the pictures and fill in the gaps:

Discuss in pairs.

iii Add the following words onto the picture to show what they refer to:

helm
keel
rigging
deck

Use a dictionary to help you, if necessary.

iv When referring to the front of a ship sailors use the word f_____.
When referring to the back sailors use the word a ____.

v The leader of the ship is called the c ____ and his men are called the cr____.

Compare your answers in pairs.

3.1.2
Anticipation

i Did you know

– that most whales move in family groups?
– that a baby whale, the calf, is born tail first, because if the head emerged first it might drown?

ii What differences are there between whales and fish? Focus on the following:

size

skin

tail

breathing

iii Can you name one species of whale and answer the following questions:

What does it usually eat?
How does it detect prey?
How fast can it move?
How long does it stay beneath the surface?

iv What products are gained from whales?
Do you agree with whaling (i.e. catching whales)? Give reasons.

v Can you tell a story about a whale? (e.g. Jonah and the whale).

3.1.3 *The following section contains short extracts from a novel called* Moby Dick. *Moby Dick is the name of a huge white sperm whale which is being hunted by Captain Ahab on his ship the* Pequod. *Captain Ahab lost a leg in an earlier battle. The final chase, which these extracts describe, lasts three days.*

i Read the following passage.

Captain Ahab has offered a doubloon (a gold coin) to the man who 'raises' Moby Dick from the sea. Tashtego is a Red Indian.

The Chase – First Day

'There she blows! – there she blows! A hump like a snowhill! It is Moby Dick!'

Fired by the cry which seemed simultaneously taken up by the three lookouts, the men on deck rushed to the rigging to behold the famous whale they had so long been pursuing. Ahab had now gained his final perch, some feet above the other lookouts … From this height the whale was now seen some mile or so ahead, at every roll of the sea revealing his sparkling hump, and regularly jetting his silent spout into the air. To the credulous mariners it seemed the same silent spout they had so long ago beheld in the moonlit Atlantic and Indian Oceans.

'And did none of ye see it before?' cried Ahab, hailing the perched men all around him.

'I saw him almost that same instant, sir, that Captain Ahab did, and I cried out,' said Tashtego.

'Not the same instant; not the same – no, the doubloon is mine, Fate reserved the doubloon for me. I only; none of ye could have raised the White Whale first. There she blows! there she blows! – there she blows! There again! – there again!'

ii Improving understanding

Who says 'There she blows!' at the beginning? What does it mean? Who is 'she'?

Describe where everyone is standing. Who claims he saw the whale first?

iii Language

What do you think the following mean? (Look at the context and try to guess):

hump	lookout
fired	sparkling
beheld	credulous
perch	

What tense is 'seemed'? What tense is 'had gained'? What does the 'had' tense show?

iv Reactions

Read the whole passage again and try to describe your feelings in either single words or phrases. Did you feel any of the following?

excited

nervous

astonished

suspicious

full of wonder

irritated that you don't know what's happened up to now

keen to know what is going to happen next

v Interpretation

How would you describe Captain Ahab? It will help you to look in particular at the beginning and the end of the passage. Look also at the exchange with Tashtego and the length of Ahab's utterances at the end.

3.1.4 Read the following extracts which continue the narrative about the first day's chase. Answer the questions after each and discuss in pairs.

Note: whalers get into smaller boats for the actual attack on the whale.

i

<table>
<tr>
<td>
GLOSSARY
foe (l.1): enemy
meadow (l.3): field of grass
nigh (l.4): near
prey (l.4): victim
fleecy (l.6): woolly
foam (l.7): small bubbles on surface of sea
</td>
<td>
... slowly they neared the foe. As they neared him, the ocean grew still more smooth; seemed drawing a carpet over its waves; seemed a noon-meadow, so serenely it spread. At length the breathless hunter came so nigh his seemingly unsuspecting prey, that his entire dazzling hump was distinctly visible, sliding along the sea as if an isolated thing, and continually set in a revolving ring of finest, fleecy, greenish foam.
</td>
<td>5</td>
</tr>
</table>

Improving understanding

Who are 'they'?

Who is 'the foe'?

What has happened?

What is the surface of the sea compared to?

Why is the hunter 'breathless'?

Why do you think Moby Dick's hump is 'dazzling'?

Where does the 'foam' come from, do you think?

Reactions and guesses

What do you think will happen?

Give at least one word which describes your feelings.

ii

<table>
<tr>
<td>
GLOSSARY
churning (l.2): agitating violently
vengeful (l.3): vindictive
wake (l.3): disturbed water left behind
</td>
<td>
But soon resuming his horizontal attitude, Moby Dick swam swiftly round and round the wrecked crew; sideways churning the water in his vengeful wake, as if lashing himself up to still another and more deadly assault.
</td>
</tr>
</table>

Improving understanding

What has happened?

What impression does the writer give of Moby Dick's attitude?

Reactions and guesses
What do you think will happen?
Give at least one word which describes your feelings.

iii
There has been a long struggle. Stubb is one of the ship's mates.

... the long tension of Ahab's bodily strength did crack, and helplessly he yielded to his body's doom: for a time, lying all crushed in the bottom of Stubb's boat, like one trodden under foot of herds of elephants.

Improving understanding
What has happened?
What state do you imagine the crew are in?

iv

'Lay it before me; – any missing men?'
'One, two, three, four, five; – there were five oars, sir, and here are five men.'

Improving understanding
Guess who is speaking the first utterance.
What do you think 'lay it before me' means?
Are any men missing as a result of the struggle?

v
Ahab is now back on the main boat.

Ahab stands alone among the millions of the peopled earth, nor gods nor men his neighbours! Cold, cold – I shiver! – How now? Aloft there! D'ye see him? Sing out for every spout, though he spout ten times a second!'

The day was nearly done; only the hem of his golden robe was rustling. Soon, it was almost dark, but the look-out men still remained unset.

'Can't see the spout now, sir; – too dark' cried a voice from the air.

5

Improving understanding
What impression do you have of Ahab now?
What does 'sing out' mean?
What time of day is it?
What colour is the sky?
What is the metaphor used to describe the day?

Follow-up work
a) Describe the first day's chase in two or three sentences.
b) Discuss what you think of Ahab. Do you like him? Do you understand him? Who do you sympathise with most? Why?

3.1.5 Read and answer the questions:

i

The Chase – Second Day
They were one man, not thirty. For as the one ship that held them all; though it was put together of all contrasting things – oak, and maple, and pine wood; iron, and pitch, and hemp – yet all these ran into each other in the one concrete hull, which shot on its way, both balanced and directed by the long central keel; even so, all the individualities of the crew. This man's valour, that man's fear; guilt and guiltiness, all varieties were welded into oneness, and were all directed to that fatal goal which Ahab their one lord and keel did point to.

GLOSSARY
welded (l.7): joined

5

Improving understanding
Underline the words that show what the ship was made of (look up in the dictionary any you don't know).
What is the metaphor used to describe how the crew was working together?
Do any words show that the chase may not end successfully?

ii

GLOSSARY
booms (l.2): lifts with a deep sound
mane (l.5): long hair (on an animal's neck)
breaching (l.5): breaking out of the water

Rising with his utmost velocity from the furthest depths the Sperm Whale thus booms his entire bulk into the pure element of air, and piling up a mountain of dazzling foam, shows his place to the distance of seven miles and more. In those moments, the torn, enraged waves he shakes off seem his mane; in some cases this breaching is his act of defiance.

5

Improving understanding
Where is Moby Dick in relation to the ship?
What impression do you get of him?
Underline at least two metaphors
Do they help you 'see' what is happening?

Reactions
Which phrases in the passage do you particularly like/dislike? Can you say why?
Give one or two words or phrases which summarise your feelings about what is happening.

61

... the White Whale churning himself into furious speed, almost in an instant as it were, rushing among the boats with open jaws, and a lashing tail, offered appalling battle on every side; and heedless of the irons darted at him from every boat, seemed only intent on annihilating each separate plank of which those boats were made.

5

Improving understanding
What has happened?
Look at the context. What do you think the following mean:

> churning   appalling
> lashing   annihilating

Reactions and guesses
The previous extract is part of a longer sentence. Read it aloud quickly. What impression do you get? What do you think will happen?

As before, the attentive ship having descried the whole fight, again came bearing down to the rescue, and dropping a boat, picked up the floating mariners, tubs, oars, and whatever else could be caught at, and safely landed them on her decks. Some sprained shoulders, wrists, and ankles; livid contusions; wrenched harpoons and lances: inextricable intricacies of rope; shattered oars and planks; all these were there; but no fatal or even serious ill seemed to have befallen any one ... so Ahab was now found grimly clinging to his boat's broken half, which afforded a comparatively easy float; nor did it so exhaust him as the previous day's mishap.

5

10

Improving understanding
What has happened?
Describe the scene in your own words.
What sort of injuries were there?

Look at the context. What do you think the following mean:

> bearing down
> inextricable intricacies
> shattered
> befallen
> grimly

Reactions and guesses
Had you expected what happened?
Are you pleased, disappointed or horrified? (or none of these)
Whose side are you on?
What do you think Ahab will do now?

v

The following exchange is between Starbuck, one of the crew, and Ahab.

a)

GLOSSARY

stove to splinters (l.3): broken into small pieces of wood

mobbing (l.4): crowding around

impiety (l.8): lack of reverence

'never never wilt thou capture him, old man. – In Jesus' name no more of this, that's worse than devil's madness. Two days chased; twice stove to splinters; thy very leg once more snatched from under thee; thy evil shadow gone – all good angels mobbing thee with warnings: – what more wouldst thou have? – Shall we keep chasing this murderous fish till he swamps the last man? Shall we be dragged by him to the bottom of the sea? Shall we be towed by him to the infernal world? Oh, oh! – Impiety and blasphemy to hunt him more!'

5

b)

GLOSSARY

underling (l.4): servant

shivered (l.5): broken in small pieces

Ahab is for ever Ahab, man. This whole act's immutably decreed. 'Twas rehearsed by thee and me a billion years before this ocean rolled. Fool! I am the Fates' lieutenant; I act under orders. Look thou, underling! that thou obeyest mine. – Stand round me, men. Ye see an old man cut down to the stump; leaning on a shivered lance; propped up on a lonely foot. 'Tis Ahab – his body's part; but Ahab's soul's a centipede, that moves upon a hundred legs.

5

Improving understanding

Is Ahab speaking in a) or b)?

What does Starbuck try to persuade him to do?

Why?

How would you describe Starbuck's mood?

In what way is the hunt more than an ordinary whale hunt?

What do phrases like 'infernal world' show?

Does Ahab give in to Starbuck?

What is Ahab's view of himself?

Look at the context. What do you think the following mean?

swamps	blasphemy
dragged	immutably decreed
towed	stump
infernal world	centipede

Reactions

How would you describe Ahab? Would you choose any of the following words? Add your own words if you like.

self-pitying	comic	possessed	mad
pathetic	tragic	obsessed	

Do you feel any sympathy for him?

Describe your reaction to this exchange of opinions.

3.1.6   **i**
Ahab is talking.

> **The Chase – Third Day**
> What a lovely day again! were it a new-made world, and made for a
> summer-house to the angels, and this morning the first of its throwing
> open to them, a fairer day could not dawn upon that world. Here's
> food for thought, had Ahab time to think; but Ahab never thinks; he
> only feels, feels, feels...   5

Improving understanding
Describe the metaphor of the summer-house in your own words.
What effect does this scene have on you?

ii
This is the narrator.

> ... scarce had he pushed from the ship, when numbers of sharks,
> seemingly rising from out the dark waters beneath the hull,
> maliciously snapped at the blades of the oars, every time they dipped
> in the water; and in this way accompanied the boat with their bites.

Improving understanding
What do you think the following mean:

>   scarce had he pushed
>   snapped at the blades

Who do you think 'he' refers to?
What effect does the picture of the sharks have on you?

iii

> ... maddened by yesterday's fresh irons that corroded him, Moby
> Dick seemed combinedly possessed by all the angels that fell from
> heaven.

Improving understanding
What do you think the word 'corroded' means?
Describe the image in your own words.

Reactions and guesses
Do you feel any sympathy for Moby Dick?
What do you think is going to happen?

iv

The Parsee was one of the crew.

… Lashed round and round to the fish's back; pinioned in the turns upon turns in which, during the past night, the whale had reeled the involutions of the line around him, the half torn body of the Parsee was seen; his sable raiment frayed to shreds; his distended eyes turned full upon old Ahab.

5

The harpoon dropped from his hand.

Improving understanding
What happened on the previous day?
What effect does the Parsee's look have upon Ahab?
What do you think the following mean?

> reeled the involutions of the line
> frayed to shreds
> distended

v

… Moby Dick was now again steadily swimming forward … He seemed swimming with his utmost velocity, and now only intent upon pursuing his own straight path in the sea.

'Oh! Ahab,' cried Starbuck, 'not too late is it, even now, the third day, to desist. See! Moby Dick seeks thee not. It is thou, thou, that madly seekest him!'

5

Improving understanding
What is Moby Dick doing?
What does Starbuck try to persuade Ahab to do?

Guesses

What do you think will happen?

vi

Whether fagged by the three days' running chase, and the resistance to his swimming in the knotted hamper he bore; or whether it was some latent deceitfulness and malice in him: whichever was true, the White Whale's way now began to abate, as it seemed, from the boat so rapidly nearing him once more.

5

Improving understanding
What does the 'knotted hamper' refer to?
What's happening to Moby Dick?

Guesses

What do you think will happen?

vii

... Moby Dick sideways writhed; ... and, ... that had it not been for the elevated part of the gunwale to which he then clung, Ahab would once more have been tossed into the sea. As it was, three of the oarsmen – ... these were flung out;

Improving understanding

What has happened?

viii

From the ship's bows, nearly all the seamen now hung inactive; hammers, bits of plank, lances, and harpoons, mechanically retained in their hands, just as they had darted from their various employments; all their enchanted eyes intent upon the whale, which from side to side strangely vibrating his predestinating head, sent a broad band of overspreading semicircular foam before him as he rushed. Retribution, swift vengeance, eternal malice were in his whole aspect, and spite of all that mortal man could do, the solid white buttress of his forehead smote the ship's starboard bow, till men and timbers reeled. Some fell flat upon their faces. Like dislodged trucks, the heads of the harpooners aloft shook on their bull-like necks. Through the breach, they heard the waters pour, as mountain torrents down a flume.

'The ship! The hearse! – the second hearse!' cried Ahab from the boat, 'its wood could only be American!'

Diving beneath the settling ship, the whale ran quivering along its keel; but turning under water, swiftly shot to the surface again, far off the other bow, but within a few yards of Ahab's boat, where, for a time, he lay quiescent.

Improving understanding

What do you think the following mean?

retribution	dislodged	breach
smote	aloft	torrents

Why were the seamen inactive?
Why had they 'darted from' their previous employment?
Why are their eyes 'enchanted'?
Say what the following words refer to in different parts of the extract:
'their', 'his', 'he', 'they', 'its'.

Why does Ahab shout 'the hearse!'?
What do you think lies behind the mysterious 'its wood could only be American'
Summarise what you think is happening.

Reactions and guesses
What do you think will happen?
What are your feelings?

ix

The harpoon was darted; the stricken whale flew forward; with igniting velocity the line ran through the groove; ran foul. Ahab stopped to clear it; he did clear it; but the flying turn caught him round the neck, and voicelessly ... he was shot out of the boat, ere the crew knew he was gone... 5

For an instant, the tranced boat's crew stood still; then turned. 'The ship? Great God, where is the ship? Soon they ... saw her sidelong fading phantom ...; only the upper-most masts out of the water; while fixed by infatuation, or fidelity, or fate, to their once loftly perches, the pagan harpooneers still maintained their sinking lookouts on the 10 sea. And now, concentric circles seized the lone boat itself, and all its crew, and each floating oar, and every lance-pole, and spinning, animate and inanimate, all round and round in one vortex, carried the smallest chip of the *Pequod* out of sight.

GLOSSARY
igniting (l.2): set light (metaphorically)
groove (l.2): long channel
ere (l.4): before
tranced (l.6): unaware of anything else
concentric (l.11): having the same centre
vortex (l.13): whirlpool

Improving understanding
What do you think the following mean?

> darted
> stricken (what does it tell you about Moby Dick's probable fate?)
> ran foul
> flying turn
> sidelong faded phantom
> fixed by infatuation
> once lofty perches
> sinking lookouts

What do the following words/phrases refer to?

> they   animate
> their   inanimate
> the lone boat smallest chip

What has happened to the ship?
What happenes to Ahab?
What impression does the word 'phantom' give?
What happens to the harpoon?
What happens to the boat?
What is left?

Reactions

Do you find the story tragic, pathetic or frightening? (or none of these?)

x

GLOSSARY *shroud (l.1):* cloth wrapped around corpse before burial	… all collapsed, and the great shroud of the sea rolled on as it rolled five thousand years ago.

Improving understanding

What impression do you have of the scene now?

How does it contrast with what has happened previously? (In fact in the book we find out there was one survivor.)

Reactions

Write some words or phrases which summarise your feelings.

3.1.7 Go back and read all the extracts one after the other and get a sense of the narrative.

3.1.8
Follow-up work

Do at least *one* of the following:

i Go back again. Underline all the verb phrases which advance the action (narrative) and circle all the verb phrases that are used essentially to describe something (description). Do not include verbs that are used in dialogue.

ii Find phrases that suggest
   a) death and damnation
   b) vengeance
   c) fate

iii Find phrases and sentences that suggest
   a) Ahab's state of mind at different times
   b) Moby Dick's state at different times

   In two separate paragraphs, describe Ahab and Moby Dick in your own words.

iv In a paragraph describe the story of the chase in your own words. Share with others in your class.

3.1.9
Background

Write a summary of Herman Melville's life using these notes to help you:

i

Moby Dick 1851 – born 1819 – at seventeen, sea on a whaler – deserted – lived for months with cannibals – joined the American Navy – retired from sea 1842 – first and second novels Typee 1846, – Omoo 1847 – fame – Moby Dick – not a success in his lifetime – declined in popularity – last book Billy Budd finished day before death – not published until 1924 – essentially in conflict with idealism of age that believed in moral re-generation and greatness of American future – saw instead financial greed and exploitation of immigrants – died New York City 1891.

ii Read the following information:

Five species of whale were hunted, mainly the white whale, in Arctic waters, and the sperm whale, in tropical waters. By the early nineteenth-century the stocks of whales in the Atlantic were running low and whaling ships – mainly from New England – were fitted out for campaigns lasting several years. These ships went on voyages to the Pacific and Indian Oceans. They would only return when they had a full cargo of whale oil, used for soap-making and for oil lamps. They had crews of 30 to 50 men, who signed on not for a wage but for a share of the profits.

The whale boats ... were manned by a crew of six. They carried three harpoons, three lances, and water and provisions, in case they lost the mother ship. They had a removable mast, sail and rudder, which were fixed and replaced by five pulling oars and a steering oar for the attack. The whale was harpooned and to the harpoon was fixed a 220-fathom line coiled in a bucket; another bucket contained a spare 100-fathom line which could be added if the whale dived too deeply. The line could run out at such speed that it had to be wetted to prevent it from catching fire by friction. This fast moving line was very dangerous as it snaked out of the boat, yet it was, by custom, at that moment that the boat-steerer and steersman swapped places, as it was the latter's job to kill the whale. Sometimes the harpooned whale would tow the boat in a wild frenzied bid for escape but it seldom turned around to attack its tormentors. Eventually when it lay exhausted on the surface it was killed with a lance.

Current studies of whales and their smaller relatives, the dolphins, show that these animals are extra-ordinarily intelligent. Nowadays many species of whales killed for commercial use are on the verge of extinction.

3.1.10 Criticism

These extracts are taken from D. H. Lawrence's essay on *Moby Dick* in *Studies in Classic American Literature (1923).*

Read and think about them.

At first you are put off by the style. It reads like journalism. It seems spurious. You feel Melville is trying to put something over to you. It won't do.

And Melville really is a bit sententious: aware of himself, self-conscious, putting something over even himself.

– – –

It is an epic of the sea such as no man has equalled; and it is a book of esoteric symbolism of profound significance, and of considerable tiresomeness.

But it is a great book, a very great book, the greatest book of the sea ever written. It moves awe in the soul.

– – –

What then is Moby Dick? He is the deepest blood-being of the white race; he is our deepest blood-nature.

And he is hunted, hunted, hunted by the maniacal fanaticism of our white mental consciousness. We want to hunt him down. To subject him to our will. And in this maniacal conscious hunt of ourselves we get dark races and pale to help us, red, yellow, and black, east and west, Quaker and fire-worshipper, we get them all to help us in this ghastly maniacal hunt which is our doom and our suicide.

3.2 Predictions

3.2.1.   **i** Read the following title of a poem:

Head and Bottle

What do you think it might be about?

ii Read the first two lines:

GLOSSARY
downs (l.1): treeless hilly
    land
allysum (l.1): plant with
    yellow and white
    flowers

> The downs will lose the sun, white allysum
> lose the bees hum;

Do you want to change your prediction about the subject matter?
What tense is used?
What time of year is being referred to?
What words are stressed more than the others?
Which words rhyme?

iii Read the next two lines:

> But head and bottle tilted back in the cart
> will never part

Do you want to change your prediction?
What do you think 'tilt' means?
What is the 'head' doing?
How long will he/she go on doing it?
Does the action take place in the town or the country?
Which words are stressed more than the others?
Which words rhyme?

iv Read:

> Till I am cold as midnight and all my hours
> Are beeless flowers

Why 'beeless'?
What is being suggested here?
Indicate stress and rhyme.

v Read:

> He neither sees, nor hears, nor smells, nor thinks,
> But only drinks,
> Quiet in the yard where tree trunks do not lie
> More quietly.

What sort of drink is he drinking?
What effect does it have on him?
Explain the metaphor in your own words.
Indicate stress and rhyme.

vi Read the poem again in its entirety without stopping.

The downs will lose the sun, white allysum
lose the bees hum;
But head and bottle tilted back in the cart
will never part
Till I am cold as midnight and all my hours   5
are beeless flowers
He neither sees, nor hears, nor smells, nor thinks,
But only drinks,
Quiet in the yard where tree trunks do not lie
More quietly.   10

Was it easy to understand when you had understood all the words?
Does the writer approve of the man?
Is he marvelling or impatient?
Is the title of the poem ennobling or belittling or merely descriptive?
How did your expectations change from the beginning to the end?
What do you think of the poem?

3.2.2   *The poem is by Edward Thomas (1878-1917). He tried to make his living as a writer but*
Notes   *remained very poor. Much of his poetry and prose describes events that take place in the*
             English countryside. He was killed in the First World War.

3.3 Focus on response

We all have thoughts and feelings about what we read, even if at first they
are not very clear or definite. Later, on re-reading, our reactions are
usually clearer to us and they gain conviction.

Obviously, we respond while we are actually reading in a variety of ways
to a variety of different things – to the story, to the characters, to the effect
of the language – but after we have finished, our reflections tend to be
about the whole of what we have read.

When a text is linguistically difficult, or when it expresses and describes
that which we have little experience of, we often need to read it several
times if we are to reach deeper levels of understanding and feel confident
with it.

Many of the exercises in this Unit will encourage you to try to express your
reactions to what you read.

3.4 Reading without assistance

A negro woman
Carrying a bunch of marigolds
    wrapped
        in an old newspaper:
She carries them upright,
    bare-headed,   5
        the bulk
of her thighs
    causing her to waddle
        as she walks
looking into   10
    the store window which she passes
        on her way.
What is she
    but an ambassador
        from another world   15
a world of pretty marigolds
    of two shades
        which she announces
not knowing what she does
    other   20
        than walk the streets
holding the flowers upright
    as a torch
        so early in the morning.

William Carlos Williams (1883–1963)

This poet, like Melville, was an American. He too sometimes conveyed a sense of wonder when he wrote.

3.5 Responding to description

3.5.1 For each of the following passages:

   i Say what kind of book you think it comes from (e.g. romantic novel, biography etc.). What do you think it is about?

   ii Say what the context is (e.g. who is 'speaking'? Is it, for example, a character in a novel? What is your impression of him/her? Which country/region is it set in?)

  iii Say what the description is of, in general terms (e.g. landscape, character).

  iv Do the exercises. Read the passage as many times as you like. Take your time. Discuss your answers in pairs.

Rain filled the gutters and splashed knee-high off the pavement. Big
cops in slickers that shone like gun barrels had a lot of fun carrying
giggling girls across the bad places. The rain drummed hard on the
roof of the car and the top began to leak. A pool of water formed on
the floorboards for me to keep my feet in. It was too early in the fall
for that kind of rain. I struggled into a trench coat and made a dash
for the nearest drugstore and bought myself a pint of whiskey. Back
in the car I used enough of it to keep warm and interested. I was long
overparked, but the cops were too busy carrying girls and blowing
whistles to bother about that.

5

10

GLOSSARY
slickers (l.2): shiny
  raincoats (American)

i Improving understanding
Write T (true) F (false) DK (don't know).
Re-write the false sentences to make them true.

> The streets were full of rain.
> The 'bad places' were wet but not as wet as the other places.
> It was raining so heavily it made a great noise on the roof of the car.
> Water came into the car through the floorboards.
> It always rains like that at that time of the year.
> He drank the whiskey in the car.
> The police didn't fine him because they were preoccupied.

ii Language
Match the words on the left with the definitions on the right.

cops (American)	autumn
giggling	let in water
leak	double-breasted waterproof coat
fall (American)	shop where medical prescriptions are made up and other goods bought
trench coat	policemen
dash	laughing nervously
drugstore (American)	sudden quick movement

iii Reactions
Which of the following do you agree with?

> When I read the passage I was interested/amused.
> The writer sounds bored/cynical/intense. (Give examples.)
> Write other sentences which describe your reactions.

iv Style
Notice the writer's use of language is quite vivid. His description is precise
and full of detail ('rain ... splashed knee-high off the pavement'). It

creates a very real picture. The prose *sounds* casual and natural ('I used enough of it to keep warm and interested') but it is written with a great deal of care.

What effect does the metaphor of the 'gun barrels' have?

There are not many adjectives in this passage. What effect does that have on the description?

Find one humorous sentence. Try to explain the humour.

v Discussion
Do you like this sort of story? Why/Why not?

Passage 2

> She was an indefatigable student: constantly reading and learning; with a strong conviction of the necessity and value of education, very unusual in a girl of fifteen. She never lost a moment of time, and seemed almost to grudge the necessary leisure for relaxation and play-hours, which might be partly accounted for by the awkwardness $\quad$ 5 in all games occasioned by her shortness of sight. Yet, in spite of these unsociable habits, she was a great favourite with her school-fellows. She was always ready to try and do what they wished, though not sorry when they called her awkward, and left her out of their sports. Then, at night, she was an invaluable story-teller, frightening $\quad$ 10 them almost out of their wits as they lay in bed.

i Improving understanding
Write T (true) F (false) DK (don't know). Re-write the false sentences to make them true.

The girl was   always tired
an excellent learner
a believer in education
fifteen years old
always wasting her time
good at sports
able to see very well
popular with her classmates
a good story-teller

ii Language
What do you think the following mean in context?

grudge

awkward

frightening them almost out of their wits

iii Reactions and style
Which of the following do you agree with?

When I read the passage I was interested/encouraged/warmed.

The writer seems to be enthusiastic/too enthusiastic.
She seems to exaggerate/give an accurate picture.
The passage is easy to read/clear/wishy-washy/unconvincing.

Give examples from the passage to support your choices. Write other
sentences which describe your reactions.

iv Discussion
Is the girl's character similar to your own?

Passage 3

Dark spruce forest frowned on either side the frozen waterway. The
trees had been stripped by a recent wind of their white covering of
frost, and they seemed to lean towards each other, black and
ominous, in the fading light. A vast silence reigned over the land. The
land itself was a desolation, lifeless, without movement, so lone and   5
cold that the spirit of it was not even that of sadness. There was a hint
in it of laughter, but of a laughter more terrible than any sadness – a
laughter that was mirthless as the smile of the sphinx, a laughter cold
as the frost and partaking of the grimness of infallibility. It was the
masterful and incommunicable wisdom of eternity laughing at the   10
futility of life and the effort of life. It was the Wild, the savage, frozen-
hearted Northland wild.

i Improving understanding
Write T (true) F (false) DK (don't know). Re-write the false sentences to
make them true.

The trees were covered with frost.
It was getting light.
There seemed to be no-one there.
The narrator was laughing.
Man's life in the Wild was futile.
The Wild was laughing.

ii Language

a) Match the words with the definitions.

spruce	ancient Egyptian statue with an inscrutable look
hint	having a share
sphinx	coniferous
partaking	suggestion

b) What do you think the following words mean in context?

frowned	mirthless
ominous	masterful
reigned	incommunicable
desolation	futility

iii Reactions
Which of these sentences do you agree with? Add your own.
a) I found the passage very gloomy and depressing.
    The atmosphere is cheerless and fatalistic.
    It's quite eerie.

b) I liked it.
    I disliked it intensely.
    I know what he means.

iv Style
a) The first four sentences describe what the writer sees in front of him.
    Each sentence begins with a noun phrase. Which words in these
    sentences convey his feelings about the place?

b) In the last three sentences, he conveys his feelings more imaginatively.
    What do you think of such phrases as 'the masterful and
    incommunicable wisdom' and 'partaking of the grimness of
    infallibility'? Are they impressive or pretentious?

v Discussion
Have you ever been to a country like that? Would you like to go?

Passage 4

I was born in a large Welsh town at the beginning of the Great War –
an ugly, lovely town, or so it was and is to me: crawling, sprawling by
a long and splendid curving shore where truant boys and Sandfield
boys and old men from nowhere, beach-combed, idled, and paddled,
watched the dock bound ships or the ships steaming away into   5
wonder and India, magic and China, countries bright with oranges
and loud with lions, threw stones into the sea for the barking outcast
dogs: made castles and harbours and forts and race tracks in the
sand: and on Saturday summer afternoons listened to the brass band,
watched the Punch and Judy, or hung about on the fringes of the   10
crowd to hear the fierce religious speakers who shouted at the sea,
as though it were wicked and wrong to roll in and out like that, white
horsed and full of fishes.

One man, I remember, used to take off his hat and set fire to his hair
every now and then, but I do not remember what it proved, if it   15
proved anything at all, except that he was a very interesting man.

GLOSSARY
the Great War (l.1): the
    First World War
Sandfield (l.3): the name of
    a school
Punch and Judy (l.10): a
    traditional children's
    puppet show

---

i Language
a) Find a word which means the following:

moving slowly	moved aimlessly
spreading out	walked in the sea with no shoes on
absent from school without permission	abandoned
looked for things on the beach	edges

b) What is a brass band?

ii Reactions, tone and style

a) What impression does the writer give when he uses language like this: 'crawling, sprawling' and 'beachcombed, idled and paddled, watched'

b) What do you notice about the number of sentences? What effect does it have?

c) Which of these sentences do you agree with? Change those you disagree with so that you agree with them. Add your own. Where possible, find examples in the passage to support your argument.

Tone

The writer paints a very glamorous picture.
The scene is magical but exaggerated.
The writer is very excited and enthusiastic, almost carried away.
The tone is very light and humorous.
The last sentence is an exaggeration: it is deliberately casual to give comic effect.

Reactions

I find the passage funny.
I find it exhilarating.
It leaves me cold.

Style

The style is very vivid; it creates a very clear picture.
The writer seems to use words because he likes the sound of them not because they mean anything.
He writes very naturally.
The description is too far away from reality.
It seems to describe exactly what is intended.

iii Discussion

What memories, if any, does this passage bring back to you?

Passage 5

He was an inch, perhaps two, under six feet, powerfully built, and he advanced straight at you with a slight stoop of the shoulders, head forward, and a fixed from-under stare which made you think of a charging bull. His voice was deep, loud, and his manner displayed a kind of dogged self-assertion which had nothing aggressive in it. It seemed a necessity, and it was directed apparently as much at himself as anybody else. He was spotlessly neat, apparelled in immaculate white from shoes to hat, and in the various Eastern ports where he got his living as ship-chandler's water-clerk he was very popular.

GLOSSARY
ship chandler (l.9): a person who deals in supplies for ships

i Improving understanding

Fill in details under the following headings. Use your own words as far as possible. Look up any words you don't know in a dictionary.

HEIGHT	
WALK	
VOICE	
MANNER	
DRESS	
OCCUPATION	

ii Reactions, tone and style

Re-write this paragraph so that you agree with it.

The passage is quite a detailed description of the man but you feel vital points are missing. For example, we get no impression of his character at all even though the writer says he likes him. The style is very cool and clear but is only concerned to describe what can be seen. The writer has avoided imagery completely and this only reinforces the impression that it comes from a police report rather than a novel. It is quite well written but I don't like it very much.

Passage 6

<table>
<tr>
<td>

GLOSSARY

Tübingen (l.9): a university town in Germany
</td>
<td>

Beautiful city! So venerable, so lovely, so unravaged by the fierce intellectual life of the century, so serene! 'There are our young barbarians, all at play!' And yet, steeped in sentiment as she lies, spreading her gardens to the moonlight, and whispering from her towers the last enchantments of the Middle Age, who will deny that   5 Oxford, by her ineffable charm, keeps ever calling us nearer to the true goal of all of us, to the idea, the perfection to beauty in a word, which is only truth seen from the other side? – nearer perhaps than all the science of Tübingen. Adorable dreamer, whose heart has been so romantic! Who hast given thyself so prodigally, given thyself   10 to sides and to heroes not mine, only never to the Philistines! Home of lost causes, and forsaken beliefs, and unpopular names, and impossible loyalties!
</td>
</tr>
</table>

i Improving understanding
a) Try to explain in your own words:

'whispering from her towers the last enchantments of the Middle Age'

'which is only truth seen from the other side'

'who hast given thyself so prodigally ... only never to the Philistines!'

b) What is 'the true goal of all of us'?

c) Who or what does 'Adorable dreamer' refer to?

d) Express in your own words what the writer is trying to say about Oxford.

ii Language

Ask other people in your class (or look up in a dictionary) any words you don't know. Notice the following:

- the repetition of the word 'so'
- the use of the exclamation mark
- the use of the question 'who will deny' (known as a 'rhetorical question' because no-one is expected to answer)
- where the verbs occur/don't occur.

Comment on how all these affect the tone and style of the passage.

iii Reactions, tone and style

Re-read the passage and write a paragraph on the tone of the passage (i.e. what it sounds like to you), the style (i.e. the way it is written) and your response (i.e. what you think and feel about it).

3.5.2 Look back over the passages.

Which ones did you prefer? (Give reasons.)
Which ones didn't you like? (Give reasons.)

Discuss in pairs.

3.5.3 Match the following descriptions with the passages in 3.5.1.
Notes The opening paragraph of the novel *White Fang* by Jack London.
It takes place in Northern Canada over a hundred years ago.

From the life of Charlotte Bronte, the author of *Jane Eyre*, by Mrs Gaskell.

By Matthew Arnold, the Victorian writer and poet, from *Essays in Criticism*.

The opening paragraph of the novel *Lord Jim*, by Joseph Conrad, the story of a man condemned for abandoning his ship.

From *The Big Sleep*, by Raymond Chandler, a detective novel set in the 1930s.

From *This Sea Town was My World* by Dylan Thomas, the Welsh poet.

3.6 Responding to drama

3.6.1 Choose at least one of the following:
Anticipation 1
  i Discuss the following situation in pairs or groups:

A husband and wife are waiting for an old friend of the wife's to arrive. They haven't seen each other for years. They talk about the past and what to expect.

Improvise the situation *either* imagining the husband has met the friend *or* imagining the husband has never met the friend. You may include the friend's arrival in your improvisation.

ii In pairs or groups: each recall a friend you haven't seen for years and tell each other an imaginary story of your re-meeting. It may be someone you want to meet or someone you don't want to meet.

iii Describe in pairs a meeting between yourself and an old friend you haven't seen for years.

3.6.2
Anticipation 2

Look at this picture:

What do you think the relationship is between the three people?
One of the women is married to the man. Which one do you think it is? Why?
The play you are about to read an extract from is called *Old Times*. What do you think it might be about?

3.6.3   i This is the scene as described in the stage directions:

A converted farmhouse.

A long window up centre. Bedroom door up left. Front door up right.

Spare modern furniture.
Two sofas. An armchair.

Autumn. Night.

GLOSSARY
spare undecorative

81

ii What does the scene suggest to you?
What do you think 'up left' and 'up right' mean?

iii Read:

ACT ONE

Light dim. Three figures discerned.

DEELEY slumped in armchair, still.
KATE curled on a sofa, still.
ANNA standing at the window, looking out.

Silence.

Lights up on DEELEY and KATE, smoking cigarettes.

ANNA's figure remains still in dim light at the window.

iv What does the scene suggest to you now?

Express the following in your own words:
Light dim   slumped
discerned   curled

Any guesses as to who might be who in the photograph?

3.6.4 Read the whole extract once.
Ignore the numbers and the divisions at this stage.

1

KATE
(*Reflectively*). Dark.

Pause.

DEELEY
Fat or thin?
KATE
Fuller than me. I think.

Pause.

DEELEY
She was then?
KATE
I think so.
DEELEY
She may not be now.

Pause.

Was she your best friend?
KATE
Oh, what does that mean?

5

DEELEY
What?
KATE
The word friend ... when you look back ... all that time.   10
DEELEY
Can't you remember what you felt?

Pause.

KATE
It is a very long time.
DEELEY
But you remember her. She remembers you. Or why would she be
coming here tonight?
KATE
I suppose because she remembers me.   15

Pause.

DEELEY
Did you think of her as your best friend?
KATE
She was my only friend.
DEELEY
Your best and only.
KATE
My one and only.

Pause.

If you have only one of something you can't say it's the best of   20
anything.
DEELEY
Because you have nothing to compare it with?
KATE
Mmnn.

Pause.

DEELEY
(*Smiling*) She was incomparable.
KATE
Oh, I'm sure she wasn't.   25

2

DEELEY
I didn't know you had so few friends.
KATE
I had none. None at all. Except her.
DEELEY
Why her?

KATE
I don't know.

Pause.

She was a thief. She used to steal things. 30

DEELEY
Who from?

KATE
Me.

DEELEY
What things?

KATE
Bits and pieces. Underwear.

DEELEY *chuckles.*

DEELEY
Will you remind her? 35

KATE
Oh … I don't think so.

DEELEY
Is that what attracted you to her?

KATE
What?

DEELEY
The fact that she was a thief.

KATE
No. 40

Pause.

3

DEELEY
Are you looking forward to seeing her?

KATE
No.

DEELEY
I am. I shall be very interested.

KATE
In what?

DEELEY
In you. I'll be watching you. 45

KATE
Me? Why?

DEELEY
To see if she's the same person.

KATE
You think you'll find out through me?

DEELEY
Definitely.

Pause.

KATE
I hardly remember her. I've almost totally forgotten her.   50

Pause.

DEELEY
Any idea what she drinks?

KATE
None.

DEELEY
She may be a vegetarian.

KATE
Ask her.

DEELEY
It's too late. You've cooked your casserole.   55

4

Pause

Why isn't she married? I mean, why isn't she bringing her husband?

KATE
Ask her.

DEELEY
Do I have to ask her everything?

KATE
Do you want me to ask your questions for you?

DEELEY
No. Not at all.   60

Pause.

KATE
Of course she's married.

DEELEY
How do you know?

KATE
Everyone's married.

DEELEY
Then why isn't she bringing her husband?

KATE
Isn't she?   65

Pause

DEELEY
Did she mention a husband in her letter?

KATE
No.

DEELEY
What do you think he'd be like? I mean, what sort of man would she
have married? After all she was your best – your only – friend. You
must have some idea. What kind of man would he be?

KATE
I have no idea.

DEELEY
Haven't you any curiosity?

KATE
You forget. I know her.

DEELEY
You haven't seen her for twenty years.

KATE
You've never seen her. There's a difference.

5

Pause

DEELEY
At least the casserole is big enough for four.

KATE
You said she was a vegetarian.

Pause

DEELEY
Did she have many friends?

KATE
Oh ... the normal amount, I suppose.

DEELEY
Normal? What's normal? You had none.

KATE
One.

DEELEY
Is that normal?

Pause

She ... had quite a lot of friends, did she?

KATE
Hundreds.

DEELEY
You met them?

KATE
Not all, I think. But after all, we were living together. There were
visitors, from time to time. I met them.

DEELEY
Her visitors?

KATE
What?

DEELEY
Her visitors. Her friends. You had no friends. 90

KATE
Her friends, yes.

DEELEY
You met them.

6   *Pause*

(*Abruptly*) You lived together?

KATE
Mmmnn?

DEELEY
You lived together? 95

KATE
Of course.

DEELEY
I didn't know that.

KATE
Didn't you?

DEELEY
You never told me that. I thought you just knew each other.

KATE
We did. 100

DEELEY
But in fact you lived with each other.

KATE
Of course we did. How else would she steal my underwear from me?
In the street?

Pause

DEELEY
I knew you had shared with someone at one time ...

Pause

But I didn't know it was her. 105

KATE
Of course it was.

Pause

DEELEY
Anyway, none of this matters.

What do you sense about

   i the relationship between Kate and Deeley?

   ii Kate's relationship with the woman they are talking about, Anna?

  iii Deeley's relationship with Anna?

Discuss in pairs.

3.6.5
Extension

i Rehearse the passage in pairs with each of you taking one part. Practise section by section. Pay particular attention to the speed (slow with lots of pauses) the rhythm and intonation of the voice.

ii (Optional)
With others in your group act it out in sections (there are six sections for six pairs). You may use the text to refer to. Try and imagine yourself in the situation.

3.6.6
Understanding and interpretation

i Complete the following sentences:

Kate and Anna haven't met for _____

Kate thinks Anna is a _____

because _____

Anna is a _____ woman.

Kate has cooked a _____

ii Write T (true) F (false) DK (don't know). Re-write the false sentences so that they are true. Add sentences of your own.

Kate
Kate is looking forward to meeting her old friend.
Anna was Kate's only friend.
She has almost forgotten Anna.
Kate thinks Deeley and Anna have never met.
She doesn't want Deeley to find out too much.
We are not sure whether Kate likes Anna or not.
She is trying to play down the importance of the meeting.
She thinks Anna never drinks.

Deeley
We don't know whether Deeley has met Anna or not.
He is looking forward to seeing her.
He is not interested in Kate's reaction to the meeting.
He is only curious about Anna.
He wants to know what kind of man she's married.
He didn't realise Anna and Kate had lived together.

iii Which of the following words do you think describe Kate's mood? Add your own.

gloomy	resentful	solitary
sad	lonely	friendly
pensive	bored	

iv Which of the following words do you think describe Deeley's mood? Add your own.

nosey	resentful	polite
cold	curious	friendly

v Discussion

Is there any tension in the scene? Why? How do you know?
Where is Anna during the scene?
Are all the feelings clear? Are they ambiguous?
Do they change?
Do you think Deeley does know Anna?
Do you think Kate is indifferent to Anna's coming?
Is Anna really married?

Look at the line 'To see if she's the same person'.
Is it ambiguous? What could it mean?
Why do you think Deeley says: 'Anyway none of this matters'?

3.6.7 Read the next part of the play.

ANNA

Queuing all night, the rain, do you remember? My goodness, the Albert Hall, Covent Garden, What did we eat? To look back, half the night, to do things we loved, we were young then of course, but what stamina, and to work in the morning, and to a concert, or the opera, or the ballet, that night, you haven't forgotten? And then riding on top 5 of the bus down Kensington High Street, and the bus conductors, and then dashing for the matches for the gasfire and then I suppose scrambled eggs, or did we? Who cooked? Both giggling and chattering, both huddling to the heat, then bed and sleeping, and all the hustle and bustle in the morning, rushing for the bus again for 10 work, lunchtimes in Green Park, exchanging all our news, with our very own sandwiches, innocent girls, innocent secretaries, and then the night to come, and goodness knows what excitement in store, I mean the sheer expectation of it all, the looking-forwardness of it all, and so poor, but to be poor and young, and a girl, in London then ... 15 and the cafes we found, almost private ones, weren't they? Where artists and writers and sometimes actors collected, and others with dancers, we sat hardly breathing with our coffee, heads bent, so as not to be seen, so as not to disturb, so as not to distract, and listened and listened to all those words, all those cafes and all those people, 20 creative undoubtedly, and does it still exist I wonder? Do you know? Can you tell me?

Slight pause

DEELEY
We rarely get to London.

Kate stands, goes to a small table and pours coffee from a pot.

GLOSSARY
Albert Hall (l.2): a concert hall in London
Covent Garden (l.2): a famous opera house in London
huddling (l.9): getting close together
hustle and bustle (l.10): noisy activity

i Understanding and interpretation

Who is Anna talking to and about?

Say in your own words, what impression Anna tries to give of their early life together?

How do you react to it? Do you believe her?

Is she being nostalgic – does it move you? – or is there a suggestion of falsity and fantasy? What does she remind you of?

ii Style and effect

How many whole sentences are there in her speech?

Towards the end what repetitions of phrases are there?

What effect do they have?

What effect does Deeley's remark have?

iii Discussion

How do you think the play will develop?

Discuss in pairs.

3.6.8 This is a further extract from later on in the play. Read:

KATE

What do you think attracted her to you?

DEELEY

I don't know. What?

KATE

She found your face very sensitive, vulnerable.

DEELEY

Did she?

KATE

She wanted to comfort it, in the way only a woman can.   5

DEELEY

Did she?

KATE

Oh yes.

DEELEY

She wanted to comfort my face, in the way only a woman can?

KATE

She was prepared to extend herself to you.

DEELEY

I beg your pardon?   10

KATE

She fell in love with you.

DEELEY

With me?

KATE

You were so unlike the others. We knew men who were brutish, crass.

GLOSSARY
crass (l.14): stupid

90

> DEELEY
> There really are such men, then? Crass men?   15
> KATE
> Quite crass.

i Understanding and interpretation

What has happened?

What do you now know about the relationship between the three characters?

What did Anna think of Deeley?

How would you describe Kate's attitude?

How would you describe Deeley's attitude?

When you read it aloud, how would you describe your reading? (e g hysterical, excited, flat, bored)

How far do you think the characters are pretending with each other?

ii Style and effect

What effect do the following utterances have?

> Did she?
>
> Oh yes
>
> I beg your pardon?
>
> With me?
>
> There really are such men, then?

Do you find the exchange intense? If so, in what way?

3.6.9
Follow-up work

Either: Write 1–2 paragraphs summarising your impression of the extracts and the effect they had on you.
Or:
In pairs, invent a story about a strange meeting. Make some notes but do not write it out completely. Tell another pair.

3.6.10
Notes

Harold Pinter, the author of this play, was born in 1930. He has written many plays for the stage and television and has scripted many films.

3.7 Responding to poetry

3.7.1
Language work

In pairs:
Write down in English the names of as many birds and as many trees as you can.
What's the difference between a 'deciduous' and an 'evergreen' tree?

3.7.2
Anticipation

Imagine you are an explorer on a ship. You come across an undiscovered land on the other side of the world. Write down one or two sentences that describe your feelings. Share your sentences with others in your class.

3.7.3 Read the following as many times as you like. You will not at this stage be asked any questions. Simply see if any of its power comes across to you.

Marina

Quis hic locus, quae
regio, quae mundi plaga?

What seas what shores what grey rocks and what islands
What water lapping the bow
And scent of pine and the woodthrush singing through the fog
What images return
O my daughter.   5

Those who sharpen the tooth of the dog, meaning
Death
Those who glitter with the glory of the hummingbird, meaning
Death
Those who sit in the stye of contentment, meaning   10
Death
Those who suffer the ecstasy of the animals, meaning
Death

Are become unsubstantial, reduced by a wind,
A breath of pine, and the woodsong fog   15
By this grace dissolved in place

Obviously, the meaning is not explicit. There is no single, 'right' interpretation. The poem suggests many things.

i   Jot down on a piece of paper any associations it offers to you. Fold it up. Try not to worry about unknown vocabulary at this stage.
ii Put your paper in the room with everyone else's. Make sure they are jumbled up.
iii Take one of them. Discuss the ideas on it with your colleagues. If possible, do this in small groups.

3.7.4   Read the following information:
Notes

Marina was the name of the daughter of Pericles in Shakespeare's play of the same name. Marina – as her name suggests – was born at sea and was lost to her father. She was miraculously found by him when she had become a woman.

T. S. Eliot was born in 1888 in St. Louis, Missouri. After a Harvard education he came to England as a bank clerk in 1915. He became a naturalised British citizen in 1927 and in 1940 won the Nobel Prize for literature. He died in 1965.

The Latin quotation is from Seneca's Hercules Furens. *It means 'What place, what region of the world is this?' Hercules has woken up in a daze after having killed his wife and children. He slowly realises the horror of what he has done.*

T. S. Eliot spent part of his youth sailing off the coast of Saint Ann. The island Eliot is thought to have at least partly in mind is Rogue Island, Maine, New England.

Discuss the poem again in pairs in the light of this information.

Match the words on the left with the definitions on the right. Use the poem to help you.

lap	coniferous tree
scent	shine brightly and intermittently
pine	small tropical bird
woodthrush	enclosure for pigs
glitter	without solidity
hummingbird	splash softly against
stye	a feeling of satisfaction
contentment	beauty, suggesting a favour from God
unsubstantial	pleasant smell
grace	type of song bird

Which of the following do you agree with. You may modify any you don't agree with.

I like the poem.

It is very personal.

The narrator is both T. S. Eliot and Pericles.

The poem suggests the landing in the New World when America was 'discovered'.

In the opening, the poet creates a sense of wonder.

The poem's 'meaning' cannot be exactly explained.

The second section beginning 'Those' suggests four of the seven deadly sins: greed, pride, sloth and lust.

The images that 'return' are the images of death.

The images of death suggest the world we live in.

The images of death relate to Hercules' horror at unnatural death.

The poem suggests hope in that the images of death dissolve when faced with rebirth.

The word 'woodsong' is an invented word. It suggests that the song of the woodthrush and the pinewood have dissolved into one another.

The word 'grace' suggests the place is blessed by God.

Discuss in pairs.

Now read the rest of the poem. Try to understand as much as you can.

What is this face, less clear and clearer
The pulse in the arm, less strong and stronger –
Given or lent? more distant than stars and nearer than the eye

Whispers and small laughter between leaves and hurrying feet   20
Under sleep, where all the waters meet.

Bowsprit cracked with ice and paint cracked with heat.
I made this, I have forgotten
And remember.

GLOSSARY
Bowsprit (l.22): strong pole pointing out from the front of the ship

rigging (l.25): ropes and sails

canvas (l.25): strong cloth used for the sails

garboard strake (l.28): wood next to the lowest part of the ship

seams (l.28): joins

caulking (l.28): making watertight

granite (l.33): very hard rock

The rigging weak and the canvas rotten   25
Between one June and another September.
Made this unknowing, half conscious, unknown, my own.
The garboard strake leaks, the seams need caulking.
This form, this face, this life
Living to live in a world of time beyond me; let me   30
Resign my life for this life, my speech for that unspoken,
The awakened, lips parted, the hope, the new ships.

What seas what shores what granite islands towards my timbers
And woodthrush calling through the fog
My daughter.   35

Which lines sound like an old man talking? Do any lines suggest memories of childhood? What is he saying in 'let me Resign my life for this life'? Who or what does 'this life' refer to?

3.7.8
Background
Compile a biography card for T. S. Eliot.
Find out what else he wrote.

3.8 Conclusion

3.8.1   Discuss the Unit in pairs. What did you enjoy most?

UNIT 4

How it's written (1)

4.1 Use of detail to create atmosphere

4.1.1
Language work

Use a dictionary if necessary:

i Write down the past tense of the following verbs:

hear
rise
cling

ii What is the difference in meaning between:

nightmare
dream

Which has a negative suggestion?

iii Which of the following verbs suggests the most noise?
Which the least noise? Put them in order of volume:

mutter
yell
whisper
shout

Which can also be used as a noun?

iv What is the difference in meaning between the following verbs?

sob   wail
mourn   cry
moan

Which can also be used as a noun?

v The following verbs have a similar meaning:

grip   snatch   seize

What are the differences between them?
Which can also be used as a noun?

vi The following verbs have a similar meaning:

shudder   shiver

What is the difference between them?

Discuss your answers in pairs.

In pairs, tell each other a ghost story you know or a vivid dream you have had. If you don't know a ghost story you may make one up. You may use the following picture sequence to stimulate ideas for either a dream or a ghost story:

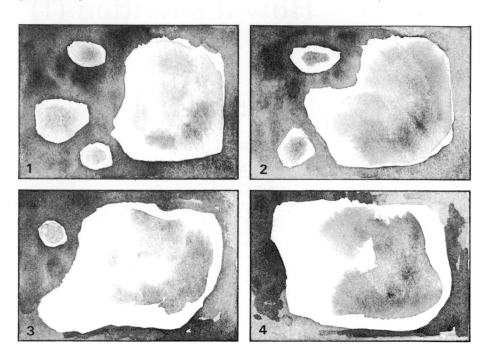

4.1.3 The story so far:

The year is 1801. The setting is the bleak landscape of the Yorkshire Moors. Mr Lockwood, a rather affected and foolish city gentleman, has called upon Mr Heathcliff, his new landlord, at his home, Wuthering Heights. A heavy snowstorm prevents his leaving the strange oppressive atmosphere he finds himself in and he is forced to spend the night at the house. He is an unwelcome guest – an intruder. He is asked to sleep in a kind of oak cupboard with sliding panelled doors into the room and a window to the outside. His fitful sleep is interrupted by dreams of the diary of Catherine Earnshaw (or Catherine Linton, her married name) that he has tried to read.

4.1.4 **i** Read the passage quickly. Try to find the answers to the following questions:

Who is telling the story?
Who was he dreaming of?
Was she young or old?
What did she try and do?
Why was the dream horrible?
What did he try and do to protect himself?
Why did he cry out?
What effect did his cry have?

Compare your answers in pairs.

This time, I remembered I was lying in the oak closet, and I heard distinctly the gusty wind, and the driving of the snow; I heard, also, the fir bough repeat its teasing sound, and ascribed it to the right cause: but it annoyed me so much, that I resolved to silence it, if possible; and, I thought, I rose and endeavoured to unhasp the casement. The hook was soldered into the staple: a circumstance observed by me when awake, but forgotten. 'I must stop it, nevertheless!' I muttered, knocking my knuckles through the glass, and stretching an arm out to seize the importunate branch; instead of which, my fingers closed on the fingers of a little, ice-cold hand! The intense horror of nightmare came over me: I tried to draw back my arm, but the hand clung to it, and a most melancholy voice sobbed, 'Let me in – let me in!' 'Who are you?' I asked, struggling, meanwhile, to disengage myself. 'Catherine Linton,' it replied, shiveringly (why did I think of Linton? I had read Earnshaw twenty times for Linton); 'I'm come home: I'd lost my way on the moor!' As it spoke, I discerned, obscurely, a child's face looking through the window. Terror made me cruel; and, finding it useless to attempt shaking the creature off, I pulled its wrist on to the broken pane, and rubbed it to and fro till the blood ran down and soaked the bedclothes: still it wailed, 'Let me in!' and maintained its tenacious grip, almost maddening me with fear. 'How can I?' I said at length. 'Let me go, if you want me to let you in!' The fingers relaxed, I snatched mine through the hole, hurriedly piled the books up in a pyramid against it, and stopped my ears to exclude the lamentable prayer. I seemed to keep them closed above a quarter of an hour; yet, the instant I listened again, there was the doleful cry moaning on! 'Begone!' I shouted, 'I'll never let you in, not if you beg for twenty years.' 'It is twenty years,' mourned the voice: 'twenty years. I've been a waif for twenty years!' Thereat began a feeble scratching outside, and the pile of books moved as if thrust forward. I tried to jump up; but could not stir a limb; and so yelled aloud, in a frenzy of fright. To my confusion, I discovered the yell was not ideal: hasty footsteps approached my chamber door; somebody pushed it open, with a vigorous hand, and a light glimmered through the squares at the top of the bed. I sat shuddering yet, and wiping the perspiration from my forehead.

Reactions

ii Describe to each other your reactions to what you read in at least two sentences. Do they include words like 'cruel', 'horrible' and 'intense'? What other words have you used in your descriptions?

iii Read the passage again carefully. You may need this glossary:
closet (l.1): closed cupboard *gusty (l.2):* blowing in strong rushes *ascribed (l.3):* attributed *unhasp the casement (l.5–6):* unfasten the window *hook (l.6):* curved piece of metal, used for keeping a window closed *soldered (l.6):* sealed by metal *staple (l.6):* U-shaped loop of metal *importunate (l.9):* persisting in making some kind of demand *pane (l.19):* glass in the window *doleful (l.27):* miserable *waif (l.29):* homeless person

iv Improving understanding

Answer the following questions:

a) What was the weather like?

What does Mr Lockwood at first think is causing the noise that disturbs him?

Why do you think his knuckles are not described as bleeding when he knocks them through the glass?

How does Mr Lockwood 'deceive' the hand?

How long has Catherine been dead?

What effect did the nightmare have on Mr Lockwood?

b) Is Mr Lockwood awake or asleep?

Why do you think the hook was soldered into the staple?

Do you think Catherine is a ghost or part of Mr Lockwood's nightmare?

Why do you think Catherine calls herself Linton and not Earnshaw when her face is that of a child?

Why do you think she is trying to get into the house?

Who do you think comes into the room at the end?

What do you know about his character from the passage?

What do you imagine the story of *Wuthering Heights* – the title of the novel – is about?

4.1.5
Language

i Find the words you explored in 4.1.1. How are they used?

ii Write down phrases which contain a verb which advances the *action* of the narrative e.g. 'I heard distinctly' (but not 'ascribed it' which details the consequence of the action, or 'was soldered' which describes a state of affairs.)

iii Find words in the passage which mean the following:

said in a sad voice

said as a question

said in a low, unclear voice

answered

said in a long high-pitched tone, as though in misery

said in a loud voice

4.1.6
Style and effect

This passage is a very important part of Chapter 3 in the novel. Before this point the atmosphere of menace has been restrained – although present – conveyed through a series of small actions, tones of voice and various attitudes. Here, we are taken to the centre of the novel's 'problem' even though it concerns events which happened many years before and the restrained menace changes into an atmosphere of unreality and horror. The writer, Emily Bronte, conveys this not just by words, which merely tell you of the horror, but by portraying small details which make you feel it.

i Underline words/phrases which make you feel the atmosphere (e.g. 'lying in the oak closet' – a closet is enclosed and creates a feeling of claustrophobia.) Give reasons for your choice.

ii Circle any words/phrases that tell you explicitly what Mr Lockwood's feelings were.

4.1.7
Extension

Do you know the story of *Wuthering Heights*? Does anybody in your class? If not can you guess how it will continue? Try to get hold of a copy and read as much as you can.

This is the part of Yorkshire where it is supposed to be set:

What impression does it make on you?

4.1.8
Background

i This is a painting of Emily Brontë, the author, by her brother, Branwell:

Consider the passage you have just read, look at the picture and discuss in pairs what you think Emily's character might have been like.

ii Read the following appreciation of Emily by Ellen Nussey, her sister Charlotte's friend:

> Her extreme reserve seemed impenetrable, yet she was intensely lovable. She invited confidence in her moral power. Few people have the gift of looking and smiling, as she could look and smile – one of her rare expressive looks was something to remember through life, there was such a depth of soul and feeling, and yet shyness of revealing herself, a strength of self-containment seen in no other – She was in the strictest sense a law unto herself, and a heroine in keeping to her law.... Emily was a child in spirit for glee and enjoyment, or when thrown entirely on her own resources to do a kindness. She could be vivacious in conversation and enjoy giving pleasure – A spell of mischief also lurked in her on occasions, when out on the moors – She enjoyed leading Charlotte where she would not dare to go of her own free will – C. had a mortal dread of unknown animals and it was Emily's pleasure to lead her into close vicinity and then to tell her of what she had done, laughing at her horror with great amusement.
>
> Emily did not easily make friends and it used to be a matter of surprise to Charlotte that she made an exception in my favour ...

Look up any words you want to know the meaning of in a dictionary. Does it confirm what you thought? How could you summarise her character?

iii Compile a biography card. Add a sentence entitled CHARACTER using the passage above. Include the following information on the card:

Born in 1818. Died of tuberculosis in 1848. Fourth child of a clergyman. Brought up by aunt after mother's death. Published under pseudonym, as did her sisters Charlotte and Anne.

Consult an encyclopaedia for anything else you wish to find out.

4.2 Building up tension

4.2.1
Continuing the story of Macbeth

Macbeth has killed Duncan, and become King but he is still not contented. Banquo has been promised by the witches that his children will be kings, and so Macbeth has had Banquo murdered. It is reported to him that Banquo's throat has been cut and that he is safe in a ditch ... 'with twenty trenched gashes in his head' and so Macbeth returns to the banquet he is giving for all his noblemen.

4.2.2   **i** Listen to the extract as many times as you like. Try not to worry if there are a few words you don't really understand. You are simply going to put the following sentences in the correct order:

1 Macbeth asks Banquo's ghost to speak.
2 Lady Macbeth accuses Macbeth of not being manly.

3 The ghost enters and sits in Macbeth's place.
4 Lady Macbeth mocks Macbeth for making faces at an empty chair.
5 Macbeth says he would prefer to reproach Banquo for being unkind in not coming to the banquet than have to pity him because he has had an accident.
6 Lady Macbeth says Macbeth's fear is not real fear and that his behaviour is shameful.
7 Ross tries to make excuses for Macbeth's strange behaviour.
8 Banquo's ghost shakes his blood-stained hair at Macbeth.
9 Macbeth says he is brave to look at such a terrible sight.
10 Ross asks Macbeth to join them.
11 Macbeth is visibly shocked for the first time.
12 Macbeth says he is horrified to think that the dead can come back to life.
13 Lady Macbeth accuses Macbeth of being afraid, just as he was before the murder of Duncan.
14 Lennox asks Macbeth to sit down.
15 Lady Macbeth tells the company to carry on eating and not to take any notice of Macbeth.
16 Macbeth wants to know who is playing a trick on him.
17 Macbeth says he wishes he had all the country's nobility, including Banquo, under one roof.
18 Macbeth says he cannot sit down because the table is full.
19 Lady Macbeth makes excuses for Macbeth's strange behaviour by saying it is a temporary condition which he has had since childhood.
20 Macbeth denies that he killed Banquo.

LENNOX	May it please your Highness sit?	
	(The ghost of BANQUO *enters, and sits in* MACBETH'S *place.)*	
MACBETH	Here had we now our country's honour roofed,	
	Were the graced person of our Banquo present;	
	Who may I rather challenge for unkindness	
	Than pity for mischance!	5
ROSS	His absence, sir,	
	Lays blame upon his promise. Please it your Highness	
	To grace us with your royal company.	
MACBETH	The table's full.	10
LENNOX	Here is a place reserved, sir.	
MACBETH	Where?	
LENNOX	Here, my good lord. What is't that	
	Moves your Highness?	
MACBETH	Which of you have done this?	15
LORDS	What, my good lord?	

MACBETH	Thou canst not say I did it: never shake
	Thy gory locks at me.
ROSS	Gentlemen, rise; his Highness is not well.
LADY MACBETH	Sit, worthy friends: my lord is often thus, 20
	And hath been from his youth: pray you, keep seat;
	The fit is momentary; upon a thought
	He will again be well. If much you note him
	You shall offend him and extend his passion.
	Feed and regard him not. Are you a man? 25
MACBETH	Ay, and a bold one, that dare look on that
	Which might appal the devil.
LADY MACBETH	O proper stuff!
	This is the very painting of your fear;
	This is the air-drawn dagger which, you said 30
	Led you to Duncan. O! these flaws and starts –
	Imposters to true fear – would well become
	A woman's story at a winter's fire.
	Authorized by her grandam. Shame itself!
	Why do you make such faces? When all's done 35
	You look but on a stool.
MACBETH	Prithee, see there! behold! look! lo!
	How say you?
	Why, what care I? If thou canst nod, speak too.
	If charnel-houses and our graves must send 40
	Those that we bury back, our monuments
	Shall be the maws of kites. *(Ghost disappears)*

ii Work in pairs. Write the numbers of the sentences on pages 100–1 in the correct order. The first one is 14.

iii Look at the passage and write next to each line who the speaker is speaking to. (e.g. LENNOX: May it please your Highness sit? MACBETH) Where the person spoken to changes in the middle of a line, put both names.

iv Go back over the passage. Express in your own words what the following mean:

Here had we now our country's honour roofed.
His absence, sir, lays blame upon his promise.
Thou canst not say I did it.
The fit is momentary.
If you much note him, You shall offend him.
This is the very painting of your fear.
This is the air-drawn dagger which led you to Duncan.
When all's done, You look but on a stool.
If thou canst nod, speak too.

Discuss in pairs.

v GLOSSARY (ar = archaic language) *appal (l.27):* shock   (ar) *o proper stuff (l.28):* What a fine thing this is! (ironical) *flaws (l.31):* outbursts *authorized (l.34):* confirmed   (ar) *grandam (l.34):* grandmother   (ar) *prithee (l.37):* please   (ar) *lo! (l.37):* look *charnel-houses (l.40):* place in which the bones of the dead are kept *maw (l.42):* stomach *kite (l.42):* bird of prey

vi Improving understanding

Look again at the extract and try to answer the following questions:

When does the ghost enter?

When does Macbeth first realise that Banquo's ghost is in the room?

Is Macbeth sincere in the lines:

'Here had we now our country's honour roofed,
Were the graced person of our Banquo present;
Who may I rather challenge for unkindness
Than pity for mischance!' (Give reasons.)

At this stage does he think Banquo is dead and buried?

What is the irony in the words 'Than pity for mischance?'

Why does Macbeth say 'the table's full'?

What is Lady Macbeth trying to do in the lines:

'Sit worthy friends . . . regard him not'?

Do you think Lady Macbeth shouts or whispers the line:

'Are you a man?'? (Give a reason.)

Can you describe what the ghost looks like from this extract?

What is Lady Macbeth trying to do in the lines:

'O proper stuff . . . but on a stool'?

Does she succeed?

Can Lady Macbeth and the other guests see the ghost?

Discuss in pairs.

vii Style and effect

Discuss in groups how Shakespeare builds up the tension in the extract. Include such things as:

Macbeth's mood at the beginning of the extract.	Macbeth's private horror.
The probable reason for the mood.	What Lady Macbeth and the other guests can see.
His role as host of the banquet.	Lady Macbeth's reaction.
The atmosphere at the beginning.	The effect of the incident on the banquet.
The appearance of the ghost.	The atmosphere at the end.

4.2.3

Follow-up work/ extension

Choose *one* of the following:

i Compare the extract from *Macbeth* with the extract from *Wuthering Heights* by adding to the following lists.

SIMILARITIES	DIFFERENCES
Both are about a ghost.	In the novel, one narrator tells the story; in the play the dialogue is shared.

Use a separate piece of paper.

ii Compare the ghost of Banquo with the ghost of Hamlet's father (2.5.3):

iii Discuss the following in pairs:

    a) Do you think Banquo's ghost should actually appear on the stage or should it be confined to Macbeth's imagination.

    What advantages are there in the audience imagining their own kind of ghost?

    Do you find it odd that Catherine Linton has the face of a child but says she's been wandering for twenty years? How do *you* think she looks?

    b) What thoughts and feelings does the *Macbeth* extract arouse in you?

    Describe the effect you think this scene has in a theatrical performance.

    Do you now believe in ghosts?!

iv Find out how *Macbeth* continues. How does it finish? (You may use a reference book, ask others in your class, or ask your teacher!)

4.3 Predictions

4.3.1 When we read a sentence quickly we concentrate on the words which carry most meaning. For example, look at the sentence:

> **As soon as I saw the elephant I knew ..... that I ought not to shoot him.**

Here, we probably focus on the words, 'saw', 'elephant', 'knew', 'ought not', 'shoot'. They carry more meaning than the words, 'I', 'the', 'to', 'him'. We don't ignore this second group of words – they help to make the meaning clearer – but we don't notice them as much as we notice the words in the first group. This helps us to read the whole sentence more easily.

  i Underline the most important words in the following:

> **It is a serious matter to shoot a working elephant – it is comparable to destroying a huge and costly piece of machinery – and obviously one ought not to do it if it can possibly be avoided.**

  ii In pairs, compare your answers.

4.3.2 There are often clues in the first part of a sentence – and the whole context – which help us guess what is to come in the second part, e.g.

And at that distance, peacefully eating, the elephant looked …

We suspect the writer is going to add to his reasons for feeling he should not shoot the elephant. The phrase will probably be linked with 'peacefully eating'. Nothing much new is added by the phrase which in fact follows: 'no more dangerous than a cow'.

   i The writer's problem was that the elephant was in a period of 'must' (i.e. a period of excitement for male elephants when they become dangerous). He thought the period was almost finished and the elephant would soon be harmless. The trouble was a huge crowd of expectant onlookers was following him hoping for a kill.

  ii Can you continue the following phrases?

     'I did not in the least want …'
     'an immense crowd blocked the road for …'
     'all certain that the elephant …'
     'They did not like me, but with the magical rifle in my hands …'
     'And suddenly I realised that I …'
     'The people …'

 iii Compare in pairs. Look in the Key in the back of the book to discover what was actually written. What helped you make your guesses?

    These extracts are from *Shooting an Elephant* by George Orwell.

4.3.3   **i** What are your feelings about hunting or shooting wild animals?
Discussion
   ii Are there any species at risk of extinction in your own country? Discuss.

4.4 Focus on 'style'

'Style' refers to the way writers express themselves. Sometimes, a writer's language is over-elaborate and self-conscious and tries to impress the reader without having much connection with the meaning of *what* is being expressed. In other words, the writer is showing off. At the other extreme, the language is sometimes flat and dull and seems not to have been written by a personal, individual voice at all. At its best a writer's language expresses his/her individual thoughts and feelings sincerely and interestingly, so that *what* is being said cannot be distinguished from *how* it is being said.

There is no definitive list of technical effects that a writer can use. Some writers, anyway, invent their own. They use whatever they can to say what they have to say.

4.5 Reading without assistance

Read the following poem and share with others in your class your response to its meaning and style.

Homage to a Government

Next year we are to bring the soldiers home
For lack of money, and it is all right.
Places they guarded, or kept orderly,
Must guard themselves, and keep themselves orderly.
We want the money for ourselves at home
Instead of working. And this is all right.   5

It's hard to say who wanted it to happen,
But now it's been decided nobody minds.
The places are a long way off, not here,
Which is all right, and from what we hear
The soldiers there only made trouble happen.   10
Next year we shall be easier in our minds.

Next year we shall be living in a country
That brought its soldiers home for lack of money.
The statues will be standing in the same
Tree-muffled squares, and look nearly the same.   15
Our children will not know it's a different country.
All we can hope to leave them now is money.   *Philip Larkin (1922–85)*

Do you think governments should keep permanent armies abroad?

4.6 Rhythm and sound

Rhythm and sound help to convey a writer's meaning and make it memorable.

4.6.1 **i** Read the following:

GLOSSARY
wilderness (l.1): deserted space
lighted on (l.1): found
den (l.2): resting place for wild animals
behold (l.3): look
brake (archaic word) *(l.8):* broke

As I walked through the wilderness of this world, I lighted on a certain place, where was a den; and I laid me down in that place to sleep: and as I slept I dreamed a dream. I dreamed, and behold I saw a man clothed with rags, standing in a certain place, with his face from his own house, a book in his hand, and a great burden upon his   5
back. I looked, and saw him open the book, and read therein; and as he read, he wept and trembled: and not being able longer to contain, he brake out with a lamentable cry; saying, 'What shall I do?'

---

ii In pairs, paraphrase the passage orally. Does the story seem to be about the real world or do you think it is a fantasy? Give reasons.

iii Underline the main verbs. What tense are they in? Circle the adjectives. Are there a lot? What effect does this have?

iv Which words join phrases together (e.g. 'as', 'and', 'but')? What do you notice? What effect does it have?

v How many sentences are there? Which words in a sentence begin with the same consonant sound? (the repetition of a consonant sound in several words close together is called *alliteration*). Does it add anything to the interest of the story in sound or meaning?

vi Which words are repeated? What effect does it have?

vii What difference would it have made to the story-telling if the writer had said; 'I saw a man who was reading a book and carrying a burden on his back. He looked unhappy and asked what he should do'?

viii Read the passage aloud. What feelings does the rhythm arouse in you?

4.6.2 **i** Read the following:

GLOSSARY
thy (l.1): your
gross (l.2): impenetrable
gentiles (l.4): people with no religion

'Arise, shine, for thy light is come, and the glory of the Lord is risen upon thee. For behold, the darkness shall cover the earth, and gross darkness the people: but the Lord shall arise upon thee, and his glory shall be seen upon thee. And the gentiles shall come to thy light, and kings to the brightness of thy rising.'

5

ii In pairs, paraphrase the passage orally. Where do you think it comes from?

iii What forms are the verbs in? Why do you think these forms are used?

iv Circle the nouns. What do many of them have in common? What effect does it have?

v Which words join phrases together? What do you notice? What effect does it have?

vi Which words contain the vowel sound /ai/ as in 'arise'? (repetition of a vowel sound for poetic effect is called *assonance*). Does it add anything to the beauty or clarity of the expression?

vii Which words are repeated? What effect does it have?

viii The sentences (and half-sentences) contain clauses which balance each other. (e.g. 'And the gentiles shall come to thy light/and kings to the brightness of thy rising') Underline the clauses which balance each other. What effect does it have?

ix Read the passage aloud. What feelings does the rhythm arouse in you?

4.6.3   **i** Listen to the following:

Mr and Mrs Veneering were bran-new people in a bran-new house in a bran-new quarter of London. Everything about the Veneerings was spick and span new. All their furniture was new, all their friends were new, all their servants were new, their plate was new, their carriage was new, their harness was new, their horses were new, their pictures were new, they themselves were new, they were as newly married as was lawfully compatible with their having a bran-new baby, and if they had set up a great-grandfather, he would have come home in matting from the Pantechnicon, without a scratch upon him, French polished to the crown of his head.

For, in the Veneering establishment, from the hall-chairs with the new coat of arms, to the grand pianoforte with the new action, and upstairs again to the new fire-escape, all things were in a state of high varnish and polish. And what was observable in the furniture, was observable in the Veneerings – the surface smelt a little too much of the workshop and was a trifle sticky.

ii In pairs, help each other to understand the passage. In general, what is it about?

iii What does the name of the characters tell you about them?

iv Which word is constantly repeated? What does it help to tell you about the writer's attitude towards the Veneerings?

v How many sentences are there? What do you notice? How is the third sentence constructed? What effect does it have?

vi Can you find any phrases which balance each other?

vii How would you describe the writer's style in this passage?

4.6.4 **i** Listen to the following:

Alone, alone, all, all alone,
Alone on a wide, wide sea!
And never a saint took pity on
My soul in agony.

The many men, so beautiful!   5
And they all dead did lie:
And a thousand thousand slimy things
Lived on; and so did I.

I look'd upon the rotting sea,
And drew my eyes away;   10
I look'd upon the rotting deck,
And there the dead men lay.

I look'd to heaven, and tried to pray;
But or ever a prayer had gusht,
A wicked whisper came, and made   15
My heart as dry as dust.

I closed my lids, and kept them close,
And the balls like pulses beat;
But the sky and the sea, and the sea and the sky,
Lay like a load on my weary eye,   20
And the dead were at my feet.

GLOSSARY
slimy (l.7): unpleasantly
   soft, wet and dirty
rotting (l.9): decaying
or ever (l.14): before
gusht (modern spelling:
   gushed) *(l.14):* flowed
   out strongly

ii The sailor has killed an albatross – a bird which usually brings good luck to seamen if it is allowed to follow them. His shipmates are dead and he is alone on the boat.

In pairs, try to summarise in your own words what he did and what his feelings were.

iii Underline the main verbs. What tense are they in?

Circle the adjectives. What do you notice? Would you say the poem was narrative, descriptive, neither or both? Give examples to support your choice.

iv Find examples of: alliteration; assonance; repetition; simile. Which of these devices do you think most affects the force of these stanzas?

v Listen to the tape. How many beats do most lines have? 4, 5 or 6 syllables? What effect does this have? Which lines are not regular? What effect does that have?

vi Which ends of lines rhyme with each other (e.g. 'sea'/'agony')? Is the scheme regular or irregular? What effect does it have?

vii Most of the stanzas have four lines. The last has five. Does the extra line add anything to the weight or tone of the poem?

viii Do you like the poem? Give reasons.

4.6.5 i Read the following:

> Some natural tears they drop'd, but wip'd them soon;
> The World was all before them, where to choose
> Their place of rest, and Providence their guide:
> They hand in hand with wandring steps and slow,
> Through Eden took their solitarie way.   5

  ii Adam and Eve are leaving the Garden of Eden. Discuss in pairs what impression the writer creates.

  iii Comment on the rhythm and the rhyme and the word order (e.g. how many syllables are there in each line? What effect does it have?).

4.6.6 i Listen to the following:

DESDEMONA	… let him confess a truth.	
OTHELLO	He hath confessed.	
DESDEMONA	What, my lord?	
OTHELLO	That he hath used thee.	
DESDEMONA	How? unlawfully?	5
OTHELLO	Ay.	
DESDEMONA	He will not say so.	
OTHELLO	No; his mouth is stopped: Honest Iago hath ta'en order for't.	
DESDEMONA	O! my fear interprets. What! is he dead?	10
OTHELLO	Had all his hairs been lives, my great revenge Had stomach for them all.	
DESDEMONA	Alas! he is betrayed and I undone.	
OTHELLO	Out, strumpet! Weepest thou for him to my face?	
DESDEMONA	O! banish me, my lord, but kill me not!	15
OTHELLO	Down, strumpet!	
DESDEMONA	Kill me to-morrow; let me live to-night!	
OTHELLO	Nay, if you strive –	
DESDEMONA	But half an hour!	
OTHELLO	Being done, there is no pause.	20
DESDEMONA	But while I say one prayer!	
OTHELLO	It is too late.	

(He smothers her.)

GLOSSARY
ta'en (l.9): (modern spelling taken)
strumpet (l.14): prostitute (i.e. here = an unfaithful wife)

  ii At the end of this extract Othello murders his wife, Desdemona, certain that she has been unfaithful to him and that Cassio, her supposed lover, has been put to death by Iago after confessing his guilt. In pairs, summarise what happens in this extract.

  iii The dialogue is written in blank verse (i.e. the lines do not rhyme) of approximately ten syllables. The ten syllable line is sometimes uttered by one character and sometimes by more than one. Do you think this breaking up of the line creates a sense of urgency? Find examples.

iv Describe in pairs the effect of the scene (e.g. is it powerful?)

4.6.7
Notes

4.6.1 *The opening of* The Pilgrim's Progress *(1678) by John Bunyan (1628–1688) a non-conformist preacher. It draws upon the Bible as its inspiration and in this extract there are references to the books of Isaiah, Psalms and Acts.*

4.6.2 *This is an extract from the* Book of Isaiah *in the Authorised version of the Bible (1611), the language and rhythm of which had a huge influence on subsequent English literature.*

4.6.3 *An extract from* Our Mutual Friend *(1864–68) by Charles Dickens.*

4.6.4 *From the* Rime of the Ancient Mariner *(1797) by Coleridge (1772–1834). The metre is in ballad form, a simple, direct narrative form in short stanzas.*

4.6.5 *The end of* Paradise Lost *(1667) by John Milton (1608–1674).* Paradise Lost *is written in blank verse.*

4.6.6 *From* Othello *(1603–4) by William Shakespeare.*

4.7 Balancing description and narrative

4.7.1
Anticipation

i Discuss this picture in pairs:

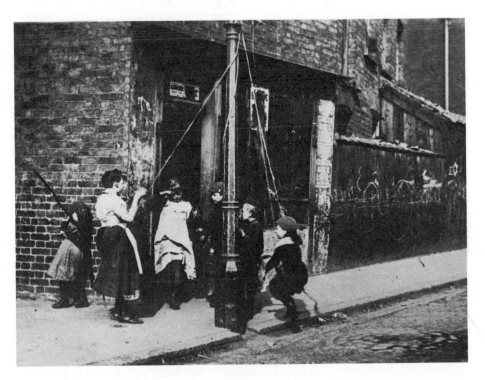

What do you think the children are doing?

ii List the games you know that children play in the street. How are they played? Have you played them? Which was your favourite?

iii What are the following games: hopscotch   leapfrog

4.7.2 The following story is called *The Great Leapfrog Contest* by the American writer William Saroyan. It has been slightly shortened. Make guesses as to what it might be about.

4.7.3 Try to find answers to these questions in the passage that follows:

In what sense was Rosie living in the 'wrong' neighbourhood?
How many were there in the family?
Was Rosie the oldest?
In what ways was Rosie unusual?
Did she win all the fights with boys?

Read:

Rosie Mahoney was a tough little Irish kid whose folks, through some miscalculation in directions, or out of an innate spirit of anarchy, had moved into the Russian-Italian-and-Greek neighbourhood of my home town, across the Southern Pacific tracks, around G Street.

She wore a turtle-neck sweater, usually red. Her father was a 5
bricklayer named Cull and a heavy drinker. Her mother's name was Mary. Mary Mahoney used to go to the Greek Orthodox Catholic Church on Kearny Boulevard every Sunday, because there was no Irish Church to go to anywhere in the neighbourhood. The family seemed to be a happy one. 10

Rosie's three brothers had all grown up and gone to sea. Her two sisters had married. Rosie was the last of the clan. She had entered the world when her father had been close to sixty and her mother in her early fifties. For all that, she was hardly the studious or scholarly type. 15

Rosie had little use for girls, and as far as possible avoided them. She had less use for boys, but found it undesirable to avoid them. That is to say, she made it a point to take part in everything boys did. She was always on hand, and always the first to take up any daring or crazy idea. Everybody felt awkward about her continuous presence, 20
but it was no use trying to chase her away, because that meant a fight in which she asked no quarter, and gave none.

If she didn't whip every boy she fought, every fight was at least an honest draw, with a slight edge in Rosie's favour. She didn't fight girl-style, or cry if hurt. She fought the regular style and took advantage of 25
every opening. It was very humiliating to be hurt by Rosie, so after a while any boy who thought of trying to chase her away, decided not to.

Answer in pairs. Help each other with any important sentences you don't understand. There is no glossary for this story; try not to worry about the meaning of every word.

   i The opening of the story is largely descriptive. Under the following headings write out the phrases from the story that build up a picture of Rosie and her family:

     PARENTS   CLOTHES   CHARACTER   BEHAVIOUR

     Underline the adjectives.

   ii What tense is the story written in?
  iii Underline the verbs which describe the action.
  iv What connection does the narrator have with the story?

4.7.4 Try to find answers to these questions in the passage that follows:

Did the boys manage to frighten her away from the neighbourhood?
Was Rex born in the neighbourhood?
What did the others think of Rex?

Read on:

As a matter of fact, she was just naturally the equal of any boy in the neighbourhood, and much the superior of many of them. Especially after she had lived in the neighbourhood three years. It took her that long to make everybody understand that she had come to stay and that she was going to stay.   5

She did, too; even after the arrival of a boy named Rex Folger, who was from somewhere in the south of Texas. This boy Rex was a natural-born leader. Two months after his arrival in the neighbourhood, it was understood by everyone that if Rex wasn't the leader of the gang, he was very nearly the leader. He had fought and   10 licked every boy in the neighbourhood who at one time or another had fancied himself leader. And he had done so without any noticeable ill-feeling, pride, or ambition.

As a matter of fact, no-one could possibly have been more good-natured than Rex. Everybody resented him, just the same.   15

Answer in pairs. Help each other with any important sentences you don't understand.

   i Tick the adjectives which describe Rex:

wilful	strong	proud	modest
shy	dominant	pleasant	

   ii The story begins to change from description to narrative. Which phrases signal the change?

4.7.5 Try to find answers to these questions in the passage that follows:

How is this version of leapfrog unusual?
Was Rosie good at it?
How did Rex feel about not having fought Rosie?

Read on:

One winter, the whole neighbourhood took to playing a game that had become popular on the other side of the track, in another slum neighbourhood of the town: *Leapfrog*. The idea was for as many boys as cared to participate, to bend down and be leaped over by every other boy in the game, and then himself to get up and begin leaping over all the other boys, and then bend down again until all the boys had leaped over him again, and keep this up until all the other players had become exhausted. This didn't happen, sometimes, until the last two players had travelled a distance of three or four miles, while the other players walked along, watching and making bets.   10

Rosie, of course, was always in on the game. She was always one of the last to drop out, too. And she was the only person in the neighbourhood Rex Folger hadn't fought and beaten.

He felt that that was much too humiliating even to think about. But inasmuch as she seemed to be a member of the gang, he felt that in   15
some way or another he ought to prove his superiority.

Answer in pairs. Help each other with any sentences you don't understand.

  i How does the story change more obviously from general description to narrative? Which parts of the passage could still be called descriptive?

  ii Which verbs describe the action? Are there more or fewer verbs than adjectives? Compare with the previous extracts.

4.7.6 You are going to answer the following questions:

How did the contest between Rosie and Rex begin?
Why wasn't it a fight?
Read on:

One summer day during vacation, an argument between Rex and Rosie developed and Rosie pulled off her turtle-neck sweater and challenged him to a fight. Rex took a cigarette from his pocket, lighted it, inhaled, and told Rosie he wasn't in the habit of hitting women – where he came from that amounted to boxing your mother.   5
On the other hand, he said, if Rosie cared to compete with him in any other sport, he would be glad to oblige her. Rex was a very calm and courteous conversationalist. He had poise. It was unconscious, of course, but he had it just the same. He was just a man who couldn't be hurried, flustered, or excited.   10

Answer in pairs. Help each other with any sentences you don't understand.

   i Which adjectives describe Rex?

   ii Which parts of this extract are descriptive and which parts are narrative?

4.7.7   Read on:

So Rex and Rosie fought it out in this game Leapfrog. They got to leaping over one another, quickly, too, until the first thing we knew the whole gang of us was out on the State Highway going south towards Fowler. It was a very hot day. Rosie and Rex were in great shape, and it looked like one was tougher than the other and more stubborn. They talked a good deal, especially Rosie, who insisted that she would have to fall down unconscious before she'd give up to a guy like Rex. [5]

He said he was sorry his opponent was a girl. It grieved him deeply to have to make a girl exert herself to the point of death, but it was just too bad. He had to, so he had to. They leaped and squatted, leaped and squatted, and we got out to Sam Day's vineyard. That was half-way to Fowler. It didn't seem like either Rosie or Rex was ever going to get tired. They hadn't even begun to show signs of growing tired, although each of them was sweating a great deal. [10] [15]

Naturally, we were sure Rex would win the contest. But that was because we hadn't taken into account the fact that he was a simple person, whereas Rosie was crafty and shrewd. Rosie knew how to figure angles. She had discovered how to jump over Rex Folger in a way that weakened him. And after a while, about three miles out of Fowler, we noticed that she was coming down on Rex's *neck*, instead of on his back. Naturally, this was hurting him and making the blood rush to his head. Rosie herself squatted in such a way that it was impossible, almost, for Rex to get anywhere near her neck with his hands. [20] [25]

   i Summarise the narrative in your own words.

   ii Is anything added to the characters of Rex and Rosie?

4.7.8   Read the rest of the story:

Before long, we noticed that Rex was weakening. His head was getting closer and closer to the ground. About a half mile out of Fowler, we heard Rex's head bumping the ground every time Rosie leaped over him. They were good loud bumps that we knew were painful, but Rex wasn't complaining. He was too proud to complain. [5]

Rosie, on the other hand, knew she had her man, and she was giving him all she had. She was bumping his head on the ground as solidly as she could, because she knew she didn't have much more fight in her, and if she didn't lay him out cold, in the hot sun, in the next ten minutes or so, she would fall down exhausted herself, and lose the contest.

Suddenly Rosie bumped Rex's head a real powerful one. He got up very dazed and very angry. It was the first time we had ever seen him fuming. By God, the girl was taking advantage of him, if he wasn't mistaken, and he didn't like it. Rosie was squatted in front of him. He came up groggy and paused a moment. Then he gave Rosie a very effective kick that sent her sprawling. Rosie jumped up and smacked Rex in the mouth. The gang jumped in and tried to establish order.

It was agreed that the Leapfrog contest must not change into a fight. Not any more. Not with Fowler only five or ten minutes away. The gang ruled further that Rex had had no right to kick Rosie and that in smacking him in the mouth Rosie had squared the matter, and the contest was to continue.

Rosie was very tired and sore; and so was Rex. They began leaping and squatting again; and again we saw Rosie coming down on Rex's neck so that his head was bumping the ground.

It looked pretty bad for the boy from Texas. We couldn't understand how he could take so much punishment. We all felt that Rex was getting what he had coming to him, but at the same time everybody seemed to feel badly about Rosie, a girl, doing the job instead of one of us. Of course, that was where we were wrong. Nobody but Rosie could have figured out that smart way of humiliating a very powerful and superior boy. It was probably the woman in her, which, less than five years later, came out to such an extent that she became one of the most beautiful girls in town, gave up tomboy activities, and married one of the wealthiest young men in Kings County, a college man named, if memory serves, Wallace Hadington Finlay VI.

Less than a hundred yards from the heart of Fowler, Rosie, with great and admirable artistry, finished the job.

That was where the dirt of the highway siding ended and the paved main street of Fowler began. This street was paved with cement, not asphalt. Asphalt, in that heat, would have been too soft to serve, but cement had exactly the right degree of brittleness. I think Rex, when he squatted over the hard cement, knew the game was up. But he

was brave to the end. He squatted over the hard cement and waited 45
for the worst. Behind him, Rosie Mahoney prepared to make the
supreme effort. In this next leap, she intended to give her all, which
she did.

She came down on Rex Folger's neck like a ton of bricks. His head
banged against the hard cement, his body straightened out, and his 50
arms and legs twitched.

He was out like a light.

Six paces in front of him, Rosie Mahoney squatted and waited. Jim
Telesco counted twenty, which was the time allowed for each leap.
Rex didn't get up during the count. 55

The contest was over. The winner of the contest was Rosie Mahoney.

Rex didn't get up by himself at all. He just stayed where he was until a
half-dozen of us lifted him and carried him to a horse trough, where
we splashed water on his face.

Rex was a confused young man all the way back. He was also a 60
deeply humiliated one. He couldn't understand anything about
anything. He just looked dazed and speechless. Every now and then
we imagined he wanted to talk, and I guess he did, but after we'd all
gotten ready to hear what he had to say, he couldn't speak. He made
a gesture so tragic that tears came to the eyes of eleven members of 65
the gang.

Rosie Mahoney, on the other hand, talked all the way home. She said
everything.

I think it made a better man of Rex. More human. After that he was a
gentler sort of soul. It may have been because he couldn't see very 70
well for some time. At any rate, for weeks he seemed to be going
around in a dream. His gaze would freeze on some insignificant
object far away in the landscape, and half the time it seemed as if he
didn't know where he was going, or why. He took little part in the
activities of the gang, and the following winter he stayed away 75
altogether. He came to school one day wearing glasses. He looked
broken and pathetic.

That winter Rosie Mahoney stopped hanging around with the gang,
too. She had a flair for making an exit at the right time.

i Discuss the story in pairs. What was your reaction to it? Did you like it? What do you think of Rosie? Do you admire her? Envy her? What do you think of Rex?

ii From this last extract what do we know about Rex and Rosie that is new? Can you describe their characters. How did Rex change after the contest? Did any part of the extract come as a surprise?

Notice how the characters are built up as the story proceeds.

4.7.9
Follow-up work

Choose *one* of the following:

i In your own experience, do boys and girls play well together or do they prefer different kinds of games? Discuss.

ii Do you think it's a good idea for girls to:
 – play football
 – play with mechanical toys
 – learn to do woodwork

Do you think little boys enjoy cooking or playing with dolls? If not, why not? Do you think parents and teachers ought to encourage boys and girls to get away from stereotyped roles of what games and activities are suitable for only one sex? Discuss.

iii Summarise the whole narrative in no more than 200 words.

iv Write character descriptions of Rex and Rosie in your own words.

4.8 Conclusion

4.8.1 Discuss the Unit in pairs.

UNIT 5

How it's written (2)

5.1 Using a colloquial idiom

This section relates to Byron's *Don Juan*. (Started in 1818 and left unfinished.)

5.1.1
Historical background

i Byron lived between 1788 and 1824. Individually, write down three major political events in your country during those years.

ii Compare and discuss in pairs.

iii Look at the following list:

> The Battle of Trafalgar
> Napoleon's retreat from Moscow
> The Greek Revolt
> The Crimean War
> The French Revolution
> The Unification of Italy
> The Congress of Vienna
> The American War of Independence
> The Accession of Queen Victoria

iv Agree which occurred between 1788 and 1824.

v Sequence chronologically and, if possible, put dates next to each.

vi Check your answers in the Key in the back of the book.

5.1.2
Anticipation

i Which of the following do you agree with?

> Young men should be brought up strictly, with a strong moral sense.
>
> Young women should be brought up strictly, with a strong moral sense.
>
> Moral issues are personal rather than social.
>
> Contact between young men and women before marriage should be supervised by their parents.

ii Change the words of any statement you don't agree with so that it expresses your opinion.

iii Discuss in pairs.

iv Discuss the difference between:

> comedy   farce   satire

Look the words up in a dictionary if necessary. Can you think of any examples of plays or films which are described by these words?

5.1.3 *Don Juan consists of 17 cantos. The first canto consists of 222 stanzas; the other cantos, however, are shorter. At the beginning of canto 1, Byron explains who his hero is going to be.*

Read as quickly as you can.

GLOSSARY
cloying (l.3): filling up
  excessively
gazettes (l.3): newspapers
cant (l.3): hypocritical talk
vaunt (l.5): praise
ere (l.8): before

> I want a hero, an uncommon want,
> When every year and month sends forth a new one,
> Till after cloying the gazettes with cant,
> The age discovers he is not the true one.
> Of such as these I should not care to vaunt;   5
> I'll therefore take our ancient friend Don Juan.
> We all have seen him in the pantomime
> Sent to the devil somewhat ere his time.   *Stanza 1*

We learn about his birthplace.

> In Seville was he born, a pleasant city,
> Famous for oranges and women. He
> Who has not seen it will be much to pity;
> So says the proverb, and I quite agree.
> Of all the Spanish towns is none more pretty;   5
> Cadiz perhaps, but that you soon may see.
> Don Juan's parents lived beside the river,
> A noble stream, and called the Guadalquivir.   *Stanza 8*

About his father.

GLOSSARY
hidalgo (l.2): Spanish
  nobleman
begot (l.7): fathered

> His father's name was José – Don, of course.
> A true hidalgo, free from every stain
> Of Moor or Hebrew blood, he traced his source
> Through the most Gothic gentlemen of Spain.
> A better cavalier ne'er mounted horse,   5
> Or being mounted e'er got down again,
> Than José, who begot our hero, who
> Begot – but that's to come. Well, to renew: *Stanza 9*

And about his mother.

GLOSSARY
magnanimity (l.2): quality
  of generosity and
  nobleness
wit (l.3): ability to say
  clever or amusing
  things
Attic (l.3): in classical
  Greek style
prodigy (l.6): genius
dimity (l.6): cotton fabric
  with raised pattern
muslin (l.7): fine thin
  cotton fabric

Her favourite science was the mathematical,
Her noblest virtue was her magnanimity,
Her wit (she sometimes tried at wit) was Attic all,
Her serious sayings darkened to sublimity.
In short in all things she was fairly what I call   5
A prodigy. Her morning dress was dimity,
Her evening silk, or in the summer, muslin
And other stuffs, with which I won't stay puzzling.   *Stanza 12*

But father and mother were not compatible.

GLOSSARY
insipid (l.2): dull
our first parents (l.3): Adam
  and Eve
bowers (l.4): shady places
  formed by trees

Perfect she was, but as perfection is
Insipid in this naughty world of ours,
Where our first parents never learned to kiss
Till they were exiled from their earlier bowers,
Where all was peace and innocence and bliss   5
(I wonder how they got through the twelve hours.)
Don José, like a lineal son of Eve,
Went plucking various fruit without her leave.   *Stanza 18*

They quarrelled.

'Tis pity learned virgins ever wed
With persons of no sort of education,
Or gentlemen, who, though well-born and bred,
Grow tired of scientific conversation.
I don't choose to say much upon this head,   5
I'm a plain man and in a single station,
But – oh ye lords of ladies intellectual!

GLOSSARY
henpecked (l.8): bullied

Inform us truly, have they not henpecked you all?   *Stanza 22*

Then Don Juan was born.

GLOSSARY

mischief (l.2): naughty
behaviour

doting (l.3): loving
excessively

imp (l.4): naughty child

A little curly-headed, good-for-nothing,
And mischief-making monkey from his birth;
His parents ne'er agreed except in doting
Upon the most unquiet imp on earth.
Instead of quarrelling, had they been but both in   5
Their senses, they'd have sent young master forth
To school or had him soundly whipped at home
To teach him manners for the time to come.   *Stanza 25*

Before they could divorce, Don José died. Donna Inez, his mother, had to bring up Don Juan.

GLOSSARY

Sagest (l.1): wisest

paragon (l.2): a supremely
excellent person

pedigree (l.3): ancestry

sire (l.4): father

dam (l.4): mother

scale (l.8): climb up

nunnery (l.8): convent for
women

Sagest of women, even of widows, she
Resolved that Juan should be quite a paragon,
And worthy of the noblest pedigree
(His sire was of Castile, his dam from Arragon.)
Then for accomplishments of chivalry,   5
In case our lord the king should go to war again,
He learned the arts of riding, fencing, gunnery,
And how to scale a fortress – or a nunnery.   *Stanza 38*

He grew up.

At six, I said, he was a charming child,
At twelve he was a fine but quiet boy.
Although in infancy a little wild,
They tamed him down amongst them; to destroy
His natural spirit not in vain they toiled,   5
At least it seemed so. And his mother's joy
Was to declare how sage and still and steady
Her young philosopher was grown already.   *Stanza 50*

And up.

GLOSSARY
well knit (l.2): well-formed
sprightly (l.3): lively
page (l.3): boy servant
precocious (l.7): having faculties developed unusually early
atrocious (l.8): shockingly bad

Young Juan now was sixteen years of age,
Tall, handsome, slender, but well knit; he seemed
Active, though not so sprightly as a page,
And everybody but his mother deemed
Him almost man, but she flew in a rage   5
And bit her lips (for else she might have screamed),
If any said so, for to be precocious
Was in her eyes a thing the most atrocious.   *Stanza 54*

However, there developed an attraction between him and Julia, a friend of his mother's, who was married to a man called Don Alfonso.

Juan she saw and as a pretty child,
Caressed him often. Such a thing might be
Quite innocently done and harmless styled
When she had twenty years, and thirteen he;
But I am not so sure I should have smiled   5
When he was sixteen, Julia twenty-three.
These few short years make wondrous alterations,
Particularly amongst sunburnt nations.   *Stanza 69*

Julia tried to resist the attraction.

She now determined that a virtuous woman
Should rather face and overcome temptation,
That flight was base and dastardly, and no man
Should ever give her heart the least sensation,
That is to say, a thought beyond the common   5
Preference, that we must feel upon occasion
For people who are pleasanter than others,
But then they only seem so many brothers.   *Stanza 77*

GLOSSARY
dastardly (l.3): cowardly

123

She found it difficult, as did Don Juan.

He thought about himself and the whole earth,
Of man the wonderful and of the stars
And how the deuce they ever could have birth,
And then he thought of earthquakes and of wars,
How many miles the moon might have in girth,   5
Of air balloons and of the many bars
To perfect knowledge of the boundless skies.
And then he thought of Donna Julia's eyes.   *Stanza 92*

Byron, though, does not just tell the story. He frequently digresses and philosophises:

Man's a phenomenon, one knows not what,
And wonderful beyond all wondrous measure.
'Tis pity though in this sublime world that
Pleasure's a sin and sometimes sin's a pleasure.
Few mortals know what end they would be at,   5
But whether glory, power or love or treasure,
The path is through perplexing ways, and when
The goal is gained, we die you know – and then?   *Stanza 133*

Don Alfonso got suspicious and searched Julia's room in an attempt to surprise her. He found nothing.

But Don Alfonso stood with downcast looks,
And truth to say he made a foolish figure.
When after searching in five hundred nooks
And treating a young wife with so much rigour,
He gained no point, except some self-rebukes,   5
Added to those his lady with such vigour
Had poured upon him for the last half-hour,
Quick, thick, and heavy as a thunder-shower.   *Stanza 161*

But Don Alfonso had been deceived.

No sooner was it bolted than – oh shame,
Oh sin, oh sorrow, and oh womankind!
How can you do such things and keep your fame,
Unless this world and t'other too be blind?
Nothing so dear as an unfilched good name.   5
But to proceed, for there is more behind.
With much heartfelt reluctance be it said,
Young Juan slipped, half-smothered, from the bed.   *Stanza 165*

GLOSSARY
it bolted (l.1): the door shut
unfilched (l.5): not stolen

Later, Don Alfonso made a discovery.

Alfonso closed his speech and begged her pardon,
Which Julia half withheld and then half granted
And laid conditions, he thought, very hard on,
Denying several little things he wanted.
He stood like Adam lingering near his garden,   5
With useless penitence perplexed and haunted,
Beseeching she no further would refuse,
When lo! he stumbled o'er a pair of shoes.   *Stanza 180*

GLOSSARY
withheld (l.2): kept back
lingering (l.5): waiting
  around
beseeching (l.7): begging
stumbled (l.8): tripped

Which led to a fight.

Alfonso grappled to detain the foe,
And Juan throttled him to get away,
And blood ('twas from the nose) began to flow.
At last as they more faintly wrestling lay,
Juan contrived to give an awkward blow,   5
And then his only garment quite gave way.
He fled, like Joseph, leaving it, but there
I doubt, all likeness ends between the pair.   *Stanza 186*

GLOSSARY
throttled (l.2): strangled
Joseph (l.7): refers to the
  story of Joseph and
  Potiphar's wife (the
  Book of Genesis)

There was a scandal.

Here ends this canto. Need I sing or say
How Juan naked, favoured by the night,
Who favours what she should not, found his way
And reached his home in an unseemly plight?
The pleasant scandal which arose next day, 5
The nine days' wonder which was brought to light,
And how Alfonso sued for a divorce
Were in the English newspapers, of course. *Stanza 188*

Don Juan was sent by his mother to Cadiz to escape the scandal.
Byron talks about his story and his art.

My poem's epic and is meant to be
Divided in twelve books, each book containing,
With love and war, a heavy gale at sea,
A list of ships and captains and kings reigning,
New characters; the episodes are three. 5
A panoramic view of hell's in training,
After the style of Virgil and of Homer,
So that my name of epic's no misnomer. *Stanza 200*

There's only one slight difference between
Me and my epic brethren gone before, 10
And here the advantage is my own, I ween
(Not that I have not several merits more,
But this will more peculiarly be seen).
They so embellish that 'tis quite a bore
Their labyrinth of fables to thread through,
Whereas this story's actually true. *Stanza 202*

5.1.4
Improving
understanding

i Go back over the extracts. Complete the following with a word or a
phrase. Use a separate piece of paper.
Don Juan, the _____ of the story, was born in _____. His
father, Don José, was _____ and _____. His mother, Donna
Inez, was _____. She liked to _____. Their marriage was
_____. They were incompatible because _____. As a baby,
Don Juan was _____. After Don José died, Donna Inez tried to

_____. At 12 Don Juan seemed to his mother to be _____. By 16, he was _____. Julia, a friend of his mother's, _____. She _____. However, she was determined _____. Don Juan himself tried to _____ but _____. Don Alfonso, Julia's _____, was _____ of his wife and one evening _____. Julia _____. However, Don Juan _____.
Later, Don Alfonso discovered _____. The two end up _____ and _____. There is a _____ and Don Juan is _____ by his mother.

ii Write down ten difficult questions about what happens in the extracts. The answers should not be too obvious. Use each of the following words at least once.

Do	What	Where	Who
Does	When	Why	How

In pairs ask each other the questions. Check up on the answers in the text.

5.1.5
Poetic form

The poem is written in _ottava rima_, a form not much used in English literature but popular among some Italian satirists such as Pulci, Casti and Berni.

How many lines are there in each stanza?
How many syllables in each line?
How many stresses?
What is the rhyme scheme at the end of each line?
What do you notice about the last two lines?

English writers have more commonly used the _heroic couplet_, a rhymed couplet with ten syllables and five stresses, e.g.

> More had she spoke, but yawn'd – All Nature nods:
> What mortal can resist the yawn of Gods?   _(Alexander Pope)_

5.1.6
Style and tone

i In what ways do you think Don Juan is a satire, in what ways a comedy. List the aspects of human behaviour Byron makes fun of e.g. Donna Inez' pretentious seriousness (in stanza 12).

What other targets are there of Byron's mockery, e.g. English newspapers (stanza 188)?

ii In stanzas 22, 38, 77 and 92, what effect do the last two lines have on the previous lines?

What effect do they have in 180?

What is their tone in 69 and 186? (look up the word 'bathos' in a dictionary).

iii Notice that Byron writes within a very strict form. How would you describe his _tone of voice_ in the poem? Tick the words you agree with. Add your own.

natural	conversational
manly	lively
vigorous	energetic
formal	amusing
flippant	beautiful

iv Read the following extracts from two literary critics.

1   The style of which we are speaking is, no doubt, occasionally satirical and witty and humorous – but it is on the whole far more gay than poignant, and it is characterized, exactly as good conversation is, rather by its constant ease and amenity, than by any traits either of extraordinary brilliancy, or of strong and ludicrous effect ... The   5
great charm is in the simplicity and naturalness of the language – the free but guarded use of all polite idioms, and even of all phrases of temporary currency that have the stamp of good company on them
...

2   Byron speaks as a man of the world and a gentleman, but not only is he not polite, the very essence of his manner is a   10
contemptuous defiance of decorum and propriety. His generosity is a cynical man-of-the-world good-humour, and his irreverence moves towards a burlesque comedy that, in its high spirits, is sometimes schoolboy.

Do you agree with either of them?

5.1.7
Background

i Read the following life of Byron.

Byron was born in 1788. He left Trinity College, Cambridge in 1805 and published his first volume of poems entitled Fugitive Pieces *the following year. After a short spell as a member of the House of Lords, he made his first major journey abroad from 1809-11. It included a visit to Greece. In 1812 he started his infamous affair with Lady Caroline Lamb and published the first two cantos of* Childe Harold. *In 1815, he married Annabella Milbanke but they separated the following year. The same year he left England for good after a scandal over his clandestine relationship with his half-sister, Augusta Leigh. In Switzerland the following year, he met Shelley for the first time, before moving to Italy, where he lived the life of a libertine. In 1819, he published the first cantos of* Don Juan *and in 1821 moved to Pisa. The following year he moved to Genoa. In 1823 he went on an expedition to assist the Greek revolution but died the following year from a fever.*

ii The following sequence of events is out of order. What do you think the correct order is? (e.g. No 6 should be No 1).

1 Byron takes his seat at the House of Lords.

2 *2nd January* Marriage of Byron to Annabella Milbanke. *April* Publication of *Hebrew Melodies. 10th December* Birth of Byron's daughter, Ada.

3 Byron attends Aberdeen Grammar School.

4 *16th August* Burning of Shelley's corpse on the beach at Viareggio. *September* Byron moves to Genoa. *15th October* Publication (in *The Liberal*) of *Vision of Judgement*.

5 *12th January* Birth of Byron's daughter by Claire Clairmont. *29th April* Byron visits Rome with Hobhouse. *14th June* Byron moves to La Mira. *16th June* Publication of *Manfred*. Affair with Margarita Cogni. *December* Sale of Newstead Abbey.

6 *22nd January* Birth of Byron at 16 Holles Street, London

7 *3rd May* Byron swims across the Hellespont from Sestos to Abydos.

8 *November* Byron moves to Pisa. *December* Publication of the third and fourth cantos of *Don Juan*, *The Two Foscari*, *Cain* and *Sardanapalus*.

9 *January* Byron settles at Missolonghi. *9th April* Byron, whose health has been poor for some time, catches a chill in the rain. *19th April* Death of Byron at Missolonghi. *16th July* Byron's remains are buried in Hucknall Torkard, Nottingham.

10 *21st May* Byron becomes Baron Byron of Rochdale

11 *22nd February* Publication of *Beppo*. *28th April* Publication of the fourth canto of *Childe Harold*. *May* Byron moves into the Palazzo Mocenigo in Venice. *2nd May* Allegra arrives in Venice.

12 *November* Publication of Byron's first collection of verse, *Fugitive Pieces*.

13 *14th July* Byron returns to England. *Late July* Death of Byron's mother.

14 *10th March* Publication of the first two cantos of *Childe Harold*. First meeting with Lady Caroline Lamb. *25th March* First meeting with Annabella Milbanke. Affair with Lady Caroline Lamb. Affair with Lady Oxford.

15 *15th January* Separation of Byron and his wife. *February* Publication of *The Siege of Corinth* and *Parisina*. *21st April* Signature of the separation deed. *24th April* Byron leaves England for ever. *24th May* Arrival at Geneva. *26th May* First meeting with the Shelleys. Affair with Claire Clairmont. *5th October* Byron leaves Switzerland for Italy and settles in Venice. *18th November* Publication of the third canto of *Childe Harold*. *5th December* Publication of *The Prisoner of Chillon and other poems*. Affair with Marianna Segati.

16 *15th July* Publication of the first two cantos of *Don Juan*. Byron moves to La Mira, then back to Venice.

17 Byron and Hobhouse sail from Falmouth for Greece and Turkey. They visit, among other places, Lisbon, Gibraltar, Malta, Jannina and Athens.

iii In 5.1.1. which events, if any, do you think may have influenced the society in which Byron lived?

5.2 Expressing a point of view

5.2.1 *George Mackay Brown, a poet and short story writer, in* An Orkney Tapestry *(1969) explores the history and the folklore of his native Orkney. He meditates on the changes of recent days.*

I often think we are not really interested in the past at all. There is a new religion, Progress, in which we all devoutly believe, and it is concerned only with material things in the present and in a vague golden-handed future. It is a rootless utilitarian faith, without beauty or mystery; a kind of blind unquestioning belief that men and their material circumstances will go on improving until some kind of nirvana is reached and everyone will be rich, free, fulfilled, well-informed, masterful. Why should Orcadians not believe in Progress? – everything seems to insist on it. The stone cots of their grandfathers, where men and animals bedded down under the same roof, are strewn all about the parishes and islands, beside the smart modern houses of wood and concrete. The horses are banished, but then tractors and lorries are much less trouble, much more efficient. There is no real poverty any more; tramps and vagrants and tinkers are exiled with the horses. (Only the very backward farmers nowadays don't have a car.) Progress is a goddess who, up to now, has looked after her children well. The sky is scored with television aerials. There is a family planning centre. There are drifts of books and oil paintings and gramophone records everywhere. And still the shower of good things intensifies. It is difficult to picture this goddess of plenty other than as some huge computer-figure, that will give our children what they desire easily and endlessly – food, sex, excitement – a synthetic goddess, vast and bland as Buddha, but without love or tenderness or compassion; activated only by a mania to create secondary objects that become increasingly shinier and shoddier and uglier.

I feel that this religion is in great part a delusion, and will peter out in the marsh. A community like Orkney dare not cut itself off from its roots and sources. Places like Rackwick and Eynhallow have no meaning if you try to describe or evaluate them in terms of a newspaper article. They cannot be described in that way.

GLOSSARY
nirvana (l.7): divine but inexpressible state of perfection
cots (l.9): simple cottages
strewn about (l.11): scattered
parishes (l.11): local areas
tinkers (l.14): tramps who sometimes mended pots and pans

Improving understanding
i Re-read as often as you like. Select the most important phrases that help to get across the writer's point of view (e.g. I often think *we are not really interested in the past* at all). Compare your selection in pairs. Can you summarise the argument?

ii What do you think the 'new religion' has in common with more
   orthodox religious belief?
   What phrases does the writer use to describe 'progress' (e.g. 'rootless,
   utilitarian faith')?
   Why do you think Rackwick and Eynhallow have no meaning if you
   try to 'describe or evaluate them in terms of a newspaper article'?
   Indicate what the word 'it' refers to at different places in the passage.

Language

i What verb form is used most frequently in the passage?

ii Find a word/phrase which means:

indistinct	produced artificially
functional and practical	more badly made
neat and fashionable	gradually disappear
marked	

iii Divide the following words into those which in context have a positive
    connotation (or a pleasant suggestion) and those which have a
    negative connotation.

progress	bland
blind	tenderness
shinier	roots

Which kind predominates? Is the strongest force in the passage the
positive or the negative? What is the writer for and what is he against?

Style

i Why does the word Progress have a capital 'P'?

ii Find a metaphor.

iii 'Why should Orcadians not believe in Progress?'
    Does the writer expect an answer? (If not, this is known as a 'rhetorical
    question'.)

iv Which sentences state a point of view and which exemplify it?

v 'And still ...'. Which word in this sentence carries most stress when
   spoken? What attitude does the sentence convey?

vi How would you describe the tone of the passage? (e.g. angry? sad?)

Discussion

Do you agree with the writer? Is 'progress' more bad than good?

5.2.2   *Matthew Arnold, a Victorian essayist and poet, in* Culture and Anarchy (1869) *considers the age in which he lived:*

Faith in machinery is, I said, our besetting danger; often in machinery most absurdly disproportioned to the end which this machinery, if it is to do any good at all, is to serve; but always in machinery, as if it had any value in and for itself. What is freedom but machinery? What is population but machinery? What is coal but machinery? What are railroads but machinery? What is wealth but machinery? What are even religious organisations but machinery? Now almost every voice in England is accustomed to speak of these things as if they were precious ends in themselves ...

Everyone must have observed the strange language current during the late discussions as to the possible failure of our supplies of coal. Our coal, thousands of people were saying, is the real basis of our national greatness; if our coal runs short, there is an end of the greatness of England. But what is greatness? – culture makes us ask ... If England were swallowed up by the sea tomorrow, which of the two, a hundred years hence, would most excite the love, interest, and admiration of mankind – would most, therefore, show the evidences of having possessed greatness – the England of the last twenty years, or the England of Elizabeth, of a time of splendid spiritual effort, but when our coal, and our industrial operations depending on coal, were very little developed?

GLOSSARY
besetting (l.1): continuously present
disproportioned (l.2): the wrong size for the purpose

Improving understanding

i   Re-read as often as you like. Select the most important phrases that help to get across the writer's point of view. Compare your selection in pairs. Can you summarise his argument?

ii Consider the rhetorical questions beginning 'What is coal but machinery?' Whose point of view do they express?
What do they try to achieve?
What does the writer expect you to answer to the question in the last sentence?
Indicate what the words 'it' and 'they' refer to in the passage.

iii What does the passage have in common with 5.2.1.?

Language

i   What is the difference between 'if' and 'as if'?
How many sentences or phrases begin with these words in this passage? What effect does this have?

ii Find a word in the passage which means:

   valuable   foundation   magnificent

iii Divide the following words into those which in context have a positive connotation (or a pleasant suggestion) and those which have a negative connotation:

   machinery   culture   spiritual

Style

i What effect do the following phrases have:

> 'almost every voice'
>
> 'everyone must have'
>
> 'thousands of people were saying'

ii What do you notice about the length of the sentences?

iii How could you describe the tone of the passage?

Discussion

Do you agree with the writer? Should we believe more in culture than in machinery?

5.2.3 *John Donne, the poet and Elizabethan courtier, was from 1621 the Dean of St. Pauls. This is a rather difficult extract from one of his sermons (1628).*

GLOSSARY

oppresses (l.1): keeps down

dunghill (l.1): pile of animal excrement

sears up (l.4): dries up

howlings (l.6): cries

gnashings (l.6): rubbing teeth together

emulation (l.11): trying to be better than other people

Reproach (l.13): condemnation

He that oppresses the poor, digs in a dunghill for worms; And he departs from that posture, which God, in nature gave him, that is, erect, to look upward; for his eye is always down, upon them, that lie in the dust, under his feet. Certainly, he that soars up himself, and makes himself insensible of the cries, and curses of the poor here in this world, does but prepare himself for the howlings, and gnashings of teeth, in the world to come. It is the Serpents taste, the Serpents diet, Dust shalt thou eat all the days of thy life; and he feeds but on dust, that oppresses the poor. And as there is evidently, more inhumanity, more violation of nature, in this oppression, than in emulation, so may there well seem to be more impiety, and more violation of God himself, by that word, which the holy Ghost chooses in the next place, which is Reproach, He that oppresses the poor, reproaches his Maker.

Improving understanding

i Read as often as you like. Where can the following sentiments be found – very differently expressed! – in the passage:

> Oppression of the poor is an obscenity.
>
> Man has God-given dignity
>
> If a person ignores the suffering of the poor, that person will be in purgatory after death.
>
> Ignoring such suffering is evil.
>
> It is worse to oppress the poor than to try and be better than others.
>
> Oppressing the poor is a sin against God himself.

ii Why can't the oppressor of the poor behave nobly?

What does 'the Serpent' refer to?

Do you recognise any parts of the Bible referred to?

'By that word' – which word?

What does 'in the next place' refer to?

Who is 'his Maker'?

Language

i Who does the word 'his' refer to in the passage?

ii Find a word in the passage which means:

physical attitude   unaware
upright   lack of reverence

iii Divide the following words into those which in context have a positive connotation (or a pleasant suggestion) and those which have a negative connotation:

oppresses   insensible
poor   serpent
nature   Maker
dust

Style

i Can you find any phrases which balance each other?

ii What difference would be made to the tone of the passage if the writer had used the phrase 'the person who' instead of 'he that'?

iii What effect does the repetition of 'he' and 'he that' have?
What effect does the repetition of 'more' have in the last sentence?
Does it show the passage is meant to be read aloud?

iv Find a metaphor. Is it vivid?

Discussion

Donne expresses the view that oppression of the poor is a Christian *sin*. Do you believe it is a sin? Why/Why not?

5.2.4 *John Berger, the Marxist novelist, art critic and essayist, in his book* A Fortunate Man *(1967) describes the position of a country doctor in relation to his patients in an 'economically depressed' part of England.*

Here are some extracts:

GLOSSARY

suffering ... diminution (l.2–3): being made less than they could be

frantic (l.10): wildly excited

fragmented (l.12): broken up

insatiable (l.12): unable to be satisfied

1 Do his patients deserve the lives they lead, or do they deserve better? Are they what they could be or are they suffering continual diminution? Do they ever have the opportunity to develop the potentialities which he has observed in them at certain moments? Are there not some who secretly wish to live in a sense that is impossible given the conditions of their actual lives? And facing this impossibility do they not then secretly wish to die? ...   5

2 He argues with himself in an attempt to maintain his peace of mind. The foresters are not subject to the same frantic pressures   10 as millions keeping up appearances in the suburbs. Families are less fragmented: appetites less insatiable: the standard of living of the foresters is lower but they have a greater sense of continuity. They may lack cultural opportunities individually: but

collectively they have their Parish Council, their Moat Society, their Dart Teams, etc. These all encourage a sense of community. There is less loneliness in the Forest than in many cities. They are, as they might answer themselves, as happy as can be expected … 15

3   Yet however he argues, the disquieting questions return. And the 20
harder he works, the more insistently they are posed. Whenever
he makes an effort to recognise a patient, he is forced to
recognise his or her undeveloped potentiality. Indeed in the case
of the young or early-middle-aged it is often this which prompts
the appeal for help – like the cry of a passenger who suddenly 25
realises that the vehicle in which he is travelling is not even going
near the destination he believed he was making for. If as a doctor
he is concerned with the total personality of his patients and if he
realises, as he must, that a personality is never an entirely fixed
entity, then he is bound to take note of what inhibits, deprives or 30
diminishes it. It is the inwritten consequence of his approach. He
can argue that the foresters are in some respects fortunate
compared to the majority of people in the world. But what is far
more relevant to his own preoccupations is that he knows that the
foresters are in almost all respects unfortunate compared to what 35
they could be – given better education, better social services,
better employment, better cultural opportunities, etc. …

4   … we in our society do not know how to acknowledge, to
measure the contribution of an ordinary working doctor. By
measure I do not mean *calculate* according to a fixed scale, but, 40
rather, *take the measure of*. It is not a question of comparing the
doctor with the artist or with the airline pilot or with the lawyer or
with the political stooge and then arranging them in a winning
order. It is a question of comparing them so that in the light of the
other examples we can better appreciate what the doctor is (or is 45
not) doing …

5   The doctor is a popular hero: you have only to consider how
frequently and easily he is presented as such on television. If his
training were not so long and expensive, every mother would be
happy for her son to become a doctor. It is the most idealised of 50
all the professions. Yet it is idealised abstractly. Some of the
young who decide to become doctors are at first influenced by
this ideal. But I would suggest that one of the fundamental
reasons why so many doctors become cynical and disillusioned
is precisely because, when the abstract idealism has worn thin, 55
they are uncertain about the value of the actual lives of the
patients they are treating. This is not because they are callous or
personally inhuman: it is because they live in and accept a
society which is incapable of knowing what a human life is worth
…

GLOSSARY
stooge (l.43): person who
  blindly carries out
  orders

6 Let me be quite clear. I do not claim to know what a human life is   60
worth. There can be no final or personal answer ... The question
is social. An individual cannot answer it for himself. The answer
resides within the totality of relations which can exist within a
certain social structure at a certain time. Finally man's worth to
himself is expressed by his treatment of himself ...   65

7 All that I do know is that our present society wastes and, by the
slow draining process of enforced hypocrisy, empties most of the
lives which it does not destroy: and that, within its own terms, a
doctor who has surpassed the stage of selling cures, either
directly to the patient or through the agency of a state service, is   70
unassessable.

GLOSSARY
draining (l.67): continual
taking away of essential
resources

Improving understanding

i Re-read as often as you like. Select the most important phrases from
extracts 1–3 which describe or suggest the views of the writer (or the
doctor through the writer's eyes) concerning the foresters' essential
quality of life (or lack of it). For example, 'Do his patients deserve the
lives they lead ...' (the writer clearly does not think so).

ii Select the most important phrases from extracts 4–5 which describe or
suggest the writer's views about how we regard doctors.

iii Select the phrases from extracts 6–7 which summarise the writer's
point of view.

iv What does the passage have in common with 5.2.3.? Can you
summarise the writer's whole argument?

Language

i Find a word in the passage that means:

have a right to	persistently
keep	basic
logical connexion	unfeeling
disturbing	gone beyond

ii Find a simile in the passage. Is it effective? Say why/why not.

iii What effect do the phrases 'let me be quite clear' and 'All that I do
know is' have on the tone of the writing?

iv Divide the following words into those which in context have a positive
connotation (or a pleasant suggestion) and those which have a
negative connotation:

diminution	insatiable	community
potentialities	idealised	loneliness
frantic	continuity	ordinary

Style

i How would you describe the writer's style?

ii How would you describe the tone of the extracts?

Discussion

i What professions do you most admire? Do you think there are some jobs which are undervalued or overvalued in our society? Should all kinds of work be equally valued and rewarded?

ii Would you like to be a doctor? Why/Why not?

iii Do you prefer life in the town to life in the country? Why/Why not?

5.3 Reading without assistance

Here is a poem by a writer who also opposed the social tendencies of his day. In it he expresses his sense of wonder and terror at the potential of created life. Notice how he too uses rhetorical questions.

The Tyger

Tyger Tyger, burning bright,
In the forests of the night;
What immortal hand or eye,
Could frame thy fearful symmetry?

In what distant deeps or skies,
Burnt the fire of thine eyes?
On what wings dare he aspire?
What the hand, dare seize the fire?

And what shoulder, & what art,
Could twist the sinews of thy heart?
And when thy heart began to beat,
What dread hand? & what dread feet?

What the hammer? what the chain,
In what furnace was thy brain?
What the anvil? what dread grasp,
Dare its deadly terrors clasp?

When the stars threw down their spears
And water'd heaven with their tears:
Did he smile his work to see?
Did he who made the Lamb make thee?

Tyger Tyger, burning bright,
In the forests of the night:
What immortal hand or eye,
Dare frame thy fearful symmetry?

William Blake

5.4 The sonnet

5.4.1   In the sixteenth century English writers began to translate *sonnets* from Italian, and in particular from Petrarch. The form became familiar and much used for both translation and original composition.

Characteristics of a *Petrarchan sonnet*:

  i   It consists of 14 lines

 ii   In its most regular form, each line has five 'feet' consisting of either one unstressed syllable followed by one stressed syllable or of one short syllable followed by one long syllable (a scheme called *iambic pentameter*). Each line has 10 syllables in all e.g.

the plough/man home/ward plods / his wea/ry way

 iii   The poem is divided into two parts: the *octave* (8 lines) and the *sestet* (6 lines).

 iv   Usually, the octave is divided into two groups of four lines and the sestet into two groups of three lines.

  v   Usually, between the octave and the sestet two main ideas are compared or balanced.

 vi   The rhyme scheme at the end of each line of the octave is: *abba abba*; the sestet often varies, e.g. *cdcdcd* or *cdecde*.

5.4.2   **i**   *Wordsworth, in a Petrarchan sonnet, describes a view of London, seen from Westminster Bridge in 1882. He feels that the beauty of the city at dawn, before the 'mighty heart' wakes to the noise of daytime, is as splendid as the loveliness of mountain scenery that he knows in his beloved Lake District. Dorothy Wordsworth, his sister, sets the scene as it happened:*

> … We mounted the Dover coach at Charing Cross. It was a beautiful morning. The city, St. Paul's, with the river, and a multitude of little boats, made a most beautiful sight as we crossed Westminster Bridge. The houses were not overhung by their cloud of smoke, and they were spread out endlessly, yet the sun shone so brightly, with such a fierce light, that there was even something like the purity of one of nature's own grand spectacles.

5

Wordsworth's poem begins:

> 'Earth has not anything to show more fair:'

and finishes:

> 'And all that mighty heart is lying still!'

ii In pairs, sequence the poem correctly (note, that while each line has ten syllables the rhythm is not entirely regular; this helps Wordsworth stress the important words).

GLOSSARY

garment (l.1): piece of clothing

steep (l.4): soak

glideth (l.5): moves smoothly

1 This City now doth, like a garment, wear
2 In his first splendour, valley, rock, or hill
3 Dull would he be of soul who could pass by
4 Never did sun more beautifully steep
5 The river glideth at his own sweet will:
6 A sight so touching in its majesty:
7 Dear God! the very houses seem asleep;
8 Ships, towers, domes, theatres, and temples lie
9 And all that mighty heart is lying still!
10 Earth has not anything to show more fair:
11 Open unto the fields, and to the sky;
12 All bright and glittering in the smokeless air.
13 The beauty of the morning; silent, bare,
14 Ne'er saw I, never felt, a calm so deep!

iii Check the correct sequence in the Key in the back of the book. Read the poem as many times as you like in order to understand it.

iv Notice how the eight lines of the octave are held together in one single sentence. Notice also how the sestet introduces a comparison of city and country.

5.4.3 Read another poem by Wordsworth. In it he uses the regular form of the Petrarchan sonnet to express powerful and complex emotions.

Surprised by joy – impatient as the wind
I turned to share the transport – Oh! with whom
But thee, deep buried in the silent tomb,
That spot which no vicissitude can find?
Love, faithful love, recalled thee to my mind –
But how could I forget thee? Through what power,
Even for the least division of an hour,
Have I been so beguiled as to be blind
To my most grievous loss! – That thought's return
Was the worst pang that sorrow ever bore,
Save one, one only, when I stood forlorn,
Knowing my heart's best treasure was no more;
That neither present time, nor years unborn
Could to my sight that heavenly face restore.

What feelings does the poem arouse in you?

Notes

William Wordsworth was born in 1770 and died in 1850. He was one of the major English Romantic poets and a poet of nature. His Lyrical Ballads *were first published in 1798 and his long autobiographical poem* The Prelude *in 1850 (45 years after it was completed).*

5.4.4 Another sonnet pattern is known as the Elizabethan or Shakespearian sonnet.

Characteristics of an *Elizabethan sonnet*:

- **i** It consists of 14 lines
- **ii** Each line is in *iambic pentameter*
- **iii** The poem is divided into four parts: 3 *quatrains* (4 lines each) and a final *couplet* (2 lines)
- **iv** The rhyme scheme is usually: *abab cdcd efef gg*

Shakespeare wrote at least 144 such sonnets.

5.4.5 **i** In one of his sonnets Shakespeare makes fun of conventional descriptions of a lady's beauty. Previously, the sonnet had often been used for love poetry that compared the beloved (the 'mistress') – her features, her way of speaking and moving – with all that is most beautiful in nature. Shakespeare describes his lady as being much less splendid and more 'natural'. He takes 12 lines of his sonnet to bring the subject down to earth. Finally, in the forceful couplet at the end, he turns the argument round and says that he feels she is indeed just as rare – as unequalled – as any other woman, who is falsely over-praised.

The poem begins:

> 'My mistress' eyes are nothing like the sun;'

and finishes:

> 'As any she belied with false compare'.

ii In pairs, sequence the poem correctly

GLOSSARY
belied (l.1): given a false impression of
compare (l.1): comparison
grant (l.5): admit
reeks (l.6): smells strongly and rather unpleasantly
damask'd (l.12): in the two colours of the damask rose
dun (l.13): brown in colour

1 As any she belied with false compare.
2 And in some perfumes is there more delight
3 My mistress, when she walks, treads on the ground:
4 If hairs be wires, black wires grow on her head.
5 I grant I never saw a goddess go, –
6 Than in the breath that from my mistress reeks.
7 That music hath a far more pleasing sound:
8 I love to hear her speak, yet well I know
9 My mistress' eyes are nothing like the sun;
10 And yet, by heaven, I think my love as rare
11 Coral is far more red than her lips' red:
12 I have seen roses damask'd, red and white,
13 If snow be white, why then her breasts are dun,
14 But no such roses see I in her cheeks;

iii Check the correct sequence in the Key in the back of the book. Read the poem as many times as you like in order to understand it.

iv How does the form help to support the main line of reasoning?

5.4.6 Here is another sonnet by Shakespeare. Notice the pun in the word 'lie':

> When my love swears that she is made of truth,
> I do believe her, though I know she lies,
> That she might think me some untutor'd youth,
> Unlearned in the world's false subtleties.
> Thus vainly thinking that she thinks me young, 5
> Although she knows my days are past the best,
> Simply I credit her false-speaking tongue:
> On both sides thus is simple truth supprest.
> But wherefore says she not she is unjust?
> And wherefore say not I that I am old? 10
> O! love's best habit is in seeming trust,
> And age in love loves not to have years told:
> Therefore I lie with her, and she with me,
> And in our faults by lies we flatter'd be.

What does the poem suggest to you?

5.5 The art of the novel

Unlike short stories, where the writer usually aims to be concise and pointed, the novelist can take time to build up character, to build up atmosphere so that one feels one is actually living through the experience evoked. Dialogue, description and narrative are all fully integrated.

5.5.1
Language work

What are the names in English of these swimming strokes?

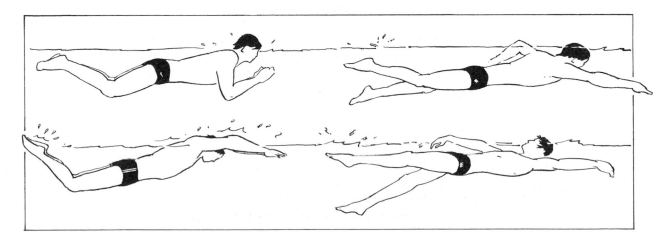

Find people in the class who have swum in at least two of the following:

the sea   a lake

a river   a swimming pool

Compare impressions. Which do they prefer? Why?

5.5.3 *Two sisters, Gudrun and Ursula, are walking by a lake, Willey Water, on a grey, moist spring morning, when they see Gerald Crich, a very efficient local industrialist – young, fair-haired, good looking, very masculine – dive into the water.*

Read:

The two girls drifted swiftly along. In front of them, at the corner of the lake, near the road, was a mossy boat-house under a walnut tree, and a little landing-stage where a boat was moored, wavering like a shadow on the still grey water, below the green, decayed poles. All was shadowy with coming summer. 5

Suddenly, from the boat-house, a white figure ran out, frightening in its swift sharp transit, across the old landing stage. It launched in a white arc through the air, there was a burst of the water, and among the smooth ripples a swimmer was making out to space, in a centre of faintly heaving motion. The whole other-world, wet and remote, he 10 had to himself. He could move into the pure translucency of the grey, uncreated water.

Gudrun stood by the stone wall, watching.

'How I envy him,' she said, in low, desirous tones.

'Ugh!' shivered Ursula. 'So cold!' 15

'Yes, but how good, how really fine, to swim out there!' The sisters stood watching the swimmer move further into the grey, moist, full space of the water, pulsing with his own small invading motion, and arched over with mist and dim woods.

'Don't you wish it were you?' asked Gudrun, looking at Ursula. 20

'I do,' said Ursula. 'But I'm not sure – it's so wet.'

'No,' said Gudrun, reluctantly. She stood watching the motion on the bosom of the water, as if fascinated. He, having swum a certain distance, turned round and was swimming on his back, looking along the water at the two girls by the wall. In the faint wash of motion, they 25 could see his ruddy face, and could feel him watching them.

'It is Gerald Crich,' said Ursula.

'I know,' said Gudrun.

And she stood motionless gazing over the water at the face which washed up and down on the flood, as he swam steadily. From his 30 separate element he saw them and he exulted to himself because of

GLOSSARY
landing-stage (l.3): platform for people getting out of boats

his own advantage, his possession of a world to himself. He was immune and perfect. He loved his own vigorous, thrusting motion, and the violent impulse of the very cold water against his limbs, buoying him up. He could see the girls watching him a way off, outside, and that pleased him. He lifted his arm from the water, in a sign to them. 35

'He is waving,' said Ursula.

'Yes,' replied Gudrun. They watched him. He waved again, with a strange movement of recognition across the difference. 40

'Like a Nibelung,' laughed Ursula. Gudrun said nothing, only stood still looking over the water.

Gerald suddenly turned, and was swimming away swiftly, with a side stroke. He was alone now, alone and immune in the middle of the waters, which he had all to himself. He exulted in his isolation in the 45 new element, unquestioned and unconditioned. He was happy, thrusting with his legs and all his body, without bond or connection anywhere, just himself in the watery world.

Gudrun envied him almost painfully. Even this momentary possession of pure isolation and fluidity seemed to her so terribly desirable that 50 she felt herself as if damned, out there on the high road.

'God, what it is to be a man!' she cried.

'What?' exclaimed Ursula in surprise.

'The freedom, the liberty, the mobility!' cried Gudrun, strangely flushed and brilliant. 'You're a man, you want to do a thing, you do it. 55 You haven't the *thousand* obstacles a woman has in front of her.'

Ursula wondered what was in Gudrun's mind, to occasion this outburst. She could not understand.

'What do you want to do?' she asked.

'Nothing,' cried Gudrun, in swift refutation. 'But supposing I did. 60 Supposing I want to swim up that water. It is impossible, it is one of the impossibilities of life, for me to take my clothes off now and jump in. But isn't it *ridiculous*, doesn't it simply prevent our living!'

She was so hot, so flushed, so furious, that Ursula was puzzled.

Nibelung (l.41): follower of Siegfried in German legend

high road (l.51): main road

Notes
This extract is from Women in Love *by D. H. Lawrence.*

i Improving understanding
Re-read the passage and answer the following questions.

    a) Where were the 'poles'? Why do you think they were 'green' and 'decayed'?

       Did Gerald know he was being watched?

What sort of swimmer was he?

How many different swimming strokes are either mentioned or implied?

b) What was Gudrun's reaction to seeing Gerald?

What was Ursula's?

How did Gerald see himself in the situation?

ii Language

Match the words on the left with the definitions on the right:

swift	exhilarated with red in the cheeks
moored	very quick
transit	slight gentle waves
ripples	sudden violent expression of feelings
translucency	fastened (for a boat)
flushed	condition where light only partly passes through
outburst	act of passing from one place to another

Look back at the passage and see how the words are used in context.

iii Descriptions

a) *Gerald*

Write down the words/phrases which describe or suggest Gerald's strength and energy (e.g. launched).

In a separate list, write down the words which describe his feelings.

b) *Gudrun*

Write down the words/phrases which describe or suggest Gudrun's response to the scene. What things does she say or do that also reveal her attitude?

c) *Ursula*

Ursula responds to both Gerald and Gudrun. Write down words or phrases which reveal her reaction. Indicate who in particular they relate to. How much of her attitude is revealed by what she says?

d)

A lot is subtly conveyed about the characters' natures from words which on the surface are not primarily used to describe them. What do the following words/phrases suggest?

Gudrun and Ursula: drifted

Gerald: 'All was shadowy' and 'a white figure ran out'
              launched
              uncreated
              invading
              the motion on the bosom of the water
              immune and perfect
              without bond or connection anywhere
              isolation and fluidity

iv **The narrator**

Lawrence does not intrude as a 'visible' narrator and yet his own sympathies come through. What character do you think he most identifies with? (Can you say why?)

v **Discussion**

How far do you identify with any of the characters? Do you agree with Gudrun that a man has more 'freedom' than a woman to do what he likes? Do you think that there should be no difference between men and women in that respect? Do you think it's a good thing to be able to do what you like?

vi **Extension**

Get hold of a copy of the novel and read the chapter which the passage comes from (Chapter IV The Diver).

5.6 Conclusion

5.6.1 Discuss the Unit in pairs.

UNIT 6

Going outside the text

6.1 Making links

6.1.1
Anticipation Look at these pictures:

  i Make guesses about the man and the girl –
       e.g. ages, character, where they live, etc.

  ii What season of the year is it?

6.1.2
Language work Look at the following words:

spring	thoughts	colder	grieve
older	express	fall	weep
sorrow	leaves	sigh	mourn

  i In pencil, cross out any words you don't understand. Then ask the other people in your class if they know what they mean. Rub out your mark as you discover the meaning.

ii   Look up any words you don't know in a dictionary.

iii Say whether each is a noun, verb or adjective (some may be more than one).

iv   Draw lines between the words that have a link in meaning, e.g. sorrow ———— sigh.

v   The words are from a poem. The first line is 'Margaret are you grieving'. Can you guess what the poem is about?

6.1.3   Listen to the poem by Gerard Manley Hopkins as many times as you like.

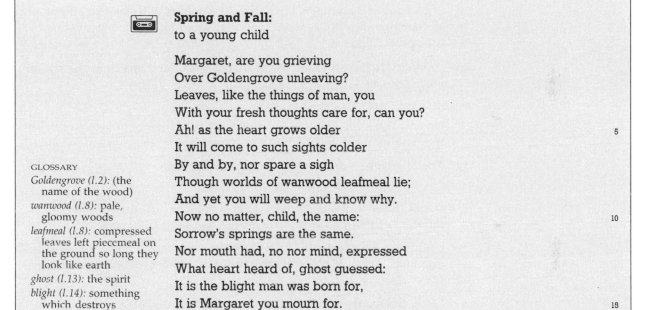

Spring and Fall:
to a young child

Margaret, are you grieving
Over Goldengrove unleaving?
Leaves, like the things of man, you
With your fresh thoughts care for, can you?
Ah! as the heart grows older   5
It will come to such sights colder
By and by, nor spare a sigh
Though worlds of wanwood leafmeal lie;
And yet you will weep and know why.
Now no matter, child, the name: 10
Sorrow's springs are the same.
Nor mouth had, no nor mind, expressed
What heart heard of, ghost guessed:
It is the blight man was born for,
It is Margaret you mourn for.   15

GLOSSARY
Goldengrove (l.2): (the name of the wood)
wanwood (l.8): pale, gloomy woods
leafmeal (l.8): compressed leaves left piecemeal on the ground so long they look like earth
ghost (l.13): the spirit
blight (l.14): something which destroys

Does the content of the poem match your expectations?

6.1.4
Improving
understanding

i   Write T (true) F (false) DK (don't know) next to each of the following statements. Re-write the false sentences to make them true.

  a) The poet's 'voice' is that of an old man.
     The poet is giving immediate expression to his thoughts.
     A younger man is speaking to an older girl.
     They are both sad.
     He is wise.
     She is picking up leaves.

  b) She is grieving because the leaves won't fall.
     He asks her if she cares about other things as she cares about leaves.
     She is innocent and he is a 'man of the world'.
     The poet thinks she won't care about falling leaves as she older.
     The poet thinks that the source of all sorrow is the s. never be described.

The poet 'says' that man is not born to suffer.
He thinks she is really weeping for him.
The poet thinks it is hard for us to express our feelings.

ii Make other statements about the poem. In pairs, discuss its 'meaning'.

iii Can you summarise what you think the poem is 'about'?

6.1.5
Language

i In pairs, try to define the meanings of the words in 6.1.2. as they are used in the poem.

ii Look in your dictionary. Find all the meanings of the word 'spring' and all the meanings of the word 'fall' that could be implied in the title of the poem. Discuss.

iii Listen to the poem again. Write marks over the words that the reader's voice stresses, e.g.

Márgaret are you gríeving.

Do you think the stresses and the rhythm of the poem help to convey the writer's meaning? Show where and how.

iv The following words were invented by the poet:

unleaving   wanwood   leafmeal

Could the writer have chosen other words? Which ones? What difference would it have made if they had been used instead?

v Underline the grammatical constructions which are not normal English grammar. Try to re-write them in 'normal' English. What effect does it have?

vi Circle the words which rhyme, e.g. grieving, unleaving

vii Write down the words which alliterate. What effect does the alliteration have?

6.1.6
Background

Listen to the story of Hopkins' life on tape and complete the chart:

BORN:_____ DIED:_____

BECAME JESUIT PRIEST:_____

POEMS FIRST PUBLISHED:_____

GENERAL DESCRIPTION OF CHARACTER:_____

GENERAL DESCRIPTION OF POEMS:_____

The tapescript is printed in the Key in the back of the book.
How do you think Hopkins' life is reflected in the poem (if at all)?

ii Look up any words you don't know in a dictionary.

iii Say whether each is a noun, verb or adjective (some may be more than one).

iv Draw lines between the words that have a link in meaning, e.g. sorrow _____ sigh.

v The words are from a poem. The first line is 'Margaret are you grieving'. Can you guess what the poem is about?

6.1.3 Listen to the poem by Gerard Manley Hopkins as many times as you like.

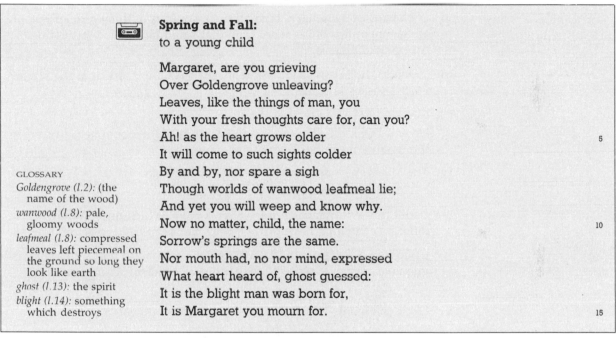

Spring and Fall:
to a young child

Margaret, are you grieving
Over Goldengrove unleaving?
Leaves, like the things of man, you
With your fresh thoughts care for, can you?
Ah! as the heart grows older   5
It will come to such sights colder
By and by, nor spare a sigh
Though worlds of wanwood leafmeal lie;
And yet you will weep and know why.
Now no matter, child, the name: 10
Sorrow's springs are the same.
Nor mouth had, no nor mind, expressed
What heart heard of, ghost guessed:
It is the blight man was born for,
It is Margaret you mourn for.   15

GLOSSARY
Goldengrove (l.2): (the name of the wood)
wanwood (l.8): pale, gloomy woods
leafmeal (l.8): compressed leaves left piecemeal on the ground so long they look like earth
ghost (l.13): the spirit
blight (l.14): something which destroys

Does the content of the poem match your expectations?

6.1.4
Improving
understanding

i Write T (true) F (false) DK (don't know) next to each of the following statements. Re-write the false sentences to make them true.

    a) The poet's 'voice' is that of an old man.
        The poet is giving immediate expression to his thoughts.
        A younger man is speaking to an older girl.
        They are both sad.
        He is wise.
        She is picking up leaves.

    b) She is grieving because the leaves won't fall.
        He asks her if she cares about other things as she cares about leaves.
        She is innocent and he is a 'man of the world'.
        The poet thinks she won't care about falling leaves as she grows older.
        The poet thinks that the source of all sorrow is the same, and it can never be described.

The poet 'says' that man is not born to suffer.
He thinks she is really weeping for him.
The poet thinks it is hard for us to express our feelings.

ii Make other statements about the poem. In pairs, discuss its 'meaning'.

iii Can you summarise what you think the poem is 'about'?

**6.1.5
Language**

i In pairs, try to define the meanings of the words in 6.1.2. as they are used in the poem.

ii Look in your dictionary. Find all the meanings of the word 'spring' and all the meanings of the word 'fall' that could be implied in the title of the poem. Discuss.

iii Listen to the poem again. Write marks over the words that the reader's voice stresses, e.g.

Márgaret are you gríeving.

Do you think the stresses and the rhythm of the poem help to convey the writer's meaning? Show where and how.

iv The following words were invented by the poet:

unleaving   wanwood   leafmeal

Could the writer have chosen other words? Which ones? What difference would it have made if they had been used instead?

v Underline the grammatical constructions which are not normal English grammar. Try to re-write them in 'normal' English. What effect does it have?

vi Circle the words which rhyme, e.g. grieving, unleaving

vii Write down the words which alliterate. What effect does the alliteration have?

**6.1.6
Background**

Listen to the story of Hopkins' life on tape and complete the chart:

BORN:_____ DIED:_____

BECAME JESUIT PRIEST:_____

POEMS FIRST PUBLISHED:_____

GENERAL DESCRIPTION OF CHARACTER:_____

GENERAL DESCRIPTION OF POEMS:_____

The tapescript is printed in the Key in the back of the book.
How do you think Hopkins' life is reflected in the poem (if at all)?

i Read the following extract:

Coldly, sadly descends
The autumn evening. The field
Strewn with its dank yellow drifts
Of withered leaves, and the elms,
Fade into dimness apace,   5
Silent.   *Matthew Arnold* from *Rugby Chapel*

ii Read the following whole poem:

Autumn in King's Hintock Park

Here by the baring bough
Raking up leaves
Often I ponder how
Springtime deceives –
I, an old woman now,   5
Raking up leaves.

Here in the avenue
Raking up leaves,
Lords' ladies pass in view
Until one heaves   10
Sighs at life's russet hue,
Raking up leaves!

Just as my shape you see
Raking up leaves,
I saw, when fresh and free   15
Those memory weaves
Into grey ghosts by me,
Raking up leaves.

Yet, Dear, though one may sigh,
Raking up leaves,   20
New leaves will dance on high –
Earth never grieves! –
Will not, when missed am I
Raking up leaves.   *Thomas Hardy (1840–1928)*

iii Both poems are about autumn, and both about leaves and yet both are
very different from the Hopkins poem. Make some statements about
the differences, e.g. The narrator in the poem by Hardy is a woman.

iv Look at the poem in 2.9.3. How does it compare?

6.1.8
Discussion

6.1.8
Discussion

i   From the three poems in this Unit, what do you think the differences
     are between autumn in England and autumn in your country.
ii   In general, do you think it is difficult to express one's feelings?
iii Which of the three poems do you prefer? Give reasons.

6.2   Recurrent themes

6.2.1
Introduction

A common theme in the literature of the sixteenth century and the first
half of the seventeenth century, deriving from Latin literature, was the
corruption of life at court and the joys of life in the country. At the same
time, the shortness of life and the ruthless passage of time were also
potent subjects (there are examples later in this book in 8.2.1).

At the end of the eighteenth century and in the nineteenth and
twentieth centuries, with the rapid industrialisation of Britain, poets and
novelists expressed their anger and despair at the increased
dehumanisation of life. Blake, Dickens and Lawrence are notable
examples. In 5.2.1 and 5.2.2, you have already met examples of writers
being sceptical about the value of 'progress'.

6.2.2

*Wordsworth (1770–1850) and his friend Coleridge (1772-1834) witnessed many huge
changes in Britain. They believed their poetry – in particular poetry about nature – could
bring people back to health and release the elemental powers within every individual.
Consequently, they are sometimes thought of as 'Romantic'. Here are some extracts from
Wordsworth's* Preface *to the* Lyrical Ballads *(1800). They are quite difficult to understand
so re-read as often as you wish.*

1 A multitude of causes, unknown to former times, are now acting
   with a combined force to blunt the discriminating powers of the
   mind, and unfitting it for all voluntary exertion, to reduce it to a
   state of almost savage torpor. The most effective of these causes
   are the great national events which are daily taking place, and   5
   the increased accumulation of men in cities, where the uniformity
   of their occupations produces a craving for extraordinary
   incident, which the rapid communication of intelligence hourly
   gratifies. To this tendency of life and manners the literature and
   theatrical exhibitions of the country have conformed themselves   10
   ...

   When I think upon this degrading thirst after outrageous
   stimulation, I am almost ashamed to have spoken of the feeble
   endeavour made in these volumes to counteract it; and, reflecting
   upon the magnitude of the general evil, I should be oppressed
   with no dishonourable melancholy, had I not a deep impression   15
   of certain inherent and indestructible qualities of the human
   mind, and likewise of certain powers in the great and permanent
   objects that act upon it, which are equally inherent and
   indestructible; and were there not added to this impression a
   belief, that the time is approaching when the evil will be   20
   systematically opposed, by men of greater powers, and with far
   more distinguished success.

GLOSSARY
blunt (l.2): lessen the
   sharpness of
torpor (l.4): inactivity
craving (l.7): strong desire
gratifies (l.9): satisfies
degrading (l.11):
   humiliating
feeble (l.12): very weak
endeavour (l.13): attempt

2 The principal object, then, proposed in *these Poems* was to
choose incidents and situations from common life, and to relate
or describe them, throughout, as far as was possible in a   25
selection of language really used by men, and, at the same time,
to throw over *them* a certain colouring of imagination, *whereby*
ordinary things should be presented to the mind in an unusual
aspect; and, further, and above all, to make these incidents and
situations interesting by tracing in them, truly though not   00
ostentatiously, the primary laws of our nature: chiefly, as far as
regards the manner in which we associate ideas in a state of
excitement. Humble and rustic life was generally chosen,
because, in that *condition*, the essential passions of the heart find
a better soil in which they can attain their maturity, are less under   35
restraint, and speak a plainer and more emphatic language;
because in that condition of life our elementary feelings coexist in
a state of greater simplicity, and, consequently, may be more
accurately contemplated, and more forcibly communicated.

3 What is a Poet? To whom does he address himself? And what   40
language is to be expected from him? *He* is a man speaking to
men: a man, it is true, endowed with more lively sensibility, more
enthusiasm and tenderness, who has a greater knowledge of
human nature, and a more comprehensive soul, than are
supposed to be common among mankind; a man pleased with his   45
own passions and volitions, and who rejoices more than other
men in the spirit of life that is in him ... To *these qualities* he has
added a disposition to be affected more than any other men by
absent things as if they were present; an ability of conjuring up in
himself passions, which are indeed far from being the same as   50
those produced by real events than anything which, from the
motion of their own minds merely, other men are accustomed to
feel in themselves ...

whereby (l.27): by means of
which
ostentatiously (l.31): by
placing unnecessary
emphasis
restraint (l.36): control
endowed with (l.42): gifted
with
conjuring up (l.49):
producing

Improving understanding

i Select the most important phrases that help get across the writer's
point of view. Compare your selection in pairs. Can you summarise his
argument?

ii Are the 'multitude of causes' new?
What examples of causes does Wordsworth give?
What effect do they have?
Are literature and the theatre immune from them?
How does Wordsworth see himself in relation to them?
What does Wordsworth place his faith in?
What did he see as ideal subject matter for poets?
Why?
What qualities does a poet possess that other human beings do not?

Language

i   What does the word 'it' refer to in different parts of the extracts?

ii Find a word which in context means:

Extract 1   able to perceive fine distinctions
              effort
              neutralise the effects of
              cannot be destroyed
              part of its essential nature

Extract 2   tell
              clearer and more ordinary
              concerning country people

Extract 3   expresses joy
              used to

iii Can you find a metaphor? Is it effective?

iv Divide the following words into those which in context have a positive connotation (or a pleasant association) and those which have a negative connotation:

Extract 1   torpor   extraordinary   human mind
              cities   stimulation   indestructible

Extract 2   common life   ordinary   ostentatiously   elementary
              imagination   unusual   humble   accurately

Extract 3   sensibility   comprehension   conjuring up
              enthusiasm   volitions

Which is the strongest force in the extracts, the positive or the negative?

Style

i   How would you describe Wordsworth's different moods and attitudes in the three extracts?

ii Is his style of writing the same in the three extracts?
What sorts of words does he use? (e.g. strong adjectives?) Are the sentences long or short? (What effect does this have?)

iii What is the function of the questions at the beginning of Extract 3?

iv Do you think his own style of writing is at variance with the style of writing he seems to believe in?

Discussion

What do you think the value of poetry is? Is poetry now dead?

6.2.3 *Matthew Arnold (1822–1888) was more gloomy. He probably did not believe that poets of 'greater powers' could 'systematically oppose' the evil. Indeed, his own poetic powers were less than those of Wordsworth. However, he too disliked the modern world and in this poem mourns the loss of religious faith:*

Dover Beach

The sea is calm to-night,
The tide is full, the moon lies fair
Upon the Straits; – on the French coast, the light
Gleams, and is gone; the cliffs of England stand,
Glimmering and vast, out in the tranquil bay.   5
Come to the window, sweet is the night air!
Only, from the long line of spray
Where the ebb meets the moon-blanch'd sand,
Listen! you hear the grating roar
Of pebbles which the waves suck back, and fling,   10
At their return, up the high strand,
Begin, and cease, and then again begin,
With tremulous cadence slow, and bring
The eternal note of sadness in.
Sophocles long ago   15
Heard it on the Aegaean, and it brought
Into his mind the turbid ebb and flow
Of human misery; we
Find also in the sound a thought,
Hearing it by this distant northern sea.   20

The sea of faith
Was once, too, at the full, and round earth's shore
Lay like the folds of a bright girdle furl'd;
But now I only hear
Its melancholy, long, withdrawing, roar,   25
Retreating to the breath
Of the night-wind down the vast edges drear
And naked shingles of the world.

Ah, love, let us be true
To one another! for the world, which seems   30
To lie before us like a land of dreams,
So various, so beautiful, so new,
Hath really neither joy, nor love, nor light,
Nor certitude, nor peace, nor help for pain;
And we are here as on a darkling plain;   35
Swept with confused alarms of struggle and flight,
Where ignorant armies clash by night.

GLOSSARY
Dover (title): is the English port nearest to France.
Straits (l.3): channel of sea between England and France
cliffs (l.4): high rock faces that run along the sea shore
moon blanch'd (l.8): made white by the moon
strand (l.11): beach
tremulous cadence (l.13): trembling sound
turbid (l.17): muddy
girdle (l.23): belt
furl'd (l.23): rolled round
withdrawing (l.25): retreating
drear (archaic) (l.27): dull
shingles (l.28): small stones on the beach
darkling (l.35): dark

153

Improving understanding

i Write T (true) F (false) DK (don't know).
Re-write the false sentences to make them true.

> The tide is out.
> It is very cloudy.
> The lights of France can be seen.
> The poet is speaking from the point of land furthest into the sea.
> He can hear the sound of waves on pebbles.
> Religious faith comes and goes; now it is in retreat.
> The poet believes the world is in a state of moral darkness and atheism.

ii Who do you imagine the poet is speaking to?
Describe the scene in your own words.
What 'classical' experience does it remind the poet of?
What is the poet's mood at the beginning of the poem?
How does it change? What changes it?
Was there more 'faith' in earlier days?
In what ways are appearances deceptive?
How does the poet picture himself at the end of the poem?

Language

i Underline two constructions where the order of words is not normal in English. What effect does this have?

ii Find a simile and a metaphor. Are they effective? Why/Why not?

iii Divide the following words into those which in context have a positive connotation (or a pleasant association) and those which have a negative connotation:

calm	sadness
fair	ebb and flow
gleams	roar
vast	shingles
tranquil	confused
grating	ignorant

Do any not fit into these two categories exactly? What is stronger in this poem, the ebb or the flow?

Style

i Which of the following negative statements do you think are true? Add your own positive sentences if you wish.

> The style is falsely poetic.
> The poet is very wishy-washy in his expression of feeling.
> The imagery is very imprecise and inaccurate.

The poet is more concerned with expressing his own melancholy than creating a picture.

The poem is self-indulgent.

The poet, particularly at the end, creates impressive sounding music rather than expresses a serious point of view.

ii Indicate parts of the poem where the sound relates to what is being expressed (e.g. *the sea is calm to-night* is a very calm opening statement).

Discussion

Are you mainly optimistic or mainly pessimistic about the future? What things make you more optimistic than pessimistic?

6.2.4 *Brian Lee, a contemporary poet, expresses his feelings about twentieth-century England in a series of satires. In one of his longer satires,* London England, An Essay in Imitation, *he is reminded of Dr Samuel Johnson's poem* London *(1738).*

GLOSSARY

Sam (l.1): Samuel Johnson

Thames (l.3): the River Thames (the river which passes through London)

Shell Towers (l.4): tall office buildings for the Shell Oil Company

cracking in the strain (l.7): breaking under tension

MPs (l.14): Members of Parliament

Fleet-street (l.15): the street in London where most of the newspapers are published

hacks (l.16): inferior journalists

isms (l.19): doctrines

... Who's tired of London's tired of life, said Sam. –
He hadn't seen an office-block, or traffic-jam,
he still found peace, by Thames's silver flood –
we've Shell Towers, dead water, stinking mud;
he still felt at home, with his family of friends   5
keeping the place from which all else extends –
he hadn't seen so many, cracking in the strain
invisible but everywhere, who tries to constrain? –
marriages breaking-up, solitude closing-in
about the separated lives of men and women –   10
independent units, always on the move –
free and professional, forgetting how to love;
he hadn't smelt this air of suppressed panic –
MPs busy quarrelling – journalists gone manic,
or read what's published these days in Fleet-street –   15
hacks spelling-out, what men would not repeat;
he'd come before all this – things are going bad –
something is rotten – people are driven mad –
as ego, and isms, distend, to replace
the absence of a something we won't face.   20

Improving understanding

Who does 'he' refer to throughout the poem?

How do Dr Johnson's times differ from our own?

What does the poet give as examples of decay?

How does he describe the atmosphere of our times?

Language

  i Divide the following words into those which in context have a positive connotation (or a pleasant suggestion) and those which have a negative connotation:

peace	separated
stinking	professional
at home	love
strain	panic
solitude	hacks

  ii What rhyme-scheme does the poem have?

  iii How would you describe the rhythm of the poem?

Style

  i Which of the following statements do you think is true? Add your own statements if you wish.

> The poem sounds 'literary' (i.e. the poet is more interested in literary form, and special literary language than in what he has to say.)
> The tone is very vigorous and conversational.
> The poet seems to be motivated by anger and disappointment.
> He is bored and cynical.
> The poem is very depressing.
> It is very stimulating.
> The poet is concerned to tell us the truth about ourselves.

  ii How far do you think the poem gains because it is in verse? (i.e. how much would be lost if it were paraphrased into a prose statement like the Wordsworth extracts?)

Discussion

Are there any things about twentieth-century society you particularly dislike? What would you change if you could?

6.2.5 Compare the Wordsworth, Arnold and Lee (Arnold is the only whole piece). What do they have in common? How do they differ? Which do you prefer? Why?

6.3 Focus on 'background'

6.3.1 What matters most is what great writers actually write. However, what we know about them as people – how they led their lives, what they thought of other people, what other people thought of *them* – can help to give what they wrote added significance.

Of course, it's difficult to get anywhere near the whole truth about *any* great writer because there is so much we don't – indeed can't – know. Writers who are truthful as artists are not always truthful in their private lives, and friends and acquaintances often have personal motives for saying what they do about them. And in some areas it probably isn't proper to enquire into the very personal details. After all, what matters is the writing, isn't it? What do you think?

The word 'background' is dangerous: it suggests something cut off from and outside the writer. The word is usually used to include not only the main political and social events of the times but also the collective beliefs of the society, its shared feelings and significant ideas.

Clearly, any one writer will have some kind of relationship with everything and everyone around him. He might seem to belong totally *to* his times, sharing everything his fellows did, or he might be battling away *against* them. Some great artists – like Blake – managed to detach themselves and follow their own paths, not always successfully.

While all artists reveal something about the society in which they live, even in the act of cutting themselves off, the greater artists create something more timeless, which subsequent generations can relate to directly. Lesser artists are often so immersed in convention that they seem to us mere representatives of their times rather than creators of living art.

Do you agree?

6.3.2   E. M. Forster in his essay *Anonymity: An inquiry* poses the question: Do you like to know who a book's by?

> The question is more profound than may appear. A poem for example: do we gain more or less pleasure from it when we know the name of the poet? *The Ballad of Sir Patrick Spens,* for example. No one knows who wrote *Sir Patrick Spens.* It comes to us out of the northern void like a breath of ice. Set beside it another ballad whose [5] author is known – *The Rime of the Ancient Mariner.* That, too, contains a tragic voyage and the breath of ice, but it is signed Samuel Taylor Coleridge, and we know a certain amount about this Coleridge. Coleridge signed other poems and knew other poets; he ran away from Cambridge; he enlisted as a Dragoon under the name [10] of Trooper Comberback, but fell so constantly from his horse that it had to be withdrawn from beneath him permanently; he was employed instead upon matters relating to sanitation; he married Southey's sister, and gave lectures; he became stout, pious and dishonest, took opium and died. With such information in our heads, [15] we speak of the *Ancient Mariner* as 'a poem by Coleridge', but of *Sir Patrick Spens* as 'a poem'. What difference, if any, does this difference between them make upon our minds? And in the case of novels and plays – does ignorance or knowledge of their authorship signify? And newspaper articles – do they impress more when they [20] are signed or unsigned?

He then answers the question:

Now comes the crucial point. While we are reading *The Ancient Mariner* we forget our astronomy and geography and daily ethics. Do we not also forget the author? Does not Samuel Taylor Coleridge, lecturer, opium eater, and dragoon, disappear with the rest of the world of information? We remember him before we begin the poem and after we finish it, but during the poem nothing exists but the poem. Consequently while we read *The Ancient Mariner* a change takes place in it. It becomes anonymous, like the *Ballad of Sir Patrick Spens*. And here is the point I would support: that all literature tends towards a condition of anonymity, and that, so far as words are creative, a signature merely distracts us from their true significance.

…

The poet wrote the poem no doubt, but he forgot himself while he wrote it, and we forget him while we read. What is so wonderful about great literature is that it transforms the man who reads it towards the condition of the man who wrote, and brings to birth in us also the creative impulse. Lost in the beauty where he was lost, we find more than we ever threw away, we reach what seems to be our spiritual home, and remember that it was not the speaker who was the beginning but the Word.

…

The personality of a writer does become important after we have read his book and begin to study it. When the glamour of creation ceases, when the leaves of the divine trees are silent, when the co-partnership is over, then a book changes its nature, and we can ask ourselves questions about it such as 'What is the author's name?' 'Where did he live?' 'Was he married?' and 'Which was his favourite flower?' Then we are no longer reading the book, we are studying it and making it subserve our desire for information. 'Study' has a very solemn sound. 'I am studying Dante' sounds much more than 'I am reading Dante'. It is really much less. Study is only a serious form of gossip. It teaches us everything about the book except the central thing, and between that and us it raises a circular barrier which only the wings of the spirit can cross. The study of science, history, etc., is necessary and proper, for they are subjects that belong to the domain of information, but a creative subject like literature – to study that is excessively dangerous, and should never be attempted by the immature.

Do you agree? Discuss these ideas in pairs.

6.3.3 On the assumption that we don't agree with E. M. Forster *completely*, we will be doing some work on background in this Unit! To support your reading of the poems, the stories and the extracts from novels and plays in this book you may find it helpful to refer to

histories of literature
political and social histories
biographies
encyclopaedias

as well as look at paintings and listen to music which come from the same period as the written text.

6.3.4 In Unit 5, you looked at extracts from *Don Juan*, some history of the times and a little about Byron's life. Here are some further exercises, amounting to quite a long project.

6.3.5 In pairs:

   i Look at these pictures of Byron from different stages of his life.

   ii From what you know of his life, put them in chronological order. Which one shows Byron at his youngest? Which at his oldest? Give reasons for your choice. (The answers are in the Key in the back of the book.)

   iii Write down some adjectives next to each picture that describe the aspects of Byron's character that the artist is trying to convey.

iv This was how the English public saw Byron at one time of his life. What does it convey? How old do you think he was, approximately?

6.3.6 In pairs:

   i Look at this picture. On the far right Byron is talking to Sir Walter Scott.

Discuss:

   ii What sort of gathering is it?
What does it show you about the society of the times?
What sorts of things do you think they might be talking about?
How does it compare with an equivalent gathering now?
How does it compare with an equivalent gathering in your own country at that time?

6.3.7 In pairs

   i Look at this picture. It is Byron's family home, which he lived in from time to time as a young man. He sold it to pay off his debts.

  ii Discuss what life might have been like there.
What do you think were the best things/the worst things about living there?

 iii Guess how many rooms there were, what they were used for, how many servants there were. Can you find out?

  iv Can you find a picture of some furniture of the times? Select the things Byron might have chosen to furnish his rooms.

6.3.8 In pairs:

   i Look at the following quotations:

> I swam in the Thames from Lambeth through the two bridges, Westminster and Blackfriars, a distance ... of 3 miles.
>
> the uncorrupted purity of his moral sense.
>
> He is extremely humble towards persons whose character he respects, and to them he would probably confess his errors ...
>
> *On marriage to Annabella:*
> 'That would have been but a *cold collation*, and I prefer hot suppers.'

I am buried in an abyss of Sensuality.

He did not look like my preconceived notion of
the melancholy poet ... His hair has already much
silver among its dark brown curls; its texture is
very silky, and although it retreats from his
temples, leaving his forehead very bare, its growth
at the sides and back of his head is abundant ...
there is something so striking in his whole appearance
that could not be mistaken for an ordinary person.
Only his own awareness of it made her aware of his limp;
she thought his voice had an accent particularly clear
and harmonious but somewhat effeminate.

I could not exist without some object
of love. I have found one with whom
I am perfectly satisfied, and who as far
as I can judge is no less so with me; our
mutual wish is *quiet* ...

Lord Byron ... looked 40. His face had
become pale, bloated and sallow. He had
grown very fat, his shoulders broad and
round and the knuckles of his hands were
lost in fat.

At twenty-three the best of life is over and its
bitters double. Secondly I have seen mankind in
various Countries and find them equally despicable.

He gives everyone an opportunity of sharing
in the conversation, and has the art of turning
it to subjects that may bring out the person
with whom he converses ... his anecdotes of life
and living characters is inexhaustible. In
spirits, as in everything else, he is ever in
extremes.

I took my gradations in the vices with
great promptitude, but they were not to
my taste ... though my temperament was
naturally burning. I could not share
in the common place libertinism of the
place and time without disgust.

I awoke one morning and found myself famous.

I am still living with my Delilah, who
has only two faults, unpardonable in a
woman – she can read and write.

ii Divide them into those you think were said *by* Byron and those said *about* him. Can you guess, from what you know, who said what?

iii Discard those you think are not helpful in giving a picture of Byron or are not *true* about him.

iv Can you sequence them chronologically?

v Make notes on what the quotations reveal and write them up into a paragraph. Show your paragraph to others in the class.

6.3.9 **i** Can you find out any more personal information about Byron's physical appearance at 18? For example, he had a clubfoot. How tall was he?

ii Can you draw a picture of what you think he may have looked like?

iii Check against any picture available.

iv How do you think his physical appearance may have affected his character?

6.3.10 **i** Find the works of a visual artist whose life overlapped with Byron's (e.g. Rowlandson, Fuseli, Blake, Constable, Turner).

ii What do they have in common with Byron's works? How do they differ?

6.4 Reading without assistance

This poem returns us to the theme of wonder we explored in Unit 3.

Full Moon and Little Frieda

A cool small evening shrunk to a dog bark and the
clank of a bucket –

Are you listening.
A spider's web, tense for the dew's touch.
A pail lifted, still and brimming – mirror   5
To tempt a first star to a tremor.

Cows are going home in the lane there, looping the
hedges with their warm wreaths of breath –
A dark river of blood, many boulders,
Balancing unspilled milk.   10

'Moon!' you cry suddenly, 'Moon! Moon!'

The moon has stepped back like an artist gazing amazed
at a work
That points at him amazed.

Ted Hughes

6.5 Personal opinion

6.5.1
Language work

i In English the 'to–infinitive' can be used as the subject of the sentence:

> e.g. To charge a lot of money would be ridiculous.

The second part of the sentence 'describes' the first. More commonly in modern English, however, an 'it' construction is used. The 'descriptive' clause begins the sentence:

> e.g. It would be ridiculous to charge a lot of money.

Change the following sentences so that they contain the more modern construction:

1 To go out in this weather would be asking for trouble.
2 To hesitate is fatal.
3 To try and help can only be thought of as a good thing.
4 To see you was a great pleasure.
5 To go out without checking your brakes would be the stupidest thing you could do.

ii A rather elegant epigrammatic construction not so commonly used nowadays is where the 'to–infinitive' is both the subject and the complement of the sentence. The second part of the sentence usually expresses a *consequence* of the first part and provides a kind of stylistic balance to the sentence:

> e.g. To be without a wife is to be without a friend.

In informal modern English this would probably be expressed by an 'if' or a 'when' construction:

> e.g. If you haven't got a wife you are short of a friend.
> *Or* When you haven't got a wife you are short of a friend.

Re-express the following sentences in more modern English:

1 To go out alone in this town is to risk your life.
2 To be woken up at dawn is to spend the rest of the day feeling tired.
3 To give all your money away is to commit an act of insanity.
4 To dress up is to make yourself presentable to the world.
5 To be an independent woman is to be thought of as not needing men.

6.5.2
Anticipation

Would you like to be rich?

i Continue this sentence in five different ways 'When you've got money ...'

ii Continue this sentence in five different ways 'When you haven't got any money ...'

Compare in pairs.

6.5.3   Listen to and read the following once:

 Literally and truly, one cannot get on well in the world without money. To be in want of it, is to pass through life with little credit or pleasure; it is to live out of the world, or to be despised if you come into it; it is not to be sent for to court, or asked out to dinner, or noticed in the street; it is not to have your opinion consulted or else rejected with contempt, to have your acquirements carped at and doubted, your good things disparaged, and at last to lose the wit and the spirit to say them; it is to be scrutinised by strangers, and neglected by friends; it is to be a thrall to circumstances, an exile in one's own country; to forego leisure, freedom, ease of body and mind, to be dependent on the good-will and caprice of others, or earn a precarious and irksome livelihood by some laborious employment; it is to be compelled to stand behind a counter, or to sit at a desk in some public office, or to marry your landlady, or not the person you would wish; or to go out to the East or West Indies, or to get a situation as judge abroad, and return home with a liver-complaint; or to be a law-stationer, or a scrivener or scavenger, or newspaper reporter; or to read law and sit in court without a brief; or to be deprived of the use of your fingers by transcribing Greek manuscripts, or to be a seal-engraver and pore yourself blind; or to go upon the stage, or try some of the Fine Arts; with all your pains, anxiety, and hopes, most probably to fail, or, if you succeed, after the exertions of years, and undergoing constant distress of mind and fortune, to be assailed on every side with envy, back-biting, and falsehood, or to be a favourite with the public for awhile, and then thrown into the background – or a gaol, by the fickleness of taste and some new favourite; to be full of enthusiasm and extravagance in youth, of chagrin and disappointment in after-life; to be jostled by the rabble because you do not ride in your coach, or avoided by those who know your worth and shrink from it as a claim on their respect or their purse; to be a burden to your relations, or unable to do anything for them; to be ashamed to venture into crowds; to have cold comfort at home; to lose by degrees your confidence and any talent you might possess; to grow crabbed, morose, and querulous, dissatisfied with every one, but most so with yourself; and plagued out of your life, to look about for a place to die in, and quit the world without any one's asking after your will. The *wiseacres* will possibly, however, crowd round your coffin, and raise a monument at a considerable expense, and after a lapse of time, to commemorate your genius and your misfortunes!

5
10
15
20
25
30
35
40

6.5.4   Try to answer these questions without looking at the glossaries below.

    i How would you describe the tone of voice of the passage?

ii In general terms, what is the writer's view of money? Do you agree with him?

iii What literary form (e.g. novel, essay, biography, etc.) do you think the passage comes from?

iv Can you guess which century it was written in?

Discuss in pairs.

6.5.5
Language

Read the passage more carefully. You may need the glossaries. The second glossary contains words you might like to remember.

GLOSSARY 1

acquirements (archaic) *(l.6):* character and ability
carped at (l.6): found fault with
thrall (l.9): slave
forego (l.10): give up
caprice (l.11): inclination to change behaviour without apparent reason
irksome (l.12): troublesome
law-stationer (l.17): person who sells articles used by lawyers
scrivener (archaic) *(l.17):* person who copies out legal letters
scavenger (archaic) *(l.17):* person employed to clean the streets
brief (l.18): document containing all the facts of a case in law
seal-engraver (l.20): person who makes seals (i.e. objects used for putting a mark on a letter to authenticate it)
pore yourself blind (l.20): lose your eyesight through studying too long
assailed (l.24): violently attacked
chagrin (l.28): humiliation
rabble (l.29): disorderly crowd
venture (l.32): go with some risk
cold comfort (l.32–33): not much consolation
crabbed (l.34): bad tempered
querulous (l.34): full of complaints
plagued (l.35): annoyed
wiseacres (l.37): boring people who pretend to be wiser than they are

GLOSSARY 2
Match the words on the left with the definitions on the right.

disparaged	insecure
wit	jealous desire to have what someone else has
scrutinised	pain and discomfort
neglected	speaking badly about an absent person
precarious	interval
compelled	intelligence
undergoing	something oppressive and difficult to bear
distress	bad tempered and gloomy
envy	ignored
back-biting	constant change
fickleness	forced
jostled	spoken contemptuously of
burden	looked at carefully
morose	experiencing
lapse	pushed roughly

List the words you would like to remember. Notice how they are used in context. Look them up in a dictionary and see if they have any other meanings.

6.5.6
Language

i Which grammatical structure is more used in the passage, the one in 6.5.1. (i) or 6.5.1. (ii)? What effect does it have on the tone?

ii What does the word 'it' refer to in different parts of the passage?

iii Which prepositions come after the following words in the passage?

compel

deprive

shrink

venture

Look in a dictionary. Are they the usual prepositions?

iv Underline the passive constructions.
What effect do they have on the passage?

v Comment on the overall construction of the paragraph. In what way is it balanced? How is the word 'or' used?

6.5.7
Follow-up work

i Read the passage again as many times as you like.

ii Summarise what you imagine to be the writer's point of view in about 75 words. Answering the following questions may help you:

Can you guess his attitude to money?
Are the consequences of not having it desirable?
How do you know?

iii Describe the writer's style in about 75 words.
Answering the following questions may help you:

Is the writer expressing his point of view explicitly?
Does he express himself concisely?
How does he get his point across? What use does he make of examples?
Is he gloomy, jovial, mocking, or dull? Or none of these?
Do you think he is enjoying writing this?
How would you describe the last sentence?

You may prefer to discuss these questions in pairs before doing any writing.

6.5.8
Discussion

What are your views on money? Is it the most important thing in life? Is it an evil?

6.5.9
Notes

The paragraph is by William Hazlitt, the essayist and critic, and comes from his essay On the Want of Money. *Hazlitt was born in 1778 and died in 1830. He was trained to follow his father into the Unitarian church but gave up the idea. Like many other thinkers of the day, for example Wordsworth and Coleridge, he was deeply influenced by the French Revolution and applauded the downfall of the autocracy in France. He deeply hated the modern or material philosophy of his day and what one critic calls the 'minimal accounts of human nature' common to many of his contemporaries. For a period he was a Parliamentary reporter.*

i Hazlitt was a contemporary of both Byron and Wordsworth. From what you know from this Unit and the previous Unit, discuss what the three writers have in common and how they differ. Focus on their:

  – attitude to the modern world
  – attitude to others
  – style of writing

ii Hazlitt died 18 years after Dickens' birth and yet they have things in common. Look back at Unit 2. Find one thing they have in common in:

  a) their working life
  b) their view of contemporary life
  c) their style

6.5.11 You might like to read what one critic has said about Hazlitt:

The works of William Hazlitt reveal a personality stubbornly individual. From early life onwards he showed his tendency to rebel against convention, and his political, literary-critical, philosophical and autobiographical writings are those of a dissenter. Whether or not De Quincey the Tory was right in saying of Hazlitt the Progressive   5
that 'his inveterate misanthropy was constitutional', Hazlitt was not so disabled by it as to be shut off from a sympathetic awareness of people and an ardent appreciation of poetry and drama. His accounts of contemporary writers in their persons and in their works are valuable despite patches of prejudice and (we believe)   10
imperceptiveness.

With a feeling for the out-of-doors which was not 'literary', and a tendency to expatiate on his love-life (in *Liber Amoris*), a tendency which seems to us unhealthily self-regarding, Hazlitt could be said to have some of the 'romantic' traits of the poets he was at pains to   15
present in the perspective of his extraordinary age.

6.6 Conclusion

6.6.1 Discuss the Unit in pairs.

UNIT 7

Making comparisons

7.1 Novels and biography

7.1.1
Anticipation

i In pairs, discuss one happy memory of school and one which you would rather forget.

ii Look at the following words and phrases. They are from a description of Jane Eyre's school days. What do they suggest to you? (Look up any words you don't know in a dictionary.) Describe what you imagine life to have been like.

irksome struggle	stiff toes
harassed	scanty supply of food
physical hardships	famished
deep snows	precious morsel of brown bread
severe cold	the exigency of hunger
numbed	blazing fire
chilblain	starved arms

7.1.2 *Jane Eyre, the orphan in Charlotte Bronte's novel of the same name, goes to school at Lowood Institution, a 'charity school' for 'charity children'.*

Read once quickly without the glossary and then read again *with* the glossary (if necessary).

My first quarter at Lowood seemed an age, and not the golden age either; it comprised an irksome struggle with difficulties in habituating myself to new rules and unwonted tasks. The fear of failure in these points harassed me worse than the physical hardships of my lot, though these were no trifles.   5

During January, February, and part of March, the deep snows, and after their melting, the almost impassable roads, prevented our stirring beyond the garden walls, except to go to church, but within these limits we had to pass an hour every day in the open air. Our clothing was insufficient to protect us from the severe cold; we had   10
no boots, the snow got into our shoes, and melted there; our ungloved hands became numbed and covered with chilblains, as were our feet. I remember well the distracting irritation I endured from this cause

GLOSSARY
comprised (l.2): consisted of
habituating (l.3): accustoming
unwonted (archaic) (l.3): unaccustomed
harassed (l.4): troubled
trifles (l.5): unimportant things

169

every evening, when my feet inflamed, and the torture of thrusting the
swelled, raw, and stiff toes into my shoes in the morning. Then the
scanty supply of food was distressing: with the keen appetites of
growing children, we had scarcely sufficient to keep alive a delicate
invalid. From this deficiency of nourishment resulted an abuse which
pressed hardly on the younger pupils: whenever the famished great
girls had an opportunity they would coax or menace the little ones out
of their portion. Many a time I have shared between two claimants the
precious morsel of brown bread distributed at teatime, and after
relinquishing to a third half the contents of my mug of coffee, I have
swallowed the remainder with an accompaniment of secret tears,
forced from me by the exigency of hunger.

Sundays were dreary days in that wintry season. We had to walk two
miles to Brocklebridge Church, where our patron officiated. We set
out cold, we arrived at church colder: during the morning service we
became almost paralysed. It was too far to return to dinner, and an
allowance of cold meat and bread, in the same penurious proportion
observed in our ordinary meals, was served round between the
services.

. . . .

How we longed for the light and heat of a blazing fire when we got
back! But, to the little ones at least, this was denied; each hearth in
the schoolroom was immediately surrounded by a double row of
great girls, and behind them the younger children crouched in
groups, wrapping their starved arms in their pinafores.

torture (l.14): severe suffering
swelled (l.15): increased in size
raw (l.15): sore and painful
invalid (l.18): person made weak from illness
hardly (l.19): severely
exigency (l.25): urgency
officiated (l.27): performed the ceremony
penurious (l.30): ungenerous
longed for (l.33): desired
hearth (l.33): part of the floor in front of the fire
pinafores (l.37): sleeveless dresses

7.1.3
Language

Guess the meanings of the following words in context:

impassable	scanty
melting	keen
stirring	coax
severe	relinquishing
inflamed	dreary
thrusting	paralysed

Discuss in pairs.

7.1.4
Improving
understanding

i In 7.1.1 which guesses did you get right and which guesses did you
get wrong about the description?

ii Read the passage again and as you do so complete the following with
as many words as you like. Use a separate piece of paper.

Jane Eyre's first term _____ to last a long time.

It was disagreeable because _____.

170

In the early part of the year the weather _____.

The children were inadequately dressed. For example, _____

_____. They were also inadequately fed, so much

so that the older girls _____.

Jane Eyre was one of the younger girls so _____.

On Sundays the children _____.

They didn't return to school after the first service because

_____ so _____.

When they got back the young girls _____

because _____.

iii How are the physical situations of the life at Lowood, the time of the year and the weather all inextricably linked with Jane's feelings?

7.1.5
Comparisons

i How does Jane Eyre's school compare with your own?

ii *Charlotte Bronte went to Cowan Bridge School. This is Mrs Gaskell's description of the school (published 1857). Mrs Gaskell was a friend of Charlotte's.*

There was another trial of health common to all the girls. The path from Cowan Bridge to Tunstall Church, where Mr Wilson preached, and where they all attended on the Sunday, is more than two miles in length, and goes sweeping along the rise and fall of the unsheltered country in a way to make it a fresh and exhilarating walk in summer, but a bitter cold one in winter, especially to children like the delicate little Brontes, whose thin blood flowed languidly in consequence of their feeble appetites rejecting the food prepared for them, and thus inducing a half-starved condition. The church was not warmed, there being no means for this purpose. It stands in the midst of fields, and the damp mist must have gathered round the walls, and crept in at the windows. The girls took their cold dinner with them, and ate it between the services, in a chamber over the entrance, opening out of the former galleries. The arrangements for this day were peculiarly trying to delicate children, particularly to those who were spiritless and longing for home, as poor Maria Bronte must have been; for her ill health was increasing, and the old cough, the remains of the whooping-cough, lingered about her.

What are the similarities between Cowan Bridge and Lowood? Make a list.

iii *Clearly, Charlotte Bronte did draw upon her school experiences for* Jane Eyre *but as Mrs Gaskell says we have to be careful about drawing exact parallels:*

Miss Bronte more than once said to me, that she should not have written what she did of Lowood in *Jane Eyre*, if she had thought the place would have been so immediately identified with Cowan Bridge, although there was not a word in her account of the institution but what was true at the time when she knew it; she also said that she had not considered it necessary in a work of fiction, to state every particular with the impartiality that might be required in a court of justice, nor to seek out motives, and make allowances for human failings, as she might have done if dispassionately analyzing the conduct of those who had the superintendence of the institution. I believe she herself would have been glad of an opportunity to correct the over-strong impression which was made upon the public mind by her vivid picture, though even she, suffering her whole life long both in heart and body from the consequences of what happened there, might have been apt, to the last, to take her deep belief in facts for the facts themselves – her conception of truth for the absolute truth.

Help each other to understand the passage. Consult a dictionary if necessary. Underline the main points in Mrs Gaskell's argument and summarise them in your own words.

iv Two obvious differences between *Jane Eyre* and Charlotte Bronte's life in this part of the book are:

– Cowan Bridge was a school for the children of clergymen, not a 'charity school' for 'charity people'

– Jane Eyre was an orphan, Charlotte Bronte wasn't, although her mother had died and she must have often *felt* like an orphan.

7.2 Comparing themes

7.2.1
Anticipation
Re-read Mrs Gaskell's description of Charlotte Bronte as a schoolgirl in 3.5.1 (Passage 2). Discuss what impressions you get of her.

7.2.2
Three weeks after Jane's entry into Lowood the Reverend Mr Brocklehurst, who governs the school according to severe religious principles, returns. He is described as 'straight, narrow, sable-clad' as he stands 'erect on the rug' with a 'grim face'. He orders the too-abundant hair of the older girls to be cut off and lectures on the sin of indulging fleshly lusts even though his wife and daughters come in dressed in silks and with their hair in curls. Jane, who is dreading his return, tries to hide but drops her slate.

Read once quickly without the glossary and then read again *with* the glossary (if necessary).

'Fetch that stool', said Mr Brocklehurst, pointing to a very high one from which a monitor had just risen: it was brought.

'Place the child upon it.'

And I was placed there, by whom I don't know. I was in no condition to note particulars. I was only aware that they had hoisted me up to the height of Mr Brocklehurst's nose, that he was within a yard of me, and that a spread of shot orange and purple silk pelisses, and a cloud of silvery plumage extended and waved below me.

Mr Brocklehurst hemmed.

'Ladies,' said he, turning to his family; 'Miss Temple, teachers, and children, you all see this girl?'

Of course they did; for I felt their eyes directed like burning-glasses against my scorched skin.

'You see she is yet young; you observe she possesses the ordinary form of childhood; God has graciously given her the shape that He has given to all of us; no single deformity points her out as a marked character. Who would think that the Evil One had already found a servant and agent in her? Yet such, I grieve to say, is the case.'

A pause – in which I began to study the palsy of my nerves, and to feel that the Rubicon was passed, and that the trial, no longer to be shirked, must be firmly sustained.

'My dear children,' pursued the black marble clergyman with pathos, 'this is a sad, a melancholy occasion; for it becomes my duty to warn you that this girl, who might be one of God's own lambs, is a little castaway – not a member of the true flock, but evidently an interloper and an alien. You must be on your guard against her; you must shun her example – if necessary, avoid her company, exclude her from your sports, and shut her out from your converse. Teachers, you must watch her; keep your eyes on her movements, weigh well her words, scrutinise her actions, punish her body to save her soul – if, indeed, such salvation be possible, for (my tongue falters while I tell it) this girl, this child, the native of a Christian land, worse than many a little heathen who says its prayers to Brahma and kneels before Juggernaut – this girl is – a liar!'

Now came a pause of ten minutes, during which I – by this time in perfect possession of my wits – observed all the female Brocklehursts produce their pocket-handkerchiefs and apply them to their optics, while the elderly lady swayed herself to and fro, and the two younger ones whispered, 'How shocking!'.

. . . .

Turning at the door, my judge said –

GLOSSARY

monitor (l.2): pupil given authority over other pupils

shot silk pelisses (l.7): long cloaks with holes for arms made of silk which has more than one colour

plumage (l.8): birds' feathers

hemmed (l.9): made a sound to call attention

scorched (l.13): burnt

palsy (l.19): paralysis

the Rubicon was passed (l.20): there was no turning back

Brahma (l.33): (a Hindu god)

Juggernaut (l.34): (an idol worshipped in Hinduism)

optics (l.37): eyes

'Let her stand half an hour longer on that stool, and let no one speak to her during the remainder of the day.'

There was I, then, mounted aloft: I, who had said I could not bear the shame of standing on my natural feet in the middle of the room, was now exposed to general view on a pedestal of infamy. What my sensations were, no language can describe; but, just as they all rose, stifling my breath and constricting my throat, a girl came up and passed me: in passing, she lifted her eyes. What a strange light inspired them! What an extraordinary sensation that ray sent through me! How the new feeling bore me up! It was as if a martyr, a hero, had passed a slave or victim, and imparted strength in the transit. I mastered the rising hysteria, lifted up my head, and took a firm stand on the stool.

45

50

martyr (l.50): person caused to suffer greatly for their beliefs

7.2.3
Language

Guess the meaning of the following words in context:

hoisted	falters
deformity	swayed
shirked	aloft
castaway	pedestal
interloper	stifling
shun	

7.2.4
Improving understanding

Read the passage again and then:

i Discuss what this picture has in common with the passage:

LATEST PARIS FASHIONS 1876.

ii Select phrases from the passage that indicate Jane's feelings. How do they change throughout the passage? Can you say what causes the changes?

iii   Select phrases that indicate Mr Brocklehurst's character.

iv   There are several contrasts in this passage:

> e.g.
>
> Mr Brocklehurst's religion
> Mr Brocklehurst's behaviour
>
> The school children
> Mr Brocklehurst's children
>
> Mr Brocklehurst's attitude to the school children
> Mr Brocklehurst's attitude to his family
>
> What happens to Jane
> Jane's feelings
>
> Jane's feeling of shame
> Jane's new-found strength

In pairs, choose two. What effect do the contrasts have? Can you guess Charlotte Bronte's purpose in making the contrasts?

7.2.5
Comparison

i   What similarities and differences are there between Mrs Gaskell's description of Charlotte Bronte in 3.5.1 (Passage 2) and your impression of Jane's character?

ii   Look back at the beginning of *Hard Times* (2.7.2 and 2.7.3). Remind yourself of when Charlotte Bronte lived and when Charles Dickens lived. List the similarities and differences between the two passages:

SIMILARITIES	DIFFERENCES

What general comments can you make about the times in which they were written?

iii   Would you like to have lived in Charlotte Bronte's time? Would you like to have gone to her school? Is/Was your school better or worse? Why?

7.3 Contrasting styles

7.3.1
Anticipation

i   Write 10 words you associate with the word FIRE.

ii   Compare in pairs.

7.3.2   *Later in the novel Jane Eyre, who knows herself to be poor and plain, goes to work as a governess in the household of Mr Rochester. From their first meeting, she is attracted to her 'Master' – violent, ugly, a kind of 'fallen angel' – even though she is sure he will marry a rich woman from his own social background. In the household are Adele, Rochester's ward (perhaps his illegitimate daughter), the housekeeper Mrs Fairfax, and a strange woman called Grace Poole.*

Read once quickly without the glossary and then read again *with* the glossary (if necessary).

This was a demoniac laugh – low, suppressed, and deep – uttered, as it seemed, at the very keyhole of my chamber door. The head of my bed was near the door, and I thought at first the goblin-laughter stood at my bedside – or rather crouched by my pillow: but I rose, looked round, and could see nothing; while, as I still gazed, the unnatural sound was reiterated: and I knew it came from behind the panels. My first impulse was to rise and fasten the bolt; my next again to cry out, 'Who is there?'

Something gurgled and moaned. Ere long, steps retreated up the gallery towards the third-storey staircase: a door had lately been made to shut in that staircase; I heard it open and close, and all was still.

'Was that Grace Poole? and is she possessed with a devil?' thought I. Impossible now to remain longer by myself; I must go to Mrs Fairfax. I hurried on my frock and a shawl; I withdrew the bolt and opened the door with a trembling hand. There was a candle burning just outside, and on the matting in the gallery. I was surprised at this circumstance: but still more was I amazed to perceive the air quite dim, as if filled with smoke; and, while looking to the right hand and left, to find whence these blue wreaths issued, I became further aware of a strong smell of burning.

Something creaked: it was a door ajar; and that door was Mr Rochester's, and the smoke rushed in a cloud from thence. I thought no more of Mrs Fairfax; I thought no more of Grace Poole, or the laugh: in an instant, I was within the chamber. Tongues of flame darted round the bed: the curtains were on fire. In the midst of blaze and vapour, Mr Rochester lay stretched motionless, in deep sleep.

'Wake! wake!' I cried. I shook him, but he only murmured and turned: the smoke had stupefied him. Not a moment could be lost: the very sheets were kindling. I rushed to his basin and ewer; fortunately, one was wide and the other deep, and both were filled with water. I heaved them up, deluged the bed and its occupant, flew back to my own room, brought my own water-jug, baptised the couch afresh, and, by God's aid, succeeded in extinguishing the flames which were devouring it.

The hiss of the quenched element, the breakage of the pitcher which I had flung from my hand when I had emptied it, and, above all, the splash of the shower-bath I had liberally bestowed, roused Mr Rochester at last. Though it was now dark, I knew he was awake; because I heard him fulminating strange anathemas at finding himself lying in a pool of water.

5
10
15
20
25
30
35
40

GLOSSARY

demoniac (l.1): devilish

goblin (l.3): as though from an evil spirit

gurgled (l.9): made a low throaty bubbling noise

ere (archaic) *(l.9):* before

shawl (l.15): large piece of material to wrap around the shoulders

matting (l.17): rough woven material used as floor covering

wreaths (l.20): rings

blaze (l.26): bright flames

stupefied (l.29): made almost unconscious

kindling (l.30): catching fire

ewer (l.30): large water jug

baptised (l.33): covered with water (baptisms are ceremonies accepting someone into the Christian church)

quenched (l.36): extinguished

pitcher (l.36): large water jug

bestowed (l.38): given (a word used for formal offerings)

fulminating (l.40): angrily shouting

anathemas (l.40): declarations (used by the Church for excommunicating the devil)

7.3.3
Language

i Which words that you associated with the word 'fire' (7.3.1 i) occurred in this passage?

ii Which other phrases in the passage are associated with fire?

iii Guess the meaning of the following words in context:

suppressed   ajar
crouched   vapour
dim   deluged

Discuss in pairs.

iv Which words suggest movement?

v Which words suggest noise?

7.3.4
Improving
understanding

i Read the passage again and as you do so answer the following questions.

Paragraphs 1 and 2:
What did Jane hear?
How many times did she hear it?
Where did it come from?
What did she see?
What did she do?
What did she hear then?

Paragraph 3:
What did she think caused the sound?
What did she do?
How was she feeling?
How do you know?
What did she notice outside the door?

Paragraphs 4, 5 and 6:
Where was the smoke coming from?
What was Jane's immediate reaction?
What danger was Mr Rochester in?
Why wouldn't he wake up?
What did Jane do?
How much water did she pour on?
What woke Mr Rochester up?
What was his reaction?

ii Describe the changes in Jane's feelings and concerns in this passage. Which expressions indicate concern for herself and which concern for others?

7.3.5
Style

Choose at least *two* of the following:

i Write down all the words associated with devils and all the words associated with the Christian religion. What do they suggest about the whole episode?

ii Jane deals with the fire quickly and efficiently. What features of style reinforce this (look at: the length of the clauses and the length of the sentences; the relative number of 'describing' verbs and 'doing' verbs; the punctuation).

iii Is there any suggestion that Jane enjoyed dealing with the situation? If so, show where and how it is conveyed.

iv Indicate the balance between narrative and description in the passage.

v What effect do you think Charlotte Bronte is trying to achieve in this scene by making Rochester so passive and Jane so active?

Discuss in pairs.

7.3.6 Comparisons

i Re-read the passage from *Wuthering Heights* in 4.1.4 by Charlotte's sister Emily.

ii Are there any similarities in the story-line with the passage from *Jane Eyre* (7.3.2)?

iii Which of the following phrases do you think come from the *Jane Eyre* passage, which from the *Wuthering Heights* passage? Check your answers. What do they suggest to you about the style of writing to be found in each?

> I was amazed to perceive the air ...
> I was surprised at this circumstance ...
> The intense horror of nightmare ...
> I became further aware ...
> I tried to jump up, but could not stir a limb ...
> Not a moment could be lost ...
> the hand clung to it ...
> terror made me cruel ...
> Impossible now to remain longer by myself ...
> 'Let me in – let me in' ...

iv Both stories are told by the first person narrator. Is it possible to say

– which narrator seems to be more involved in what is happening

– which seems to be more closely 'in character' and which more the author's own voice?

v Which of these statements do you agree with (if any)?

The *Jane Eyre* passage changes pace when Jane forgets about herself.
Charlotte Bronte writes in a self-contained manner.
There is no relaxation of tension in the *Wuthering Heights* passage.
There is too much violence and suggestion of cruelty in *Wuthering Heights*.

vi Which passage do you prefer? (Say why).

Discuss your answers in pairs.

7.4 Contrasting moods

7.4.1 Look at these two pictures:

Which time of the year do you prefer? Discuss in pairs.

7.4.2 *Jane and Rochester plan to marry but the wedding is stopped.*
The following extract describes Jane's feelings at the end of what was supposed to be her wedding day:

Jane Eyre, who had been an ardent expectant woman – almost a
bride – was a cold, solitary girl again: her life was pale; her prospects
were desolate. A Christmas frost had come at midsummer; a white
December storm had whirled over June; ice glazed the ripe apples,
drifts crushed the blowing roses; on hayfield and cornfield lay a   5
frozen shroud: lanes which last night blushed full of flowers, to-day
were pathless with untrodden snow; and the woods, which twelve
hours since waved leafy and fragrant as groves between the tropics,
now spread, waste, wild, and white as pine-forests in wintry Norway.

My hopes were all dead – struck with a subtle doom, such as, in one   10
night, fell on all the first born in the land of Egypt. I looked on my
cherished wishes yesterday so blooming and glowing; they lay stark,
chill, livid corpses that could never revive. I looked at my love: that
feeling which was my master's – which he had created; it shivered in
my heart, like a suffering child in a cold cradle: sickness and anguish 15
had seized it; it could not seek Mr Rochester's arms – it could not
derive warmth from his breast.

Match the words on the left with the definitions on the right.

ardent	glowed with light and colour
desolate	cold to the touch
whirled	empty
glazed	very pale
shroud	obtain
blushed	covering for a dead body
groves	passionate
chill	small woods
livid	coated
derive	moved rapidly around

i Which words or phrases in the passage suggest the following?

COLD AND SORROW   WARMTH AND HAPPINESS

What does the contrast illustrate?

ii Can you find any similes and metaphors? Are they effective?

iii Comment on the effect of the following:

The punctuation in the sentences beginning 'A Christmas frost ...' and 'I looked at ...'
The balance of phrases in at least one sentence.
The repetition of 'I looked' and 'it could not'
The number of adjectives to describe the one thing (e.g. 'cold' and 'solitary' to describe 'girl')
The use of the third person narrator in the first sentence.

iv Pick out some phrases from the passage to show how Charlotte Bronte uses the description of the landscape to describe Jane's feelings.

v Could Jane's feelings be equally described in sentences like this:

Jane was very unhappy because she was not going to be married. She felt lonely and miserable without Mr Rochester to comfort her.

What difference would it make?

Can you get hold of the novel and find out why the wedding was stopped?

Do you find your own feelings sometimes reflected in nature (e.g. in the weather)? Do you think landscape and the weather sometimes 'influence' your feelings?

Charlotte Bronte

Draw lines to link the following words (e.g. Born _____ 1816 _____ Thornton). Look up information in an encyclopaedia.

parsonage	*Wuthering Heights*
Jane Eyre brother	Thornton
sisters tuberculosis 1854 Maria died	
English teacher Branwell Brussels	
born Elizabeth clergyman Haworth	
married Emily drinking	
Father 1847 curate	
1816	

7.5   Plays and novels

Modal auxiliary verbs like 'can', 'may', 'must' are incomplete in themselves but are used with full verbs to express such functions as *permission, offers, probability*. Each modal may have more than one function. Match the 'modal' on the right with the words on the left. Write a sentence to illustrate. (e.g. obligation – must: *You must go. Your father's waiting for you.*)

ability	might
permission	will
possibility	can
duty	could
certainty	should
probability	may

i   Find out what a 'duel' is.

ii   In pairs, discuss:

> What do you know about duelling?
>
> When was it fashionable?
>
> Why did duels occur?
>
> What were the rules?
>
> Did they have duels in your country?
>
> Do they have them today?

7.5.3 *The Rivals by Richard Sheridan was first produced in London in 1775. It is known as a 'comedy of manners' – a play about the social conventions and behaviour of people of the period. This play takes place in Bath, a fashionable town in eighteenth-century England. The playwright's aim was to get the audience to laugh, partly at themselves. The characters usually fitted a type and this type, as in Dickens' novels, was reflected in their names.*

Four of the characters' names are:

SIR ANTHONY ABSOLUTE *(the father of Captain Absolute and a person of power and authority, of firm, 'absolute', opinions)*

SIR LUCIUS O'TRIGGER *(an Irish nobleman quick to fight with a gun)*

MRS MALAPROP *(an older lady who uses the wrong words for the occasion, confusing them with other words)*

LYDIA LANGUISH *(a young lady full of romantic dreams)*

Try to match the following quotations from the play with the characters' names:

---

1 I am sorry to say … that my affluence over my niece is very small.

2 There would he kneel to me in the snow, and sneeze and cough so pathetically! he shivering with cold and I with apprehension! and while the freezing blast numbed our joints, how warmly would he press me to pity his flame, and glow with mutual ardour! – Ah Julia, that was something like being in love!   5

3 I'll disown you. I'll disinherit you. I'll unget you! and damn me! if ever I call you Jack again!

4 I don't know what's the reason, but in England, if a thing of this kind gets wind, people make such a pother, that a gentleman can never fight in peace and quietness.   10

Discuss in pairs.

7.5.4 *This is an extract from the end of the play. Bob Acres, a country gentleman, has been persuaded by his friend Sir Lucius O'Trigger to challenge Ensign Beverley to a duel over the woman they both love, Lydia Languish. Sir Lucius loves fighting; Bob does not and is scared of being killed. Nor does Bob know that his rival 'Beverley' is really his good friend Captain Absolute in disguise.*

Listen:

Part 1

Act V

SCENE III

King's-Mead-Fields

Enter SIR LUCIUS O'TRIGGER *and* ACRES, *with pistols.*

ACRES   By my valour! then, Sir Lucius, forty yards is a good distance. Odds levels and aims! – I say it is a good distance.

SIR LUCIUS	Is it for muskets or small field-pieces? Upon my conscience, Mr Acres, you must leave those things to me. – Stay now – I'll show you. – (*Measures paces along the stage.*) There now, that is a very pretty distance – a pretty gentleman's distance.	5
ACRES	Zounds! we might as well fight in a sentry-box! I tell you, Sir Lucius, the farther he is off, the cooler I shall take my aim.	10
SIR LUCIUS	Faith! then I suppose you would aim at him best of all if he was out of sight!	
ACRES	No, Sir Lucius; but I should think forty or eight-and-thirty yards . . .	15
SIR LUCIUS	Pho! pho! nonsense! three or four feet between the mouths of your pistols is as good as a mile.	
ACRES	Odds bullets, no! – by my valour! there is no merit in killing him so near: do, my dear Sir Lucius, let me bring him down at a long shot: – a long shot, Sir Lucius, if you love me!	20
SIR LUCIUS	Well, the gentleman's friend and I must settle that. – But tell me now, Mr Acres, in case of an accident, is there any little will or commission I could execute for you?	
ACRES	I am much obliged to you, Sir Lucius – but I don't understand –	25
SIR LUCIUS	Why, you may think there's no being shot at without a little risk – and if an unlucky bullet should carry a quietus with it – I say it will be no time then to be bothering you about family matters.	30
ACRES	A quietus!	
SIR LUCIUS	For instance now, – if that should be the case – would you choose to be pickled and sent home? – or would it be the same to you to lie here in the Abbey? – I'm told there is very snug lying in the Abbey.	35
ACRES	Pickled! – Snug lying in the Abbey! – Odds tremors! Sir Lucius, don't talk so!	
SIR LUCIUS	I suppose, Mr Acres, you never were engaged in an affair of this kind before?	40
ACRES	No, Sir Lucius, never before.	
SIR LUCIUS	Ah! that's a pity! – there's nothing like being used to a thing.	

field-pieces (archaic) *(l.4)*: light cannons for use on a field of battle

a pretty distance (l.7): a very long way

Zounds! (l.9): (mild exclamation indicating indignation)

sentry-box (l.9): small shelter with an open front for sentries (i.e. soldiers who keep guard)

will or commission (l.24): duty or task

quietus (archaic) *(l.28)*: death

pickled (l.33): preserved in special liquid

Abbey (l.34): building lived in by a community of monks

snug (l.35): sheltered and secure

Odds tremors (l.36): (a mild oath; associated with fear; tremors = shakes)

Part 2

SIR LUCIUS	Pray now, how would you receive the gentleman's shot?	
ACRES	Odds files! – I've practised that – there, Sir Lucius – there. – (*Puts himself in an attitude*). A side-front, hey? Odd! I'll make myself small enough: I'll stand edgeways.	45
SIR LUCIUS	Now – you're quite out – for if you stand so when I take aim – (*Levelling at him*)	

Odds files (l.44): (a mild oath; files = rows of soldiers)

edgeways (l.46): with my side to the front

ACRES	Zounds! Sir Lucius – are you sure it is not cocked?	
SIR LUCIUS	Never fear.	50
ACRES	But – but – you don't know – it may go off of its own head!	
SIR LUCIUS	Pho! be easy. – Well, now if I hit you in the body, my bullet has a double chance – for if it misses a vital part on your right side – 'twill be very hard if it don't succeed on the left!	55
ACRES	A vital part?	
SIR LUCIUS	But, there – fix yourself so – *(placing him)* – let him see the broad-side of your full front – there – now a ball or two may pass clean through your body, and never do any harm at all.	60
ACRES	Clean through me! – a ball or two clean through me!	
SIR LUCIUS	Ay, may they – and it is much the genteelest attitude into the bargain.	
ACRES	Look'ee! Sir Lucius – I'd just as lieve be shot in an awkward posture as a genteel one; so, by my valour! I will stand edgeways.	65

Part 3

SIR LUCIUS	*(Looking at his watch)* Sure they don't mean to disappoint us – Hah! – no, faith – I think I see them coming.	
ACRES	Hey! – what! – coming! –	
SIR LUCIUS	Ay. – Who are those yonder getting over the stile?	70
ACRES	There are two of them indeed! – well – let them come – hey, Sir Lucius! – we – we – we – we – won't run.	
SIR LUCIUS	Run!	
ACRES	No – I say – we won't run, by my valour!	
SIR LUCIUS	What the devil's the matter with you?	75
ACRES	Nothing – nothing – my dear friend – my dear Sir Lucius – but I – I – I don't feel quite so bold, somehow, as I did.	
SIR LUCIUS	O fy! – consider your honour.	
ACRES	Ay – true – my honour. Do, Sir Lucius, edge in a word or two every now and then about my honour.	80
SIR LUCIUS	Well, here they're coming.	
	(Looking)	
ACRES	Sir Lucius – if I wa'n't with you, I should almost think I was afraid. – If my valour should leave me! – Valour will come and go.	
SIR LUCIUS	Then pray keep it fast, while you have it.	85
ACRES	Sir Lucius – I doubt it is going – yes – my valour is certainly going! – it is sneaking off! – I feel it oozing out as it were at the palms of my hands!	
SIR LUCIUS	Your honour – your honour! – Here they are.	
ACRES	O mercy! – now – that I was safe at Clod Hall! or could be shot before I was aware!	90

cocked (l.49): got the hammer in a firing position

broad-side (l.58): entire side

genteelest (l.62): most proper and refined

lieve (archaic) *(l.64):* rather

yonder (l.70): over there

stile (l.70): set of steps over a fence

bold (l.77): courageous

O fy! (l.78): rubbish!

valour (l.83): courage

sneaking off (l.87): disappearing in a cowardly way

oozing out (l.87): flowing out slowly

Clod Hall (l.90): (Name of Acres' house in the country. Clod = a piece of earth; suggests stupidity)

i Read or listen to Part 1 as many times as you like and answer the following questions in pairs:

> Why does Acres say 'fifty yards is a good distance'?
> Does Sir Lucius agree? How do you know?
> Explain the pun in the word 'pretty'.
> Why does Acres say 'we might as well fight in a sentry-box'?
> How does Acres try and persuade Sir Lucius to change the distance?
> How does Sir Lucius increase Acres' fear?
> How often has Acres been in a duel?
> What role is Sir Lucius to have in the duel?

ii Read or listen to Part 2 as many times as you like. Describe in your own words what happens on stage without quoting the characters or worrying about everything that is said. Indicate what – if anything! – you find funny.
Compare with your partner.

iii Read Part 3 as many times as you like and re-read the other two parts.

> – Which exchanges indicate that Acres is afraid? How is he made to seem ridiculous?
>   Which exchanges indicate Sir Lucius' character?

How would you describe the two characters? Was your opinion about Sir Lucius' name (7.5.3) confirmed? What do you think Acres' name shows?

i Underline examples of 'modal auxiliaries'. Choose three different modals and say what they express in context.

ii Re-express 'that I was' in 'that I was safe at Clod Hall' in your own words.

iii Reported speech is when we describe what is being said. So 'Is it for muskets or small field pieces?' might read 'Sir Lucius was rather sarcastic. He wanted to know whether Acres was intending to fight with muskets or small field-pieces.'

Re-express the following in reported speech:

ACRES	there is no merit in killing him so near: do, my dear Sir Lucius, let me bring him down at a long shot: – a long shot, Sir Lucius, if you love me!
SIR LUCIUS	Well, the gentleman's friend and I must settle that.

Make sure your description is expressed naturally.

i Which exchanges – if any – did you find particularly funny?

ii Is the humour in the words or in the physical action on the stage?

iii How does Sheridan convey Acres' fear?

iv Can you select some lines in which it is not clear from the language what is happening and which need a producer to interpret them on the stage? What is left to your imagination when reading them?

7.5.8
Novels and plays

Novelists usually use far more words than most dramatists. In fact, plays shouldn't be too wordy or they get boring. The novelist has to bring a scene to life in the reader's imagination usually through a combination of description, narrative and dialogue, whereas the producer and actors of a play can *interpret* a dramatist's words for the audience and give it physical reality. The dramatist therefore usually avoids putting too much description and narrative in the mouths of characters.

However, look at this exchange from *The Rivals*:

ACRES   I say it is a good distance.

SIR LUCIUS Is it for muskets or small field-pieces?

It would be deadly dull if a novelist simply rendered such an exchange in conventional reported speech (e.g. 'Acres insisted that it was a good distance although Sir Lucius wanted to know if he meant for muskets or short field-pieces'). He would have to re-create it:

e.g. Acres still tried to pretend he wasn't frightened. But he was, and he insisted that forty yards was near enough. Sir Lucius was not having it. 'Is it for muskets or small field-pieces?' he shouted indignantly, with a hint of sarcasm.

i Choose a small section of the scene from *The Rivals* and try to re-write it as though it were from a novel.

ii Try the reverse. Re-write the section of *Jane Eyre* in 7.2.2 from 'Fetch that stool' to 'melancholy occasion' as though it were from a play. (Include any stage directions you wish for the producer and actors.)

7.5.9
Notes

Richard Brinsley Sheridan (1751-1816) was the son of the actor and author Thomas Sheridan. Richard was a writer, theatre owner and manager for more than twenty years. His most important plays are: The Rivals *(1775)* The School for Scandal *(1777) and* The Critic *(1779), all 'comedies of manners' dealing with the daily life of sophisticated society. Sheridan also had an important career as a member of Parliament and proved a powerful orator in famous debates. Although his last three years were clouded by debt and sickness, he was given a splendid public funeral in 1816.*

Which of these two pictures of Sheridan is closer to your image of him? In picture b) he is the man in the dark coat next to the dog.

Picture a)

Picture b)

The caricature in picture b) shows Sheridan in his later life.
What changes seem to have taken place?

7.6 Linking sound and meaning

7.6.1 Writers frequently use the sounds of words to echo the sense of what they are trying to convey. For example:

'the stuttering rifles' rapid rattle' *(Owen)*.

Here the quickly stressed syllables 'rifles', 'rapid', 'rattle', copy the sound of gunfire as does the repetition of the 'r' and 't' sounds.

Discuss in pairs how the following link sound and meaning:

---

1 The murmuring of innumerable bees.   *(Lord Tennyson)*

2 I hear lake water lapping
   with low sounds by the shore.   *(W. B. Yeats)*

3 Leap of purple spurting from his thigh.   *(Wilfred Owen)*

4 He sipped with his straight mouth,
   Softly drank through his straight gums, into his
   slack long body,
   Silently.   (from *Snake*, by *D. H. Lawrence*)

5 There's a hammer up at Harwich and it's worked by steam.
    (David Holbrook)

7.7 Reading without assistance

7.7.1 Here is an extract from a story that returns us to the theme of boats (see Unit 3).

He laid his hand on my shoulder and gave me a slight turn, pointing with his other arm at the same time.

'There! That's your ship, Captain,' he said.

I felt a thump in my breast – only one, as if my heart had then ceased to beat. There were ten or more ships moored along the bank, and the one he meant was partly hidden from sight by her next astern. He said: 'We'll drift abreast her in a moment.'

What was his tone? Mocking? Threatening? Or only indifferent? I could not tell. I suspected some malice in this unexpected manifestation of interest.
He left me, and I leaned over the rail of the bridge looking over the side. I dared not raise my eyes. Yet it had to be done – and, indeed, I could not have helped myself. I believe I trembled.

But directly my eyes had rested on my ship all my fear vanished. It went off swiftly, like a bad dream. Only that a dream leaves no shame behind it, and that I felt a momentary shame at my unworthy suspicions.

Yes, there she was. Her hull, her rigging filled my eye with a great content. That feeling of life-emptiness which had made me so restless for the last few months lost its bitter plausibility, its evil influence, dissolved into a flow of joyous emotion.

At the first glance I saw that she was a high-class vessel, a harmonious creature in the lines of her fine body, in the proportioned tallness of her spars. Whatever her age and her history, she had preserved the stamp of her origin. She was one of those craft that, in virtue of their design and complete finish, will never look old. Amongst her companions moored to the bank, and all bigger than herself, she looked like a creature of high breed – an Arab steed in a string of cart-horses.

A voice behind me said in a nasty equivocal tone: 'I hope you are satisfied with her, Captain.' I did not even turn my head. It was the master of the steamer, and whatever he thought of her, I knew that, like some rare women, she was one of those creatures whose mere existence is enough to awaken an unselfish delight. One feels that it is good to be in the world in which she has her being.

from *The Shadow-line* by *Joseph Conrad* 1857–1924

Can you imagine what it would have been like for a captain in the
nineteenth century seeing his first ship for the first time?

7.8 Comparing different writers on the same theme

7.8.1
Topic 1 Death

i **Anticipation**
Discuss in pairs:
what images of
death are familiar
to you?
What do the following
suggest?

1

2

ii Listen and read as
many times as you like.
What does the poet seem
to be saying about death
and man's attitude to it?

Nor dread nor hope attend
A dying animal;
A man awaits his end
Dreading and hoping all;
Many times he died,   5
Many times rose again.
A great man in his pride
Confronting murderous men
Casts derision upon
Supersession of breath;   10
He knows death to the bone –
Man has created death.

W. B. Yeats

GLOSSARY
dread (l.1): great fear
casts derision upon (l.9):
  mocks at because it has
  no value
supersession (l.10): getting
  rid of

iii Improving understanding

Write T (true) F (false) DK (don't know) next to each of these sentences. Re-write the false sentences to make them true.

> Unlike man, an animal when it dies feels neither fear nor hope.
> Because he fears death, a man dies more than once.
> A great man in a battle always looks for death.

Can you summarise the poet's argument in your own words?

iv

Listen to the following poem as many times as you like. What seems to be the poet's own attitude to death?

GLOSSARY

Mighty (l.2): powerful
overthrow (l.3): destroy
Fate (l.9): the power that seems to control events; destiny
dost (archaic) *(l.10):* do ('you do' – familiar form)
dwell (l.10): live
poppy (l.11): the plant from which opium is obtained
stroke (l.12): blow
Why swell'st thou? (l.12): Why do you push your chest out in pride?

Death, be not proud, though some have called thee
Mighty and dreadful, for thou art not so;
For those whom thou think'st thou dost overthrow
Die not, poor Death, nor yet can'st thou kill me.
From rest and sleep, which but thy pictures be,   5
Much pleasure; then from thee much more must flow;
And soonest our best men with thee do go,
Rest of their bones, and soul's delivery.
Thou'rt slave to Fate, chance, kings, and desperate men,
And dost with poison, war, and sickness dwell;   10
And poppy or charms can make us sleep as well,
And better than thy stroke. Why swell'st thou then?
One short sleep past, we wake eternally,
And death shall be no more. Death, thou shalt die.   *John Donne*

v Improving understanding

Write T (true) F (false) DK (don't know). Re-write the false sentences to make them true.

The poet is telling Death that He is nothing to be afraid of and so has no reason to be proud.

Death thinks he is killing people but really they do not die.

Nothing comes from rest or sleep, which are images of death, except death.

The sooner the best men die, the sooner they will find peace and salvation.

Death is the master of Fate and superior to the things which cause death.

Drugs and magical charms give us better sleep than death.

The poet tells Death that in eternity there is no death.

Can you summarise the poet's argument in your own words?

vi Comparing poems

Say which poem the following sentences relate to. If neither, write (N). If both, write (B).

a) It is a Shakespearian sonnet.

Each line, except one, has six syllables.

Each line has ten syllables.
The rhyming scheme is *abba/abba/cddc/ee*.
It is a Petrarchan sonnet.
It contains a metaphor.
It is written in the present tense.

b) The poet is addressing death directly.
   The poet is describing the human condition as he sees it.
   Death is regarded as a person.
   The poet's mood is defiant and scornful.
   The poem sounds like a person speaking; it keeps to the rhythms
      of the human voice.
   There is a lot of repetition of sounds including examples of
      alliteration.
   The last line is epigrammatic and mysterious.

How do the poems differ? Say which you prefer and why. Which view
of death, if either, do you relate to?

7.8.2
Topic 2 Young love

i **Anticipation**
Write down words or phrases which you associate with the phrase
'young love', e.g. romantic

Discuss in pairs.

ii Read the following extract from a play as many times as you like. What
is the relationship between the boy and the girl? How do you know?

*Jo and a boy, a black naval rating, are walking on the street. They stop by
a door.*

JO:	I'd better go in now. Thanks for carrying my books.	
BOY:	Were you surprised to see me waiting outside school?	
JO:	Not really.	
BOY:	Glad I came?	
JO:	You know I am.	5
BOY:	So am I.	
JO:	Well, I'd better go in.	
BOY:	Not yet! Stay a bit longer.	
JO:	All right! Doesn't it go dark early? I like winter. I like it better	
	than all the other seasons.	10
BOY:	I like it too. When it goes dark early it gives me more time for	
	– *(He kisses her).*	
JO:	Don't do that. You're always doing it.	
BOY:	You like it.	
JO:	I know, but I don't want to do it all the time.	
BOY:	Afraid someone'll see us?	15
JO:	I don't care.	
BOY:	Say that again.	
JO:	I don't care.	

191

BOY:	You mean it too. You're the first girl I've met who really didn't care. Listen, I'm going to ask you something. I'm a man of few words. Will you marry me?
JO:	Well, I'm a girl of few words. I won't marry you but you've talked me into it.
BOY:	How old are you?
JO:	Nearly eighteen.
BOY:	And you really will marry me?
JO:	I said so, didn't I? You shouldn't have asked me if you were only kidding me up. *(She starts to go.)*
BOY:	Hey! I wasn't kidding. I thought you were. Do you really mean it? You will marry me?
JO:	I love you.
BOY:	How do you know?
JO:	I don't know why I love you but I do.
BOY:	I adore you. *(Swinging her through the air.)*
JO:	So do I. I can't resist myself.
BOY:	I've got something for you.
JO:	What is it? A ring!
BOY:	This morning in the shop I couldn't remember what sort of hands you had, long hands, small hands or what. I stood there like a damn fool trying to remember what they felt like. *(He puts the ring on and kisses her hand.)* What will your mother say?
JO:	She'll probably laugh.
BOY:	Doesn't she care who her daughter marries?
JO:	She's not marrying you, I am. It's got nothing to do with her.
BOY:	She hasn't seen me.
JO:	And when she does?
BOY:	She'll see a coloured boy.
JO:	No, whatever else she might be, she isn't prejudiced against colour. You're not worried about it, are you?
BOY:	So long as you like it.
JO:	You know I do.
BOY:	Well, that's all that matters.
JO:	When shall we get married?
BOY:	My next leave? It's a long time, six months.
JO:	It'll give us a chance to save a bit of money. Here, see … this ring … it's too big; look, it slides about … And I couldn't wear it for school anyway. I might lose it. Let's go all romantic. Have you got a bit of string?
BOY:	What for?
JO:	I'm going to tie it round my neck. Come on, turn your pockets out. Three handkerchiefs, a safety pin, a screw! Did that drop out of your head? Elastic bands! Don't little boys carry some trash. And what's this?

20

25

30

35

40

45

50

55

60

GLOSSARY
kidding me up (l.28): pretending as a joke
leave (l.55): holiday
safety pin (l.62): pin often used for fastening bandages
trash (l.64): rubbish

BOY:	Nothing 65
JO:	A toy car! Does it go?
BOY:	Hm hm!
JO:	Can I try it? *(She does.)*
BOY:	She doesn't even know how it works. Look, not like that. *(He makes it go fast.)*
JO:	I like that. Can I keep it? 70
BOY:	Yes, take it, my soul and all, everything.
JO:	Thanks. I know, I can use my hair ribbon for my ring. Do it up for me.
BOY:	Pretty neck you've got.
JO:	Glad you like it. It's my schoolgirl complexion. I'd better tuck 75 this out of sight. I don't want my mother to see it. She'd only laugh. Did I tell you, when I leave school this week I start a part-time job in a bar? Then as soon as I get a full-time job, I'm leaving Helen and starting up in a room somewhere.
BOY:	I wish I wasn't in the Navy. 80
JO:	Why?
BOY:	We won't have much time together.
JO:	Well, we can't be together all the time and all the time there is wouldn't be enough.
BOY:	It's a sad story, Jo. Once, I was a happy young man, not a care 85 in the world. Now! I'm trapped into a barbaric cult …
JO:	What's that? Mau-Mau?
BOY:	Matrimony.
JO:	Trapped! I like that! You almost begged me to marry you.
BOY:	You led me on. I'm a trusting soul. Who took me down to that 90 deserted football pitch?
JO:	Who found the football pitch? I didn't even know it existed. And it just shows how often you must have been there, too … you certainly know where all the best spots are. I'm not going there again … It's too quiet. Anything might happen to a girl. 95
BOY:	It almost did. You shameless woman!
JO:	That's you taking advantage of my innocence.
BOY:	I didn't take advantage. I had scruples.

tuck this out of sight (l.75–76): put this away so no-one can see it

cult (l.86): system of devotion

Mau-Mau (l.87): a secret society set up in Kenya in the 1950s to terrorise the European settlers

led me on (l.90): encouraged me falsely

scruples (l.98): feelings of conscience

from *A Taste of Honey* by *Shelagh Delaney*

iii Improving understanding

Write T (true) F (false) DK (don't know) next to each of these sentences. Re-write the false sentences to make them true.

The boy had walked home from school with the girl.
It is still light.
They are both very young.
She agrees to marry him.

He is not at all surprised.
He had already bought her a ring.
She is coloured.
Her mother won't mind them marrying.
He has to go back to work in the navy for six months.
The ring doesn't fit her finger so she wants to wear it round her
    neck.
She hides her ring so her mother won't see it.
Her mother's name is Helen.
The boy and girl tease each other.

Can you summarise what happens in your own words?

iv Listen to the following three extracts as many times as you like. Romeo
belongs to the Montague family, Juliet the Capulet family. The families
are at war with each other. What is the relationship between Romeo
and Juliet at this stage? How do you know?

Capulet's orchard

Enter ROMEO

1 ROMEO   He jests at scars that never felt a wound.

Enter JULIET above at a window.

GLOSSARY
Extract 1
He jests (l.1): He (referring
    to the character
    Mercutio) laughs
scars (l.1): marks left by
    wounds
yonder (l.2): over there
grief (l.5): deep
    unhappiness
her maid (l.6): (i.e. a
    servant of Diana, the
    virgin goddess of the
    moon, who was
    unmarried)
vestal (l.8): pure and
    virginal
livery (l.8): dress (as worn
    by the servants of Diana
    – sickly green in colour,
    supposedly like girls
    suffering from lack of
    blood)
fool (l.9): jester employed
    in wealthy houses
    (usually dressed in
    green)
twinkle (l.17): shine
    intermittently
spheres (l.17): (i): referring
    to the system by which
    planets revolve round
    the earth) ii): eye-
    sockets

But soft! What light through yonder window breaks?
It is the east, and Juliet is the sun.
Arise, fair sun, and kill the envious moon,
Who is already sick and pale with grief   5
That thou her maid art far more fair than she.
Be not her maid, since she is envious;
Her vestal livery is but sick and green,
And none but fools do wear it; cast it off.
It is my lady; O, it is my love!   10
O that she knew she were!
She speaks, yet she says nothing. What of that?
Her eye discourses; I will answer it.
I am too bold, 'tis not to me she speaks;
Two of the fairest stars in all the heaven,   15
Having some business, do entreat her eyes
To twinkle in their spheres till they return.
What if her eyes were there, they in her head?
The brightness of her cheek would shame those stars,
As daylight doth a lamp; her eyes in heaven   20
Would through the airy region stream so bright
That birds would sing, and think it were not night.
See how she leans her cheek upon her hand!
O that I were a glove upon that hand,
That I might touch that cheek!   25

	JULIET	Ay me!
	ROMEO	She speaks.
		O, speak again, bright angel, for thou art
		As glorious to this night, being o'er my head,
		As is a winged messenger of heaven
		Unto the white-upturned wond'ring eyes
		Of mortals that fall back to gaze on him,
		When he bestrides the lazy-pacing clouds
		And sails upon the bosom of the air.
	JULIET	O Romeo, Romeo! wherefore art thou Romeo?

winged messenger of heaven (l.30): flying messenger of the gods

white-upturned (l.31): looking upwards so that the whites are showing

bestrides (l.33): sits over

30

35

- -

2	JULIET	How cam'st thou hither, tell me, and wherefore?
		The orchard walls are high and hard to climb;
		And the place death, considering who thou art,
		If any of my kinsmen find thee here.
	ROMEO	With love's light wings did I o'erperch these walls,
		For stony limits cannot hold love out;
		And what love can do, that dares love attempt.
		Therefore thy kinsmen are no stop to me.
	JULIET	If they do see thee, they will murder thee.
	ROMEO	Alack, there lies more peril in thine eye
		Than twenty of their swords; look thou but sweet,
		And I am proof against their enmity.
	JULIET	I would not for the world they saw thee here.
	ROMEO	I have night's cloak to hide me from their eyes;
		And but thou love me, let them find me here.
		My life were better ended by their hate
		Than death prorogued wanting of thy love.
	JULIET	By whose direction found'st thou out this place?
	ROMEO	By love, that first did prompt me to enquire;
		He lent me counsel, and I lent him eyes.
		I am no pilot; yet, wert thou as far
		As that vast shore wash'd with the farthest sea,
		I should adventure for such merchandise.

Extract 2

cam'st (l.1): did you come

wherefore (l.1): why

orchard (l.2): plantation of fruit trees

kinsmen (l.4): male relatives

o'erperch (l.5): fly over

Alack (l.10): alas! (an expression of sorrow)

peril (l.10): danger

enmity (l.12): hostility

death prorogued wanting of thy love (l.17): delayed death lacking your love

he lent me counsel (l.20): he advised me

pilot (l.21): ship's navigator

wert thou (l.21): if you were

merchandise (l.23): goods

5

10

15

20

- -

3	ROMEO	Lady, by yonder blessed moon I vow,
		That tips with silver all these fruit-tree tops –
	JULIET	O, swear not by the moon, th' inconstant moon,
		That monthly changes in her circled orb,
		Lest that thy love prove likewise variable.
	ROMEO	What shall I swear by?
	JULIET	Do not swear at all;
		Or, if thou wilt, swear by thy gracious self,
		Which is the god of my idolatry,
		And I'll believe thee.

Extract 3

orb (l.4): orbit

lest (l.5): in case

5

10

	ROMEO	If my heart's dear love –
	JULIET	Well, do not swear. Although I joy in thee,

ROMEO   If my heart's dear love –

JULIET   Well, do not swear. Although I joy in thee,
              I have no joy of this contract to-night:
              It is too rash, too unadvis'd, too sudden;
              Too like the lightning, which doth cease to be   15
              Ere one can say 'It lightens.' Sweet, good night!
              This bud of love, by summer's ripening breath,
              May prove a beauteous flow'r when next we meet.

rash (l.14): badly
    considered
bud (l.17): unopened
    flower

from *Romeo and Juliet* by *William Shakespeare*

v Improving understanding

Write T (true) F (false) DK (don't know) next to each of these sentences.
Re-write the false sentences to make them true.

Extract 1

Romeo is in a good mood.
Juliet can hear what he is saying.
The scene takes place just before day-break.
Romeo is saying that Juliet is prettier than the moon.
The moon is envious of Juliet's beauty.
Romeo says that anyone who decides never to marry is a fool.
Juliet knows that Romeo loves her.
Juliet is silently praying and not speaking to Romeo.
Romeo imagines that if the stars and her eyes changed places, her cheeks
    would make the stars look inferior.
Juliet is quietly hoping that Romeo will come to her.

Extract 2

Juliet wants to know how he got there when he is supposed to be dead.
Her family will be very sorry to have missed him.
Romeo found it easy to climb the wall since he's in love.
He is not afraid of anybody else; he is more frightened of what she might
    feel.
She says that if she is kind to him he cannot be hurt.
Juliet wants him to meet her family but they won't find him in the dark.
Romeo said he would have taken any risk to reach her.

Extract 3

Romeo wants to make an oath and swear his love.
Juliet doesn't want him to because everything has happened too quickly.
She wants their love to mature more.

Can you summarise what happens in your own words?

vi Comparing plays

Say which play the following sentences relate to. If neither, write (N).
If both, write (B).
  a) Each line contains ten syllables.
      The writer makes it clear what is happening on the stage.
      It is written in 'blank verse'.

b) There is no imagery.
The moon is addressed directly.
The lovers are casual with each other.
The distance between the lovers creates tension.
It is modern.
There is no humour.

The language is ordinary and unpoetic.
The lovers show respect for their differences.
Great passion is expressed.
Nothing religious is expressed.
The language is intense.
There is cliche in the language.

How do the plays differ? Say which you prefer and why.
Are you romantic? Do you think that the way boys and girls
behave nowadays when they are in love is different from before?

7.8.3
Topic 3 Art and nature

i **Anticipation**
Look at these three paintings:

What is the relationship between the painting and the natural world in each?
What do you think each painter's intention is?
What do you think the painter's view of art is?
Which do you prefer? Why?

ii Listen and read the following lines as many times as you like. Consider the question: What is the poet's view of the relationship between art and nature?

First follow NATURE, and your Judgment frame
By her just Standard, which is still the same:
Unerring Nature, still divinely bright,
One clear, unchanged, and Universal Light,
Life, Force, and Beauty, must to all impart,   5
At once the Source, and End, and Test of Art.
Art from that Fund each just Supply provides;
Works without Show, and without Pomp presides:
In some fair Body thus th'informing Soul
With Spirit feeds, with Vigour fills the whole,   10
Each Motion guides, and every Nerve sustains;
Itself unseen, but in th'Effects, remains.

from *An Essay on Criticism* by *Alexander Pope*

iii **Improving understanding**
Write T (true) F (false) DK (don't know) next to each of these sentences. Re-write the false sentences to make them true.

The poet is telling the reader to live according to the laws of Nature.
Nature is very unfair.
Nature gives life, power and beauty to everything except art.
Nature gives life in an unobvious way, without false display.
Nature itself cannot be seen; one can only see the effects of nature.
Nature is superior to Art.

Can you summarise the poet's argument in your own words?

iv Read the following extract as many times as you like.
What is Vivian's view of the relationship between art and nature?

CYRIL *(coming in through the open window from the terrace)*
My dear Vivian, don't coop yourself up all day in the library. It is a perfectly lovely afternoon. The air is exquisite. There is a mist upon the woods, like the purple bloom upon a plum. Let us go and lie on the grass and smoke cigarettes and enjoy Nature.

VIVIAN Enjoy Nature! I am glad to say that I have entirely lost that   5
faculty. People tell us that Art makes us love Nature more than we

loved her before; that it reveals her secrets to us; and that after a careful study of Corot and Constable we see things in her that had escaped our observation. My own experience is that the more we study Art, the less we care for Nature. What Art really reveals to us is Nature's lack of design, her curious crudities, her extraordinary monotony, her absolutely unfinished condition. Nature has good intentions, of course, but, as Aristotle once said, she cannot carry them out. When I look at a landscape I cannot help seeing all its defects. It is fortunate for us, however, that Nature is so imperfect, as otherwise we should have no art at all. Art is our spirited protest, our gallant attempt to teach Nature her proper place. As for the infinite variety of Nature, that is a pure myth. It is not to be found in Nature herself. It resides in the imagination, or fancy, or cultivated blindness of the man who looks at her.

CYRIL Well, you need not look at the landscape. You can lie on the grass and smoke and talk.

VIVIAN But Nature is so uncomfortable. Grass is hard and lumpy and damp, and full of dreadful black insects. Why, even Morris's poorest workman could make you a more comfortable seat than the whole of Nature can. Nature pales before the furniture of 'the street which from Oxford has borrowed its name', as the poet you love so much once vilely phrased it. I don't complain. If Nature had been comfortable, mankind would never have invented architecture, and I prefer houses to the open air. In a house we all feel of the proper proportions. Everything is subordinated to us, fashioned for our use and our pleasure. Egotism itself, which is so necessary to a proper sense of human dignity, is entirely the result of indoor life. Out of doors one becomes abstract and impersonal. One's individuality absolutely leaves one. And then Nature is so indifferent, so unappreciative. Whenever I am walking in the park here, I always feel that I am no more to her than the cattle that browse on the slope, or the burdock that blooms in the ditch. Nothing is more evident than that Nature hates Mind. Thinking is the most unhealthy thing in the world, and people die of it just as they die of any other disease. Fortunately, in England at any rate, thought is not catching. Our splendid physique as a people is entirely due to our national stupidity. I only hope we shall be able to keep this great historic bulwark of our happiness for many years to come; but I am afraid that we are beginning to be over-educated; at least everybody who is incapable of learning has taken to teaching – that is really what our enthusiasm for education has come to. In the meantime, you had better go back to your wearisome uncomfortable Nature, and leave me to correct my proofs.

from *The Decay of Lying* a dialogue by *Oscar Wilde (1854–1900)*

Corot/Constable (l.8): (two painters who closely observed nature)
defects (l.15): faults
gallant (l.17): courageous
teach ... proper place (l.17): keep down in an inferior position
Morris (l.24): (William Morris 1834–1896, poet, artist and socialist)
'the Street which...' (l.26) (Oxford Street; a large street of shops in London)
vilely (l.28): disgustingly
browse (l.37): feed on grass
slope (l.37): side of a hill
burdock (l.37): a type of weed
ditch (l.38): long, narrow channel where water flows
bulwark (l.43): protection
proofs (l.48): first copy of a printed manuscript

v Improving understanding

Write T (true) F (false) DK (don't know) next to each of these sentences. Re-write the false sentences to make them true.

Cyril hates Nature.

Vivian feels that Art is superior to Nature and makes us lose interest in Nature.

He thinks that Nature is badly designed, boring and uncomfortable.

He is glad Nature is uncomfortable or else man would not make buildings.

He thinks egotism is caused by Nature and is the ruin of man.

He hates Nature because it gives him no distinction.

He has a high opinion of the English.

He thinks art is superior to nature.

Can you summarise Vivian's argument in your own words? Do you think they represent the writer's views?

vi Comparing ideas expressed in different genres

Say which the following sentences relate to. If neither, write (N). If both, write (B).

The writer gives us moral rules.

The tone is serious and without humour.

The tone is light.

The writer is cynical and supercilious.

The writer believes that Nature is a living organism.

The writer has a high opinion of Nature.

The writer sounds very refined and over-civilised.

The extract is amoral.

The writer sounds egotistic.

How do the poem and the prose extract differ? Say which you prefer and why.

Do you think art should represent nature? What do you think of abstract art? (Look back at the paintings in 7.8.3.(i).)

7.9 Conclusion

7.9.1   Discuss the Unit in pairs.

UNIT 8

What is it we value?

8.1 Looking at the long extract

i Separate the following 'regular' verbs into those where the final letter is doubled in the past tense (e.g. spot – spotted) and those where it is not (e.g. help – helped). Look up in a dictionary any words you don't know.

dress	skip	grab
litter	clap	roll
drop	scamper	struggle
fold	stir	clog

Do you know what the 'rules' for doubling the final letter are?

ii What are the superlative forms of the following adjectives? (e.g. beautiful: most beautiful, ugly: ugliest).

splendid	gaudy
sweet	pretty
astonishing	sick
funny	

Do you know what the 'rules' for forming the superlative are?

iii Put the verbs in the following sentences in the correct form:

1) The men looked ever so tall, with their heads (BOB) _____ and (SKIM) _____ along.

2) Faster and faster they went, all of them (DANCE) _____, the horses (LEAN) _____ more and more and the ring-master (GO) _____ round the centre-pole.

3) The horse began to jump, with two circus men (HANG) _____ on to his neck, his head (FLY) _____ in the air every jump, and the whole crowd of people (STAND) _____ up (SHOUT) _____ and (LAUGH) _____ till the tears (ROLL) _____ down.

Look up in a dictionary any words you don't know.
Why did you choose the forms you did?

201

Look at these pictures:

Tell each other about a visit you made to the circus or a story you know about the circus. Do you like circuses? What is the history of the circus in your own country?

8.1.3 *The following extract is from* Huckleberry Finn *by Mark Twain. Huckleberry Finn has run away from home to escape the cruelties of a drunken father and the pressures of a respectable society. He meets Jim, a runaway Negro slave, and together they make their way by raft down the Mississippi. Their first plan is to leave the river at Cairo, where it joins the river Ohio, and go up the Ohio to the freedom of the Northern States. But the raft is run down by a steamboat and Huckleberry spends some time as a 'captive' in the company of two cunning villains known as the King and the Duke, who try to exploit the townsfolk of the local riverside communities. In one of the towns of Arkansas he visits a circus ...*

Read. Try to answer the following questions:

Who is speaking?
How old do you think he is?
What did he see at the circus?
How was he tricked?

I went to the circus, and loafed around the back side till the
watchmen went by, and then dived in under the tent. I had my
twenty-dollar gold piece and some other money, but I reckoned I
better save it, because there ain't no telling how soon you are going
to need it, away from home and amongst strangers, that way. You
can't be too careful. I ain't opposed to spending money on circuses,
when there ain't no other way, but there ain't no use in *wasting* it on
them.

It was a real bully circus. It was the spendidest sight that ever was,
and when they all come riding in, two and two, a gentleman and lady,
side by side, the men just in their drawers and undershirts, and no
shoes nor stirrups, and resting their hands on their thighs, easy and
comfortable – there must a' been twenty of them – and every lady
with a lovely complexion, and perfectly beautiful, and looking just
like a gang of real sure-enough queens, and dressed in clothes that
cost millions of dollars, and just littered with diamonds. It was a
powerful fine sight; I never see anything so lovely. And then one by
one they got up and stood, and went a-weaving around the ring so
gentle and wavy and graceful, the men looking ever so tall and airy
and straight, with their heads bobbing and skimming along, away up
there under the tent-roof, and every lady's rose-leafy dress flapping
soft and silky around her hips, and she looking like the most loveliest
parasol.

And then faster and faster they went, all of them dancing, first one
foot stuck out in the air and then the other, the horses leaning more
and more, and the ring-master going round and round the centre-
pole, cracking his whip and shouting 'hi! – hi!' and the clown cracking
jokes behind him; and by-and-by all hands dropped the reins, and
every lady put her knuckles on her hips and every gentleman folded
his arms, and then how the horses did lean over and hump
themselves! And so, one after the other they all skipped off into the
ring, and made the sweetest bow I ever see, and then scampered out,
and everybody clapped their hands and went just about wild.

Well, all through the circus they done the most astonishing things;
and all the time that clown carried on so it most killed the people.
The ring-master couldn't ever say a word to him but he was back at
him quick as a wink with the funniest things a body ever said; and
how he ever *could* think of so many of them, and so sudden and so

5

10

15

20

25

30

35

GLOSSARY
(a- before a present
   participle = in the act
   of)
bully (l.9): good
drawers (l.11): underpants
   with legs!
stirrups (l.12): foot-rests,
   hanging down from a
   saddle, for the rider of a
   horse
a-weaving (l.18): moving
   from side to side
parasol (l.23): sunshade
knuckles (l.29): bones at a
   finger joint
hips (l.29): place where the
   bone of the leg joins the
   trunk of the body
hump themselves (l.30–31):
   form an arch
*it most killed the people
   (l.35):* the people were
   almost overcome with
   laughter
ring-master (l.36): person
   who directs the
   performance
quick as a wink (l.37): very
   quickly

pat, was what I couldn't noway understand. Why, I couldn't a thought
of them in a year. And by-and-by a drunk man tried to get into the
ring – said he wanted to ride; said he could ride as well as anybody
that ever was. They argued and tried to keep him out, but he wouldn't
listen, and the whole show come to a standstill. Then the people
begun to holler at him and make fun of him, and that made him mad,
and he begun to rip and tear; so that stirred up the people, and a lot
of men begun to pile down off of the benches and swarm towards the
ring, saying, 'Knock him down! throw him out!' and one or two women
begun to scream. So, then, the ring-master he made a little speech,
and said he hoped there wouldn't be no disturbance, and if the man
would promise he wouldn't make no more trouble, he would let him
ride, if he thought he could stay on the horse. So everybody laughed
and said all right, and the man got on. The minute he was on, the
horse begun to rip and tear and jump and cavort around, with two
circus men hanging onto his bridle trying to hold him, and the drunk
man hanging onto his neck, and his heels flying in the air every jump,
and the whole crowd of people standing up shouting and laughing till
the tears rolled down. And at last, sure enough, all the circus men
could do, the horse broke loose, and away he went like the very
nation, round and round the ring, with that sot laying down on him
and hanging to his neck, with first one leg hanging most to the
ground on one side, and then t'other one on t'other side, and the
people just crazy. It warn't funny to me, though; I was all of a tremble
to see his danger. But pretty soon he struggled up astraddle and
grabbed the bridle, a-reeling this way and that – and the next minute
he sprung up and dropped the bridle and stood! and the horse
agoing like a house afire too. He just stood up there, a-sailing around
as easy and comfortable as if he warn't ever drunk in his life – and
then he begun to pull off his clothes and sling them. He shed them so
thick they kind of clogged up the air, and altogether he shed
seventeen suits. And then, there he was, slim and handsome, and
dressed the gaudiest and prettiest you ever saw, and he lit onto that
horse with his whip and made him fairly hum – and finally skipped
off, and made his bow and danced off to the dressing-room, and
everybody just a-howling with pleasure and astonishment.

Then the ring-master he see how he had been fooled, and he *was* the
sickest ring-master you ever see, I reckon. Why, it was one of his
own men! He had got up that joke all out of his own head; and never
let on to nobody. Well, I felt sheepish enough, to be took in so, but I
wouldn't a been in that ring-master's place, not for a thousand dollars.
I don't know; there may be bullier circuses than what that one was,
but I never struck them yet. Anyways it was plenty good enough for
me; and wherever I run across it, it can have all my custom, every
time.

pat (l.39): easily
holler (l.44): shout
cavort around (l.53): jump
  about
bridle (l.54): leather bands
  put on a horse's head to
  control its movements
*like the very nation (l.58–
  59):* like hell
  (exclamation: nation =
  damnation)
sot (l.59): drunkard
astraddle (l.63): with a leg
  on either side
a-reeling (l.64): moving
  unsteadily
fairly hum (l.72): move
  feverishly
a-howling (l.74): laughing
fooled (l.75): tricked
sickest (l.76): most upset
  and disgusted
sheepish (l.78): foolish
struck (l.81): found

8.1.4
Improving understanding

i   In pairs, discuss answers to the questions in 8.1.3.

ii Which clothes were the following wearing?

HORSEMEN	HORSEWOMEN

iii Answer these questions:

Fairly easy questions:

How did Huckleberry Finn get into the circus?
Why didn't he pay?
What was the first thing he saw?
What did the following do:

– the horsemen
– the horsewomen
– the clown

Why did Huckleberry Finn admire the clowns?
What did the drunk do when he came into the ring?
What was the reaction of the audience?
How do you know the man wasn't really drunk?

More difficult questions:

In what ways is Huckleberry Finn a typical boy?
Is he unusual in any way?
What are Huckleberry Finn's feelings about the circus? How do you know?
In what way is Huckleberry Finn a detached spectator? How does it show?
In what instances does Huckleberry Finn's perception of what he sees differ from our perception of what we imagine happened?
In what way was it not the ring-master who was 'fooled' but Huckleberry Finn?

Summarise what the ring-master does during the time that Huckleberry Finn is there.

8.1.5
Language

i   Find in the passage the words and sentences used in 8.1.1.
How do your answers compare? Beware: Huckleberry Finn does not always use 'correct' English!

ii What are the following in 'correct' English:

I better	I couldn't noway understand
ain't no	the whole show come
they all come riding in	the ringmaster he made
I ever see	there wouldn't be no
they done	it warn't

What effect does this 'incorrect' English have?

iii Some language is written as it was spoken (e.g. 'must a' been' instead of 'must have been'). Find other examples.

8.1.6
Style   Huckleberry Finn's character is revealed not by the author's description of him, but through what he says and the way he says it.

  i Underline the 'connecting words' (e.g. 'and',' but', etc.) Are they few or many in number? Are there many complex sentences? What effect does it have?

  ii Find examples of where Huckleberry Finn exaggerates. What effect do the superlatives (e.g. 'splendidest', which in 'correct' English is 'most splendid') have?

  iii Which words or phrases
    a) make him sound   – American (e.g. 'bully')
                            – a child
                            – innocent
    b) vividly convey what is being described

  iv Which paragraph is more descriptive than narrative? Contrast the main verbs in that paragraph with the main verbs in another paragraph. Which paragraph advances the action most?

  v What effect do the verbs ending in -ing have?

  vi Summarise in your own words how the writer's style conveys Huckleberry Finn's character. Share your summary with other people in your class.

8.1.7
Evaluation   It is very difficult to generalise about a whole novel on the basis of a single extract. However, which of the following do you agree with on the basis of your reading?:

'Huckleberry Finn manages to evoke the lost world of boyhood with all the horror and loveliness it once possessed for the child who lived it.'

'rough, coarse, inelegant, dealing with a series of experiences not elevating'

'How can it be at once so terrifying and so comfortable to read ... it is a funny book.'

'good, clean quite undangerous fun'

'Huck is a cheat and a fraud.'

'One reads *Huckleberry Finn* and hears ... a voice which is not Twain's but genuinely Huck's.'

'Huck's own essential goodness'

'Twain was not merely writing prose. He was recording the speech of a way of life. *Huckleberry Finn* is one of the most aural novels in the language, and in order for it to be so Twain had to depart from the polite cadences of educated grammar and take us into the sensuous unexpectedness of living words and forms.'

'Huckleberry Finn has the universality of all major art.'

Discuss in pairs.

8.1.8

Background

Write a summary of Mark Twain's life using these notes to help you:

Born – Florida, Missouri 1835 – father, lawyer – became printer's apprentice – licensed pilot on Mississippi, 1859 – left outbreak Civil War – army volunteer, gold prospector, timber speculator – journalist – real name Samuel Clemens – first book 1865 Jumping Frog *– travelling reporter: Sandwich Islands, Mediterranean, Middle East – first major literary success 1869:* Innocents Abroad *– married Olivia Langdon 1870 – lived Hartford Connecticut 17 years –* Tom Sawyer *1876 –* Huckleberry Finn *(1884/5) – combined writing, public lecturing, foreign travelling – reputation humorist/philosopher – intellectual pessimism and despair of human nature combined with success   bankrupt 1894 by failure in type-setting and publishing companies – daughter Susie died – wife died 1904 – daughter Jean 1909 – died Redding, Connecticut 21 April 1910.*

8.2 Placing poems next to each other

8.2.1

Listen to the following poems. They were all written in the seventeenth century and have a similar theme. While listening, try to think what that theme is and ask yourself which of the following most accurately describes it.

1 I am old and only love can give me pleasure in my final years.
2 Time has no mercy. Fight it and stay young.
3 Life is short. You should love me while you can because soon it will be too late.
4 Don't be shy. There is plenty of time for us to learn to love each other.
5 Love-games are the best way of passing the time.

Λ

Come my Celia, let us prove,
While wee may, the sports of love;
Time will not be ours for ever:
He, at length, our good will sever.
Spend not then his gifts in vaine.   5
Sunnes that set, may rise againe:
But, if once wee lose this light,
'Tis, with us, perpetuall night.
Why should we deferre our joyes?
Fame, and rumor are but toyes.   10
Cannot we delude the eyes
Of a few poore houshold spyes?
Or his easier eares beguile?
So removed by our wile?
'Tis no sinne, loves fruit to steale,   15
But the sweet theft to reveale:
To bee taken, to be seene,
These have crimes accounted beene.

GLOSSARY
prove (l.1): experience
sever (l.4): cut off
deferre (l.9): (modern spelling: defer) postpone
delude (l.11): deceive
beguile (l.13): cheat
wile (l.14): trick
accounted beene (l.18): been considered

B

Gather ye Rose-buds while ye may,
Old Time is still a flying:
And this same flower that smiles today,
To morrow will be dying.
The glorious Lamp of Heaven, the Sun,   5
The higher he's a getting;
The sooner will his Race be run,
And neerer he's to setting.

That Age is best, which is the first,
When Youth and Blood are warmer;   10
But being spent, the worse, and worst
Times, still succeed the former.

Then be not coy, but use your time;
And while ye may, goe marry:
For having lost but once your prime,   15
You may for ever tarry.

C

Had we but World enough, and Time,
This coyness Lady were no crime.
We would sit down, and think which way
To walk, and pass our long Loves Day.
Thou by the *Indian Ganges* side   5
Should'st rubies find: I by the Tide
Of *Humber* would complain. I would
Love you ten years before the Flood:
And you should if you please refuse
Till the Conversion of the *Jews*.   10
My vegetable Love should grow
Vaster than Empires, and more slow.
An hundred years should go to praise
Thine Eyes, and on thy Forehead Gaze.
Two hundred to adore each Breast: 15
But thirty thousand to the rest.
An Age at least to every part,
And the last Age should show your Heart.
For Lady you deserve this State;
Nor would I love at lower rate.   20

But at my back I alwaies hear
Times winged Charriot hurrying near:
And yonder all before us lye

Desarts of vast Eternity.
Thy beauty shall no more be found;   25
Nor, in thy marble Vault, shall sound
My echoing Song: then Worms shall try
That long preserv'd Virginity:
And your quaint Honour turn to dust;
And into ashes all my Lust.   30
The Grave's a fine and private place,
But none I think do there embrace.

Now therefore, while the youthful hew
Sits on thy skin like morning dew,
And while thy willing Soul transpires   35
At every pore with instant Fires,
Now let us sport us while we may;
And now, like am'rous birds of prey,
Rather at once our Time devour
Than languish in his slow-chapt pow'r.   40
Let us roll all our Strength, and all
Our sweetness, up into one Ball:
And tear our Pleasures with rough strife,
Thorough the Iron gates of Life.
Thus, though we cannot make our Sun   45
Stand still, yet we will make him run.

marble (l.26): hard, limestone rock

Vault (l.26): burial chamber

quaint (l.29): old-fashioned; odd; pleasing (also the female pudenda)

Lust (l.30): sexual desire

hew (l.33): (modern spelling: hue) complexion

dew (l.34): moisture (suggesting: freshness)

transpires (l.35): gives off vapour from the skin

sport us (l.38): enjoy ourselves

Rather (l.39): it is better to

devour (l.39): eat up greedily

languish (l.40): lose life and vitality

slow-chapped power (l.40): (chap = jaw) power of slowly devouring jaws

strife (l.43): conflict

Thorough (l.44): through

8.2.2
Improving awareness

i Circle any of the poems (A, B or C) to which you think the following sentences may refer. Some refer to more than one. You may change the wording of any you don't agree with.

The poet seems to be talking to one young girl in particular.   A B C
The poem is a poem of seduction.   A B C
It is a love poem.   A B C

The poet's arguments are:

The crime is not to enjoy love but to be seen enjoying love.   A B C
You will not have your beauty in the grave.   A B C
The more quickly one is at one's peak the more quickly one dies.   A B C
You should get away from those that have been sent to keep an eye on you.   A B C
Once you have lost your youth you will forever be waiting for love.   A B C
There would be nothing wrong with your resisting my advances if life lasted much longer.   A B C
Let us consume time rather than let time consume us.   A B C
Each line of the poem has eight syllables.   A B C
The rhyme scheme is *aa/bb/cc* etc.   A B C

The poem has the natural rhythms of someone actually speaking.   A B C
The poem is both solemn and light at the same time.   A B C
It has moments of mystery and remoteness.   A B C
It is full of genuine feeling.   A B C
The poem sounds graceful.   A B C
The poem sounds rather trivial.   A B C

ii   Who or what do you think the following are or refer to?

Poem A

He (line 4)	our joyes (line 9)
gifts (line 5)	his easier eares (line 13)
this light (line 7)	sweet theft (line 16)

Poem B

this same flower (line 3)

his Race (line 7)

that Age (line 9)

Poem C

This coyness (line 2)

Thou (line 5)

the youthful hew (line 33)

iii   Find examples in the poems of

– the use of the imperative (e.g. 'Come my Celia')
– hypothetical expression (e.g. 'Had we but World enough …')
– future reference (e.g. 'Tomorrow will be dying')
How do they affect each poet's manner of address?

iv   Look at the third poem.

How do the three main parts of the poem differ?
What is the effect of the exaggeration (hyperbole) in the first part?

Select at least three of the following phrases and comment on their effect in the poem.

I would love you ten years before the Flood
My vegetable love
But at my back
Desarts of vast Eternity
My echoing Song
Worms shall try that long preserv'd Virginity
The Grave's a fine and private place
amorous birds of prey
all our Strength, and all our sweetness
tear our Pleasures
yet we will make him run

Compare your answers in pairs.

Which poem is the most profound? Can you say why? Which interests you most? Do you find any of the poems immoral? How would you feel if you were the person addressed in each poem? Is the poem only of interest to the person spoken to? Can you say that one poem is better than another or are they just different?

Poem A : *Song – to Celia* by Ben Jonson (published 1616)

Poem B : *To the Virgins, to make much of Time* by Robert Herrick (published 1648)

Poem C : *To his Coy Mistress* by Andrew Marvell (published 1681)

The 'theme' of the poems is an ancient one e.g. Asclepiades (c270 B.C.): 'You would keep your virginity? What will it profit you? You will find no lover in Hades, girl. It is among the living that we taste the joys of Kypris. In Acheron, child, we shall only be bones and dust'. Jonson's poem is a 'creative translation' from Catullus (84–54 B.C.).

8.3 Focus on evaluation

Most of us, when we read, know what we like and what we don't like, what we prefer and what we think little of. How far, though, are we able properly to assess the value of what we read? Some of the exercises in this Unit are designed to help you towards this.

8.3.1 One of the jobs of critics is to make evaluations. It is up to us to decide how far we agree with them.

Read the following critics' opinions about some of the writers illustrated in previous Units. Can you guess which writer each critic is talking about? (Look in the Key in the back of the book for the answers.) Could the comments equally apply to other writers? Do you agree with them?

1 Her courage in speaking out and acting on behalf of her expectations and rights in love, is the positive force for life against the many manifestations of self-deception and oppression in the novel.

2 His poetry is honoured for the rare precision and intensity of its language … It celebrates the intricate, bountiful order of nature, and attunes the English tongue to some of the voices of the classical past – Homer, Virgil, Ovid and Horace.

3 This short, strong poem has at least five 'thoughts', all significant in any serious contemplation of the poet's theme. All the thoughts

are given explicit utterance; they are declared statements, they are not contained or potently implied and suggested in images. To have made a poem out of propositions, stated with such bareness, is the poet's triumph. Perhaps that is not perfectly accurate, for the poem doesn't exist for the propositions merely; we don't feel that the poem sprang from 'ideation' at all; although the poem is in a sense made of thought and thoughts, and although the thoughts are in themselves significant, it is the presence of something else that gives the deep impressiveness and that makes us feel we are in contact with a kind of poetic thought and not merely with stated, general ideas.

4 He speaks of love, of fame, of politics, and of poetry; and in so doing he voices explicitly that sardonic but finally compassionate sense of the human comedy which equally informs his presentation of the incidents of his plot.

8.3.2 Critical opinions, though, need to be more than opinion. Just because somebody says something doesn't make it so. They need to express the truth about the nature of what is being assessed. Unless we trust critics completely we will have to test their usually generalised opinions against what is being talked about. Really, a case is more persuasive if it is well-illustrated and carefully argued.

  i Read the following poem by Shelley (1792-1822) as many times as you like.

Ozymandias

GLOSSARY
Ozymandias (title): The Greek name for the Egyptian Pharoah – Rameses II.
trunkless (l.2): without the upper part of the body (the trunk)
shattered (l.4): broken to pieces
visage (l.4): face
wrinkled (l.5): curled, to express displeasure
sneer (l.5): contemptuous smile
fed (l.8): nourished
pedestal (l.9): base of the statue
ye (archaic) *(l.11):* you
Mighty (l.11): rulers of the world
colossal (l.13): very big
wreck (l.13): ruin
boundless (l.13): without end

I met a traveller from an antique land
Who said: Two vast and trunkless legs of stone
Stand in the desert ... Near them, on the sand,
Half sunk, a shattered visage lies, whose frown,
And wrinkled lip, and sneer of cold command,   5
Tell that its sculptor well those passions read
Which yet survive, stamped on these lifeless things,
The hand that mocked them, and the heart that fed:
And on the pedestal these words appear:
'My name is Ozymandias, king of kings: 10
Look on my works, ye Mighty, and despair!'
Nothing beside remains. Round the decay
Of that colossal wreck, boundless and bare
The lone and level sands stretch far away.

Written 1817

Shelley is describing what a traveller to a far-off land is supposed to have told him about a broken statue he had seen of a cruel and powerful king. From the poem it is not clear, nor is it important, whether the traveller actually existed, or whether Shelley actually saw the statue. He wishes to make a more philosophical point.

The poem is a sonnet in that it has fourteen lines of ten syllables each and is loosely divided into two parts. (The first eight lines and the second six). However, unlike many sonnets, there is no real break in thought nor is there a very strict rhyme scheme.

The first image we have of the statue is of 'two vast and trunkless legs of stone' standing in a desert. This startling image suggests the immensity of the king's importance and power. The fact that he had such a statue built to him also suggests his vanity and his belief that he would be remembered and feared for ever. We then move on to the image of the broken 'visage' 'half sunk' in the sand, suggesting that his reign, and with it his power, is finished. We also learn of his unpleasant and unfeeling arrogance from the words 'frown', 'wrinkled lip', 'sneer' and 'cold'. The poet notes that the sculptor had understood and satirised his character (his 'passions') and captured it in his art, where it survives, even though the sculptor ('the hand that mocked' the passions) and the king ('the heart that fed' them) are dead.

In the second 'part' of the poem Shelley tells us of the inscription at the base of the statue, which once again confirms the king's arrogance although now the words sound ironical because all that remains of the king's power is the 'colossal wreck' of a statue. The final image in the last two lines suggests eternity, immense and empty, and contrasts with the temporary nature of man's vanity and pride.

Shelley, in this poem, manages to persuade us of his theme partly through his choice of the central image of the broken statue in the desert but also very strongly through the rhythms and the compressed language used to express the image. Although the expression is controlled within the sonnet form the rhythms are very close to the irregular rhythms of the human voice where the use of stress helps to focus attention on what is important.

The opening sounds a little like an incantation ('I met a traveller from an antique land...') which contrasts nicely with the heavy rhythms of 'Two vast and trunkless legs of stone' which suggest the huge size of the statue. The verb phrase 'Stand in the desert' is kept back until the next line and passes quickly away, again to act as a contrast. We are then led through a series of short phrases 'near them', 'on the sand' etc. to the main focus of attention, the 'shattered visage'. The lines are linked both rhythmically and through the use of alliteration and near-alliteration (*s*and, *s*unk, *s*hattered, vi*s*age, fro*w*n, *w*rinkled). The phrase 'which yet survive' achieves prominence in a grammatically complex construction through its position at the beginning of the seventh line and has a dramatic, almost melodramatic, effect. The final contrast between the inscription, which now seems ironical and very silly, and the 'lone and level sands' also comes out in the rhythms. The rhythms of the inscription make its arrogance sound futile. This is emphasised by the calm and unhurried rhythms of the final two lines, linked together by a series of alliterative pairs (*b*oundless and *b*are, *l*one and *l*evel, *s*ands and *s*tretch).

The poem very powerfully portrays the folly of human vanity which thinks itself so important.

iii   How is the assessment structured? (i.e. How does it start? How does it finish? What is the focus of each paragraph? Does one thing lead into another?)

Is it well argued and well illustrated? Give reasons for your answer.

iv   Evaluate the following poem as far as you can. Plan your essay in outline first. What will you put in each paragraph?

A Poison Tree

I was angry with my friend:
I told my wrath, my wrath did end.
I was angry with my foe:
I told it not, my wrath did grow.

And I watered it in fears,   5
Night and morning with my tears;
And I sunned it with smiles,
And with soft deceitful wiles.

And it grew both day and night,
Till it bore an apple bright;   10
And my foe beheld it shine,
And he knew that it was mine,

And into my garden stole
When the night had veiled the pole:
In the morning glad I see   15
My foe outstretched beneath the tree.   *William Blake*

8.4 Personification

You may have noticed that writers often
– give human characteristics to things and to abstract ideas.
– represent an abstract quality or an idea in the form of a person.

8.4.1 Are the following examples of the first or the second of these, or neither?
What effect does the technique have?

---

1 Busy old fool, unruly Sun,
  Why dost thou thus,
  Through windows, and through curtains, call on us.   *(John Donne)*

2 Love bade me welcome
  Yet my heart drew back
  Guilty of dust and sin.   *(George Herbert)*

3 O sleep! O gentle sleep!
  Nature's soft nurse, how have I frighted thee,
  That thou no more wilt weigh my eyelids down
  And steep my senses in forgetfulness.   *(William Shakespeare)*

4 Words strain
  Crack and sometimes break, under the burden,
  Under the tension, slip, slide, perish,
  Decay with imprecision, will not stay in place,
  Will not stay still.   *(T. S. Eliot)*

5 Overnight, very
  Whitely, discreetly,
  Very quietly.

  Our toes, our noses
  Take hold on the loam
  Acquire the air.   *(Sylvia Plath* from a poem called *Mushrooms)*

Can you find examples of personification in previous Units?

8.5 Reading without assistance

This soliloquy comes from the last Act of *Macbeth*. What does it tell us about Macbeth's emotional state? What has changed since he saw Banquo's ghost (4.2.2)?

MACBETH   To-morrow, and to-morrow, and to-morrow,
Creeps in this petty pace from day to day,
To the last syllable of recorded time;
And all our yesterdays have lighted fools
The way to dusty death. Out, out, brief candle!   5
Life's but a walking shadow; a poor player,
That struts and frets his hour upon the stage,
And then is heard no more: it is a tale
Told by an idiot, full of sound and fury,
Signifying nothing.   10

(from *Macbeth* by *William Shakespeare*)

8.6 Comparing the same theme in two different literary forms

8.6.1
Anticipation

Re-read the extract from Hazlitt (6.5.3).

8.6.2 Listen to the following. They are extracts (abridged) from the opening of Ben Jonson's play *Volpone* (1606). The rich Volpone (the Fox) and his servant Mosca (the Fly) are seen together.

VOLPONE   Good morning to the day; and next, my gold!
Open the shrine, that I may see my saint.

(MOSCA draws a curtain, and reveals piles of gold, plate jewels, etc.)

Hail, the world's soul, and mine!

. . .

O thou son of Sol
(But brighter than thy father), let me kiss,   5
With adoration, thee, and every relic
Of sacred treasure in this blessed room.

. . .

Dear saint,
Riches, the dumb god that giv'st all men tongues;
Thou canst do nought and yet mak'st men do all things;   10

GLOSSARY
shrine (l.2): place in which devotion is paid to a saint
Hail (archaic) *(l.3):* (a respectful greeting)
relic (l.6): object once belonging to a saint
dumb (l.9): not having power of speech
canst (archaic) *(l.10):* can
nought (archaic) *(l.10):* nothing

The price of souls; even hell, with thee to boot,
Is made worth heaven. Thou art virtue, fame,
Honour, and all things else. Who can get thee,
He shall be noble, valiant, honest, wise –

MOSCA   And what he will, sir. Riches are in fortune   15
A greater good than wisdom is in nature.

VOLPONE   True, my beloved Mosca. Yet I glory
More in the cunning purchase of my wealth,
Than in the glad possession, since I gain
No common way.   20

.   .   .

MOSCA   And besides, sir,

.   .   .   .

You will not lie in straw whilst moths and worms
Feed on your sumptuous hangings and soft beds:
You know the use of riches, and dare give now,
From that bright heap, to me, your poor observer,   25

.   .   .

VOLPONE   Hold thee, Mosca;

(Gives him money.)

.   .   .

(Exit MOSCA.)

What should I do …
I have no wife, no parent, child, ally,
To give my substance to; but whom I make
Must be my heir: and this makes men observe me;   30
This draws new clients daily to my house,
Women and men of every sex and age,
That bring me presents, send me plate, coin, jewels,
With hope that when I die (which they expect
Each greedy minute) it shall then return   35
Tenfold upon them; whilst some, covetous
Above the rest, seek to engross me whole,
And counter-work the one unto the other,
Contend in gifts, as they would seem in love:
And which I suffer, playing with their hopes,   40
And am content to coin them into profit,
And look upon their kindness, and take more,
And look on that; still bearing them in hand,
Letting the cherry knock against their lips,
And draw it by their mouths, and back again.   45

to boot (l.11): in addition
cunning (l.18): clever
sumptuous (l.23): luxurious
hangings (l.23): curtains, tapestries
heap (l.25): pile
ally (l.28): partner
substance (l.29): wealth
my heir (l.30): the person who inherits my property
plate (l.33): precious metal
tenfold (l.36): times ten
covetous (l.36): greedy
engross (l.37): possess
contend (l.39): compete
coin (l.41): make money

i What do you think the names Volpone (the Fox) and Mosca (the Fly) are meant to tell you about their characters?

ii Select lines or phrases from the passage to support the following statements about Volpone.

> He is more interested in clever ways of making money than in enjoying it once he has acquired it.
>
> He has no family or friends to leave his money to when he dies.
>
> He enjoys sleeping in a very luxurious bedroom.
>
> He is willing to give some of his money to Mosca occasionally.
>
> His 'friends' bring him rich gifts in the hope of inheriting a great deal from him after his death.
>
> Volpone takes their presents each time they bring them.
>
> He tempts them by teasing them into false hopes that they shall one day have his money.
>
> The 'friends' fight with one another about who seems to love him best and who can bring the most costly presents.

iii Volpone 'worships' his gold. Which words or phrases suggest his 'religious' attitude. Do you find them blasphemous? In what ways are they ironical?

iv What does the image of 'the cherry' convey?

v Which of the following words, if any, do you think describe Volpone's character:

imaginative	resourceful	deceitful	vicious
lively	outrageous	unpleasant	
fascinating	mean	perverse	delightful

Is he a 'villain' or a 'good' character?

vi What do you imagine Volpone and Mosca look like (their physical characteristics, their clothes)? What do you imagine Volpone's room looks like? Do you know anyone whose attitude to money is similar to Volpone's?

The plot of *Volpone* is revealed in the opening lines. Volpone and Mosca try and trap the money seekers who are waiting for him to die in a series of lively and farcical situations where his victims are repeatedly disappointed. In the end, Volpone is unmasked and brought before a court of law. Jonson declared his play was meant to 'mix profit with pleasure'.

i In what way is the above extract from the play 'pleasurable'? What do you think Jonson's moral purpose (our 'profit') was?

ii How did Hazlitt achieve his purpose in his essay on money?

iii Can you compare the extract from *Volpone* with the extract from Hazlitt?

iv Jonson was a contemporary and friend of Shakespeare. Can you see any differences between Jonson's dramatic style and Shakespeare's?

8.6.5 The poem *Come my Celia* (8.2.1.) is Volpone's song to Celia later in the play. What does this add to your views of *Volpone*, the play?

8.6.6 *Ben Jonson was born in Westminster in 1572, the son of a minister. He was a leader among* **Notes** *London poets and wits and from 1615–31 wrote masques for the court which were highly regarded by King James. Among his other plays are* Every Man in his Humour, The Alchemist *and* Sejanus. *He died in 1637.*

8.7 Relating prose-rhythms and meaning

8.7.1 **i** Look at these pictures:
Anticipation

ii Describe the different kinds of running portrayed.
What are they called in English?
Do these kinds of running exist in your country?
Can you name one athlete famous for each kind, in your country?
Do you like running? Why/Why not?

8.7.2 *The following is a slightly abridged extract from* The Loneliness of the Long Distance Runner *a modern novel by Alan Sillitoe. The hero – or really anti-hero – is in Borstal, a type of penal institution for young offenders meant to help reform them. He is a superb long-distance runner and is admired by his officers. It is 'sports day' and the next event is the big cross-country race.*

8.7.3 Try to find answers to these questions in the passage that follows.

Why weren't parents there?
What sort of day was it?
Why was the governor going to be disappointed?
Why did Roach 'lift his hand'?

Read:

The sports ground looked a treat: with big tea-tents all round and
flags flying and seats for families – empty because no mam or dad
had known what opening day meant – and boys still running heats for
the hundred yards, and lords and ladies walking from stall to stall,
and the Borstal Boys Brass Band in blue uniforms ...   5

The blue sky was full of sunshine and it couldn't have been a better
day ...

'Come on, Smith,' Roach the sports master called to me, 'we don't
want you to be late for the big race, eh? Although I dare say you'd
catch them up if you were.'... So the big race it was, for them,   10
watching from the grandstand under a fluttering Union Jack, a race
for the governor, that he had been waiting for, and I hoped he and all
the rest of his pop-eyed gang were busy placing big bets on me,
hundred to one to win, all the money they had in their pockets, all the
wages they were going to get for the next five years and the more   15
they placed the happier I'd be. Because here was a dead cert going
to die on the big name they'd built for him, going to go down dying
with laughter whether it choked him or not. My knees felt the cool
soil pressing into them, and out of my eye's corner I saw Roach lift his
hand... then the gun went and I was away.   20

GLOSSARY
a treat (l.1): lovely
opening day (l.3): a day when the Borstal was open to the public
heats (l.3): races to decide who is in the final
Union Jack (l.11): U.K. national flag
pop-eyed (l.13): staring
a dead cert (l.16): someone sure to win
choked (l.18): upset

---

i Discuss your answers in pairs.

ii In context, guess what the following mean:

fluttering
bets

8.7.4 Try to find answers to these questions in the passage that follows:

How could the runners measure the distance as they were running?
What position was Smith in over the first stile?
What is his technique for winning?
Had he changed his mind about how he would finish the race?

Read on:

We went once around the field and then along a half-mile drive of
elms, being cheered all the way, and I seemed to feel I was in the
lead as we went out by the gate and into the lane, though I wasn't
interested enough to find out. The five-mile course was marked by
splashes of whitewash gleaming on gateposts and trunks and stiles   5
and stones, and a boy with a waterbottle and bandage-box stood
every half-mile waiting for those that dropped out or fainted. Over the
first stile, without trying, I was still nearly in the lead but one; and if
any of you want tips about running, never be in a hurry, and never let
any of the other runners know you are in a hurry even if you are. You   10
can always overtake on long-distance running without letting the
others smell the hurry in you; and when you've used your craft like
this to reach the two or three up front then you can do a big dash
later that puts everybody else's hurry in the shade because you've not
had to make haste up till then. I ran to a steady jog-trot rhythm, and   15
soon it was so smooth that I forgot I was running, and I was hardly
able to know that my legs were lifting and falling and my arms going
in and out, and my lungs didn't seem to be working at all, and my
heart stopped that wicked thumping I always get at the beginning of
a run. Because you see I never race at all; I just run, and somehow I   20
know that if I forget I'm racing and only jog-trot along until I don't
know I'm running I always win the race. For when my eyes recognise
that I'm getting near the end of the course – by seeing a stile or
cottage corner – I put on a spurt, and such a fast big spurt it is
because I feel that up till then I haven't been running and that I've   25
used up no energy at all. And I've been able to do this because I've
been thinking; and I wonder if any of the other lads are on to the
same lark, though I know for a fact that they aren't. Off like the wind
along the cobbled footpath and rutted lane, smoother than the flat
grass track on the field and better for thinking because it's not too   30
smooth, and I was in my element that afternoon knowing that nobody
could beat me at running but intending to beat myself before the day
was over …

GLOSSARY

elms (l.2): types of tree
whitewash (l.5): lime and
  water mixture for
  making outside surfaces
  white
trunks (l.5): main stems of
  trees
bandage-box (l.6): box with
  dressings for wounds
onto the same lark (l.27–28):
  playing the same game
cobbled (l.29): made of
  round stones
rutted (l.29): worn down
  by continual use

i Discuss your answers in pairs.

ii In context guess what the following mean:

drive	fainted
cheered	tips
gleaming	craft
stile	dash
in the lead	spurt

8.7.5 Try to find answers to these questions in the passage that follows:

How far was Smith from the lead?
When did he feel most alone?
What did the loneliness mean to him?
How important was the 'winning post' to his running?
What did the winner receive?
In what ways was Smith rebelling?

Read on:

I trotted on along the edge of a field bordered by the sunken lane, smelling green grass and honeysuckle, and I felt as though I came from a long line of whippets trained to run on two legs, only I couldn't see a toy rabbit in front and there wasn't a collier's cosh behind to make me keep up the pace. I passed the Gunthorpe runner whose shimmy was already black with sweat and I could just see the corner of the fenced-up copse in front where the only man I had to pass to win the race was going all out to gain the halfway mark. Then he turned into a tongue of trees and bushes where I couldn't see him any more, and I couldn't see anybody, and I knew what the loneliness of the long-distance runner running across country felt like, realising that as far as I was concerned this feeling was the only honesty and realness there was in the world and I knowing it would be no different ever, no matter what I felt at odd times, and no matter what anybody else tried to tell me.

The runner behind me must have been a long way off because it was so quiet, and there was even less noise and movement than there had been at five o'clock of a frosty winter morning. It was hard to understand, and all I knew was that you had to run, run, run, without knowing why you were running, but on you went through fields you didn't understand and into woods that made you afraid, over hills without knowing you'd been up and down, and shooting across streams that would have cut the heart out of you had you fallen into them. And the winning post was no end to it, even though crowds might be cheering you in, because on you had to go before you got your breath back, and the only time you stopped really was when you tripped over a tree trunk and broke your neck or fell into a disused well and stayed dead in the darkness forever. So I thought: they aren't going to get me on this racing lark, this running and trying to win, this jog-trotting for a bit of blue ribbon, because it's not the way to go on at all, though they swear blind that it is. You should think about nobody and go your own way, not on a course marked out for you by people holding mugs of water and bottles of iodine in case you fall and cut yourself so that they can pick you up – even if you want to stay where you are – and get you moving again.

GLOSSARY
honeysuckle (l.2): climbing shrub with sweet-smelling flowers
whippets (l.3): small, slim very fast dogs
a collier's (l.4): a coal miner's
cosh (l.4): short heavy stick covered with leather
shimmy (l.6): vest
copse (l.7): group of small trees
well (l.28): deep hole in the earth used to reach water
swear blind (l.31): assert emphatically
iodine (l.33): a chemical used as an antiseptic

    i Discuss your answers in pairs.

    ii In context, guess what the following mean:

trotted	going all out
sunken	had you fallen
keep up the pace	disused

8.7.6   Try to find answers to these questions in the passage that follows:

Did he go into the lead?
What did winning the race represent to him?
Could he win?
Why does he choose not to win?

Read on:

GLOSSARY
broad (l.3): wide
greyhound (l.4): type of fast
   racing dog
bramble (l.14): covered
   with a prickly, fruit-
   bearing shrub
coppers (slang) (l.19): police
wall-barred (l.21): like wall-
   bars (a piece of
   apparatus on the walls
   of a gymnasium)
mugs (slang) (l.22): faces

On I went, out of the wood, passing the man leading without knowing
I was going to do so. Flip-flap, flip-flap, jog-trot, jog-trot, crunchslap-
crunchslap, across the middle of a broad field again, rhythmically
running in my greyhound effortless fashion, knowing I had won the
race though it wasn't half over, won it if I wanted it, could go on for   5
ten or fifteen or twenty miles if I had to and drop dead at the finish of
it, which would be the same, in the end, as living an honest life like
the governor wanted me to. It amounted to: win the race and be
honest, and on trot-trotting I went, having the time of my life, loving
my progress because it did me good and set me thinking which by   10
now I liked to do, but not caring at all when I remembered that I had
to win this race as well as run it. One of the two, I had to win the race
or run it, and I knew I could do both because my legs had carried me
well in front – now coming to the short cut down the bramble bank
and over the sunken road – and would carry me further because they   15
seemed made of electric cable and easily alive to keep on slapping
at those ruts and roots, but I'm not going to win because the only way
I'd see I came in first would be if winning meant that I was going to
escape the coppers after doing the biggest bank job of my life, but
winning means the exact opposite, no matter how they try to kill or   20
kid me, means running right into their white-gloved wall-barred
hands and grinning mugs and staying there for the rest of my natural
long life of stone-breaking anyway, but stone-breaking in the way I
want to do it and not in the way they tell me.

    i Discuss your answers in pairs.

    ii In context, guess what the following mean:

short cut	grinning
slapping	stone-breaking

8.7.7
Style

Look back over the extract.

i Select phrases/sentences which show

– the attitude of the officers to Smith's ability
– Smith's resentment
– Smith's refusal to win

ii Where does the writer show Smith's pleasure in running? Is there any sense of tension between this pleasure and his resentment of authority?

iii Select phrases which show that Smith is talking directly and personally to the reader. What effect does this have on you? Can you find examples of very colloquial English?

iv As the extract goes on the writer helps us to feel both the sensation of running and Smith's tiredness. These are conveyed by such things as

– sentence length
– the use of conjunctions (particularly 'and', 'but' and 'because')
– the rhythm of the prose
– grammatical inaccuracy
– the sound of the words

Find at least one example of each and show how it helps us to feel what Smith is feeling. Can you find any other techniques that have the same effect?

v What effect do the following repetitions have 'all the ...' (8.7.3) 'couldn't' (8.7.5) 'run, run, run' (8.7.5) 'this' (8.7.5).

8.7.8
Discussion

Have you ever felt like Smith in wanting to rebel against authority? Can you describe a situation from your own experience – or describe an imaginary situation – in which someone chooses his/her own way of doing things even though he/she disappoints parents, teachers or friends?

8.8 Conclusion

8.8.1 Go back over the Unit and comment on the passages and exercises.

UNIT 9

Looking at literary form

9.1 Reading a poem

9.1.1
Anticipation

i Look at these pictures:

ii Which of the following adjectives apply to the birds in

PICTURE 1	PICTURE 2	PICTURE 3

graceful	noisy	innocent
beautiful	romantic	strong
web-footed	pure	powerful
heavy in flight	ugly when they walk	majestic

iii These words/phrases appear in the poem which follows:

mount (verb)	October	twilight
water	mysterious	
my heart is sore		scatter
drift (verb)	autumn	
swans		not grown old

Look up any you don't know in a dictionary.
Can you guess from the vocabulary what the poem might be about?

9.1.2 *The poem is by W. B. Yeats. He describes some wild swans he saw in Coole Park in Ireland.*

See if you can answer the following questions:

What time of year is it?
What time of day is it?
What is the weather like?
Has the poet seen these or similar swans before?
Is he happy?

Listen:

The trees are in their autumn beauty,
The woodland paths are dry,
Under the October twilight the water
Mirrors a still sky;
Upon the brimming water among the stones   5
Are nine-and-fifty swans.

The nineteenth autumn has come upon me
Since I first made my count;
I saw, before I had well finished,
All suddenly mount   10
And scatter wheeling in great broken rings
Upon their clamorous wings.

I have looked upon those brilliant creatures,
And now my heart is sore.
All's changed since I, hearing at twilight,   15
The first time on this shore,
The bell-beat of their wings above my head,
Trod with a lighter tread.

GLOSSARY
brimming (l.5): full and fast flowing
scatter (l.11): go in different directions
wheeling (l.11): circling
clamorous (l.12): noisy
sore (l.14): sad
bell-beat (l.17): heavy sound, a little like a bell
trod (l.18): walked
tread (l.18): way of walking

Unwearied still, lover by lover,
They paddle in the cold   20
Companionable streams or climb the air;
Their hearts have not grown old;
Passion or conquest, wander where they will,
Attend upon them still.

But now they drift on the still water,   25
Mysterious, beautiful;
Among what rushes will they build,
By what lake's edge or pool
Delight men's eyes when I awake some day
To find they have flown away?   30

paddle (l.20): walk in
  shallow water
rushes (l.27): tall plants
  which grow by the side
  of a lake

9.1.3
Improving
understanding

i Write T (true) F (false) DK (don't know) next to each of the following statements. Re-write the false sentences to make them true.

Both the water and the sky are calm.
The last time he counted the swans was 19 years ago.
They flew off silently as a group the first time he counted them.
The poet feels he has aged considerably since the last time he was here.
They are the same swans although they, too, have grown older.
The poet is regretting the difference between himself and the swans.
The poet wonders where they will be when one day he wakes up and they have gone.
The poet is imagining his death.

Discuss your answers in pairs.

ii Are the swans only birds or are they also a symbol of something else?
e.g. youth
     changelessness
     the mystery of life
     everlasting life

If so, does it make the poem more powerful and disturbing?

iii Why are the streams 'companionable' as well as 'cold'?

iv What does the phrase 'lover by lover' add to the meaning of the poem?

9.1.4
Style

A

i What difference would it have made to the poem if the poet had said
  a) 'fifty-nine' swans instead of 'nine and fifty'
  b) 'I am nineteen years older since I first counted them' instead of 'the nineteenth autumn has come upon me since first I made my count'.

227

ii Try to paraphrase the lines: 'I saw ... clamorous wings'. What is lost?

iii The words 'clamorous' and 'bell-beat' describing the swans' wings appeal to the ear. What kind of sound is made?

iv What sort of question is the one in the final stanza? What effect does it have?

v Look carefully at the rhythm of the poem. Notice how each stanza seems to build up to a climax. How is this achieved? Although there is a regularity in the rhyme scheme and the number of lines in each stanza, the pattern of stress varies according to the meaning. Listen again to the recording and mark the strong stresses of one stanza.

B

i How is the word 'still' used in the poem?

ii What words or phrases does the poet use to describe the swans'

   a) beauty
   b) movement in the water or in flight?

9.1.5
Follow-up work

Either: Write a short description of any bird(s) or animal(s) you have watched closely and describe your feelings about them.
Or: Look back at *The Thought Fox* (1.11.2) and write a paragraph on the different ways Yeats and Hughes treat the creatures they are describing in their poetry.

9.1.6
Notes

William Butler Yeats was born near Dublin in 1865, the son of a famous painter. His early years were spent both in Dublin and London but in 1896 he returned to Ireland to become a leader of the Celtic Renaissance. Yeats was passionately affected by the political events of the time in Ireland and deeply aware of Irish history. Believing in the public role of a poet and the social importance of literature, he helped found the Irish National Theatre Society. He also published books of Irish legends and fairy tales. His great poems were published between 1919 and 1929. In 1923 he was awarded the Nobel Prize for Literature. He died in 1939.

9.2 Saying it in verse/saying it in prose

9.2.1
Anticipation

Which texts in previous Units have been concerned with ghosts?

9.2.2

In 1893 Yeats published a book of short stories The Celtic Twilight. *Here is one of them.*

9.2.3   **i** Read the story as many times as you like.

There was a doubter in Donegal, and he would not hear of ghosts or fairies, and there was a house in Donegal that had been haunted as long as man could remember, and this is the story of how the house got the better of the man. The man came into the house and lighted a fire in the room under the haunted one, and took off his boots and set ^{5} them on the hearth, and stretched out his feet and warmed himself. For a time he prospered in his unbelief; but a little while after the night had fallen, and everything had got very dark, one of his boots began to move. It got up off the floor and gave a kind of slow jump towards the door, and then the other boot did the same, and after that ^{10} the first boot jumped again. And thereupon it occurred to the man that an invisible being had got into his boots, and was now going away in them.

When the boots reached the door they went upstairs slowly, and then the man heard them go tramp, tramp round the haunted room over ^{15} his head. A few minutes passed, and he could hear them again upon the stairs, and after that in the passage outside, and then one of them came in at the door, and the other gave a jump past it and came in too. They jumped along towards him, and so on, until they drove him out of the room, and finally out of the house. In this way he was ^{20} kicked out by his own boots, and Donegal was avenged upon its doubter. It is not recorded whether the invisible being was a ghost or one of the Sidhe, but the fantastic nature of the vengeance is like the work of the Sidhe who live in the heart of fantasy.

GLOSSARY
Donegal (l.1): a county in the North-West of Ireland
the Sidhe (l.23): the fairy people of Ireland

ii Find a word or phrase in the passage which means:
      someone who doesn't believe
      gained a victory over
      inhabited by ghosts
      floor in front of the fireplace
      from that moment on
      had taken vengeance

iii Select the words/phrases that give essential information about the narrative (e.g. 'a doubter in Donegal'). What have you left out? Why?

iv In pairs, re-tell the story in your own words as far as possible. If you can, record it.

v Compare your story with the original. Did you add a lot? Did you miss out a lot? What were the differences?

i   Was it easier to paraphrase the four lines in *Wild Swans of Coole* than to re-tell the story of the doubter? Why/Why not? Is the language more tightly organised in the poem or the story?

ii What similarities of style are there between the poem and the story? (Look at, for example, 'go tramp, tramp round the haunted room').

iii Why do you think Yeats chose to express himself in verse (in *Wild Swans of Coole*) and in prose (in the *Celtic Twilight*)?

iv Can you make one or two generalisations about the differences between verse and prose and the advantages of one over the other?

9.3 Reading prose

i   Do you prefer the heat or the cold?

ii Tell each other about the hottest day you have known.

iii Write down a list of words you associate with 'heat'.

9.3.2   These three passages are partly about 'heat'.

Passage 1

Read:

GLOSSARY
Precinct (American) (l.4): division of a city made for police control
slashes (l.6): long strokes (suggesting violent cutting)
rhinestone (l.7): colourless artifical gemstone
saffron (l.7): orange-yellow
asphalt (l.11): browny-black substance used for surfacing roads
dungarees (l.15): a workman's one-piece suit usually made from blue denim

July.
Heat.
In the city, they are synonymous, they are identical, they mean one and the same thing. In the 87th Precinct, they strut the streets with a vengeance, these twin bitches who wear their bleached blond hair and their bright-red lipstick slashes, who sway on glittering rhinestone slippers, who flaunt their saffron silk. Heat and July, they are identical twins who were born to make you suffer.   5

The air is tangible. You can reach out to touch it. It is sticky and clinging, you can wrap it around you like a viscous overcoat. The   10 asphalt in the gutters has turned to gum, and your heels clutch at it when you try to navigate the streets. The pavements glow with a flat off-white brilliance, contrasting with the running black of the gutter, creating an alternating pattern of shade and light that is dizzying. The sun sits low on a still sky, a sky as pale as faded dungarees. There is   15 only a hint of blue in this sky for it has been washed out by the intensity of the sun, and there is a shimmer over everything, the shimmer of heat ready to explode in rain.

i Language

Match the words on the left with the definitions on the right.

strut	female dogs (slang: immoral, spiteful women)
twin	sticky
bitches	light evening shoes worn by ladies
bleached	move from side to side
sway	capable of being touched
slippers	grip
flaunt	walk with a pompous and affected air
tangible	suggestion
viscous	parade ostentatiously
gum	two related and similar
clutch	light which shines unsteadily
hint	a sticky substance
shimmer	whitened by chemicals

ii Improving understanding
Complete the following with as many words as you like.

The writer says that in the city it is always _____ in July. He uses the metaphor of _____ to describe _____. His attitude towards that time of the year is one of _____. The trouble is the _____ is humid and sticky and the weather is so hot the roads _____. The light from the pavements is _____. The sun is so brilliant that the sky _____. Perhaps _____.
Use a separate piece of paper.

iii Style
a) What verb form is used predominantly? Does it have any interesting effect?
b) Are there a lot of adjectives in the passage? What effect does it have?
c) What do you notice about the length of the sentences?
d) Can you find examples of alliteration?

iv Context
What kind of book does the passage come from?
What clues have you got for making your decision?
Who do you think the narrator is?
Where do you think the story takes place?

Read:

GLOSSARY

placards (l.2): boards with headlines (used as advertising)

wicker (l.3): made from thin flexible twigs, usually of willow

gauze (l.7): light-weight, often transparent fabric (also: a thin mist)

lumber (l.11): heavy movement

battlements (l.13): high defensive walls

bayonets (l.16): steel blades attached to the end of guns

Since it was a very hot night and the paper boys went by with placards proclaiming in huge red letters that there was a heat-wave, wicker chairs were placed on the hotel steps and there, sipping, smoking, detached gentlemen sat. Peter Walsh sat there. One might fancy that day, the London day, was just beginning. Like a woman who had slipped off her print dress and white apron to array herself in blue and pearls, the day changed, put off stuff, took gauze, changed to evening, and with the same sigh of exhilaration that a woman breathes, tumbling petticoats on the floor, it too shed dust, heat, colour; the traffic thinned; motor-cars, tinkling, darting, succeeded the lumber of vans; and here and there among the thick foliage of the squares an intense light hung. I resign, the evening seemed to say, as it paled and faded above the battlements and prominences, moulded, pointed, of hotel, flat, and block of shops, I fade, she was beginning, I disappear, but London would have none of it, and rushed her bayonets into the sky, pinioned her, constrained her partnership in her revelry.

5

10

15

i Language

Match the words on the left with the definitions on the right.

sipping	taken off quickly and casually
detached	making a ringing sound
fancy	letting fall
slipped off	carved into shape
array	moving suddenly and rapidly
tumbling	drinking a little at a time
shed	got rid of
tinkling	imagine
darting	held down
faded	merry making
moulded	dress in a decorative way
pinioned	gradually disappeared
revelry	emotionally distanced

ii Improving understanding

Rewrite the following completing the gaps with as many words as you like. Use a separate piece of paper

The newspapers said _____. It was _____ although it seemed like _____ because _____. Men were sitting _____. It was less _____ than during the _____. There were fewer _____ and more _____. From among the trees in the _____ there _____. Against the sky you could see _____.

iii Style

a) Which two verb tenses are used predominantly? There is a change from one to the other: what effect does it have?

b) What do you notice about:

– the length and construction of the sentences?
– the number of verbs in relation to the number of adjectives?

c) Can you find examples of a simile, a metaphor and personification? Are they effective in context?

iv Context

What kind of book do you think the passage comes from? Does the passage tell you more about Peter Walsh or about a London evening? Does it help you guess anything at all about the narrator of the story? Do you think it comes from a modern book? What clues are there to help you with your decisions?

Passage 3

Read:

There is a tin roof on the kitchen. It leaks only when the rain is very heavy and then only along the juncture with the roof of the main house. The difficulty is more with heat. The room is small: very little more than big enough to crowd in the stove and table and chairs: and this slanted leanto roof is quite low above it, with no ceiling, and half the tin itself visible. The outdoor sunlight alone is in the high nineties during many hours of one day after another for weeks on end; the thin metal roof collects and sends this heat almost as powerfully as a burning-glass; wood fires are particularly hot and violent and there is scarcely a yard between the stove and one end of the table: between the natural heat, the cumulated and transacted heat striven downward from the roof, and the heat of the stove, the kitchen is such a place at the noon meal that, merely entering it, sweat is started in a sheet from the whole surface of the body, and the solar plexus and the throat are clutched into tight kicking knots which relax sufficient to admit food only after two or three minutes.

GLOSSARY

leanto (l.5): resting on the side of the house

in the high nineties (l.6): between 95–100 degrees Fahrenheit

burning-glass (l.9): lens which concentrates the sun's rays to a point of intense heat

solar plexus (l.14): network of nerves in the abdomen

i Language

a) Match the words on the left with the definitions on the right:

leaks	on an incline
juncture	massed up
slanted	pushed with difficulty
scarcely	conducted
cumulated	thin layer
transacted	lets in water
striven	seized
sheet	join
clutched	hardly

b) Answer the following questions:

'It' is used three times in the passage. What does it refer to each time?
What does 'alone' mean in the passage?
What does 'this heat' refer to?
What does 'merely' mean?

ii Improving understanding
Complete the following with as many words as you like.

The writer starts by describing a _____ which lets in _____ when
_____. When it is hot outside the _____ is even _____
because _____. When a wood fire is lit in the stove, it is so hot that
_____.

iii Style
a) What verb tense is used predominantly? How does it relate to what seems to be the writer's purpose?

b) Which convey the writer's purpose more – the nouns, the verbs or the adjectives? Are any of them used unusually? If so, what effect does it have?

c) What do you notice about the length and construction of the sentences?

iv Context
What kind of book do you think the passage comes from? Is it modern? Which part of the world is it set in? What do you think the attitude of the narrator is? What clues are there to help you with your decisions?

9.3.3
Comparisons

Look at the three passages again and answer the following questions:

i What do the passages have *in common* and how are they *different*?

ii Do any have anything in common with verse? Could you imagine any being written as verse?

iii Do you think prose has any advantages over verse?

iv Which passage do you prefer? Give reasons.

9.3.4
Notes

Match the following descriptions with the passages you have just read:

i From *Let Us Now Praise Famous Men* by James Agee, published in 1941. This is a book which sets out to describe the daily life of the poor tenant farmers in Alabama, U.S.A. during the Depression.

ii From *See Them Die* by Ed McBain, published in 1960, an American detective novel.

iii From *Mrs Dalloway* by Virginia Woolf, published in 1925, a novel in which six lives are shown in a cross-section of time.

9.3.5
Follow-up work

Write one or two paragraphs describing a hot day in the town or place where you live.

9.4 Focus on literary form

Look back at 1.5.1. Clearly, verse and prose are different modes of expression and serve different purposes. Verse tends to be more personal and suggests what cannot be expressed explicitly in prose. It frequently aims to *create* a feeling in the reader rather than *explain* it.

However, Byron, for example, wishes *his* verse to be entertaining as well as express his personal feelings and attitudes. In fact, good verse is rarely 'personal' only to the poet.

Also, verse is not limited to poems. Plays like *Macbeth* are written in verse. And there are also many different kinds of prose. Prose might be used to explain something or put across a point of view explicitly but in novels and short stories it can create and suggest a whole range of thought and feeling. It can also be written 'poetically' (as verse can sometimes be written 'prosaically'.)

Novels tend to be comprehensive and wide-ranging and short stories tend to focus on one small incident. However, it is very difficult to generalise.

9.4.1 Read what two great writers have said about poetry:

Poetry is, as a rule, either the voice of the far future, exquisite and ethereal, or it is the voice of the past, rich, magnificent. When the Greeks heard the *Iliad* and the *Odyssey*, they heard their own past calling in their hearts, as men far inland sometimes hear the sea and fall weak with powerful, wonderful regret, nostalgia; or else their own 5 future rippled its time-beats through their blood, as they followed the painful, glamorous progress of the Ithacan. This was Homer to the Greeks: their Past, splendid with battles won and death achieved, and their Future, the magic wandering of Ulysses through the unknown.

. . . . . .

But there is another kind of poetry: the poetry of that which is at hand: 10 the immediate present. In the immediate present there is no perfection, no consummation, nothing finished. The strands are all flying, quivering, intermingling into the web, the waters are shaking the moon.

D. H. Lawrence

I have said that poetry is the spontaneous overflow of powerful 15 feelings: it takes its origin from emotion recollected in tranquillity: the emotion is contemplated till, by a species of reaction, the tranquillity gradually disappears, and an emotion, kindred to that which was before the subject of contemplation, is gradually produced, and does itself actually exist in the mind. 20

William Wordsworth

GLOSSARY
ethereal (l.2): lacking material substance
rippled (l.6): pushed in small waves
strands (l.12): threads
quivering (l.13): vibrating slightly
intermingling (l.13): mixing together
web (l.13): network
recollected (l.16): remembered
kindred (l.18): similar

Help each other to understand the extracts. Do you agree or disagree with the ideas expressed?

9.4.2 Read what D. H. Lawrence had to say about the novel:

Now here we see the beauty and the great value of the novel. Philosophy, religion, science, they are all of them busy nailing things down, to get a stable equilibrium. Religion, with its nailed-down One God, who says *Thou shalt, Thou shan't,* and hammers home every time; philosophy, with its fixed ideas; science with its 'laws': they, all of them, all the time, want to nail us on to some tree or other. 5

But the novel, no. The novel is the highest example of subtle inter-relatedness that man has discovered. Everything is true in its own time, place, circumstance, and untrue outside of its own place, time, circumstance. If you try to nail anything down, in the novel, either it kills the novel, or the novel gets up and walks away with the nail. 10

Morality in the novel is the trembling instability of the balance. When the novelist puts his thumb in the scale, to pull down the balance to his own predilection, that is immorality.

GLOSSARY
stable (l.3): fixed and established
equilibrium (l.3): balance
scale (l.13): tray of an instrument used for weighing
predilection (l.14): preference

9.5 Reading without assistance

Yeats and Lawrence were very aware of the power of nostalgia. In the following passage, a writer looks back at his past.

When he was at school his mother used to meet him for a meal in the middle of the day. Sometimes they had lunch in a 'cook-house', sometimes in the park:

My mother used to bring fine lunches. She must have spent the morning on them. Above all she would bring ginger puddings, which I adored, in our white pudding-basin wrapped in an old towel to keep warm. For me it was like magic, on a cold day, to sit on one of the green slatted benches, and see the towel and then the pudding-cloth come off, and the steam from the pudding fume up. We had plates and spoons, and cornflour sauce and all sometimes: she could see how much this dish made me happy, and she brought it over and over. It was while eating one of these puddings that I first heard the cuckoo: and the note of the cuckoo and the taste of ginger still go together in my mind. Several times we ate our lunch there in the snow, and sharp, sharp cold. When I think of these times I recall the 5 10 bite of the cold and the hot taste and warm colour of the pudding together too. There were jays as well as the cuckoo; strange and exotic they seemed, and slow-moving – as indeed they are. Once, but only once, we saw the cuckoo that we so often heard. This bird seemed mysterious to me, so often close yet so seldom seen. I thought about the cuckoo a little as one might about the phoenix, as if there were only one.

15

My mother had what at any rate used once to be the country feeling for all living creatures: whether you like them or not, and quite probably you do not, they are immediately and vividly *there*, as much as any human being. After the time of this book, and when I was nine and we lived further out and in a more rural place, she once woke me up in the middle of the night, and what she wanted me for was to look through her bedroom window at the garden – it was mauve with the moonlight, I see it still – and listen to a nightingale, sitting on a bush not twenty feet away. It meant so much to her, partly because it was the first nightingale she had heard for twenty years: the move we had made was bringing back to her some of the things she had lost when she lost the world of her childhood. I shall never cease to be grateful for how she did such things for me: she was more romantic than was good for her – or others – but the simple fact is that it is better to care than not to care.

20

25

30

From *A London Childhood* by *John Holloway, 1966*

What actually *is* nostalgia? What part of your early life – if any – do you feel nostalgic about? Does everybody feel nostalgic? Is nostalgia harmful?

9.6 The limerick

The limerick is a humorous – and often indecent! – verse form consisting of five lines, with the first, second and fifth lines rhyming and the third and fourth lines rhyming. For example:

There was a young man of Bengal
Who went to a fancy-dress ball
He went just for fun
Dressed up as a bun
And a dog ate him up in the hall.

5

Is it funny? Can you mark the main stresses? What is the pattern? Can *you* write a limerick?

9.7 The ballad

The ballad is a narrative composition in rhyming verse. Look back at the extract from the *Rime of the Ancient Mariner* (4.6.4.) A Rime is a ballad. Originally, in the late Middle Ages, ballads were folk poems designed to be set to music and sung.

Here are two stanzas from an early English ballad with the second line 'echoed' in each, naming the herbs that might be sold at a local fair or market.

Scarborough Fair

Are you going to Scarborough Fair?
Parsley, Sage, Rosemary and Thyme.
Remember me to one who lived there,
For once she was a true love of mine.

Tell her to make me a cambric shirt –   5
Parsley, Sage, Rosemary and Thyme –
Without any seam or needlework.
She shall be a true love of mine.

GLOSSARY
cambric (l.5): fine cotton
seam (l.7): line joined by sewing

9.7.1 Listen:

 Song

The stranger lighted from his steed,
And ere he spake a word,
He seiz'd my lady's lilly hand,
And kiss'd it all unheard.

The stranger walk'd into the hall,   5
And ere he spake a word,
He kiss'd my lady's cherry lips,
And kiss'd em all unheard.

The stranger walk'd into the bower, –
But my lady first did go, –   10
Aye hand in hand into the bower,
Where my lord's roses blow.

My lady's maid had a silken scarf,
And a golden ring had she,
And a kiss from the stranger, as off he went   15
Again on his fair palfrey.   *John Keats (1795–1821)*

GLOSSARY
lighted (l.1): got off
steed (poetic) *(l.1):* horse (a spirited horse used for war)
ere (archaic) *(l.2):* before
lilly (l.3): (modern spelling: lily) white
bower (archaic) *(l.9):* lady's bedroom (also a shelter in the garden made of plants and flowers)
palfrey (archaic) *(l.16):* horse (a light horse not used for war).

i   Who is the narrator? How do you know? Can you tell the story in your own words?

ii What is the purpose of the first line in the first three stanzas?
What does the change in stress and word order imply in the second line of the third stanza?
How is the third stanza different from the first two?
What is the importance of the last stanza to the story?

iii Does the vocabulary change as the 'song' progresses?
What does it show?
The poem is a ballad. How is it different from *Scarborough Fair?* (Look at, for example, the number of lines, the rhythm, the rhyme and the tone.)

iv Do you know anything similar to a ballad or a limerick in your own language?

9.7.2 'Modern' poets also make use of the ballad. Listen:

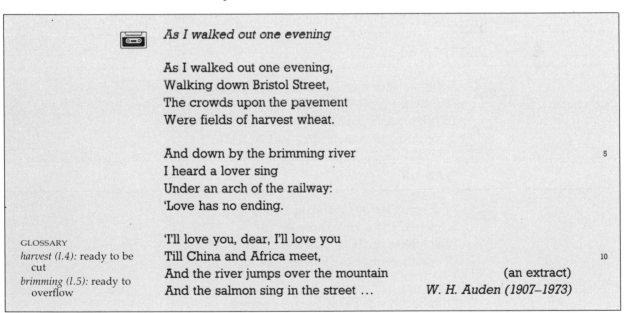

As I walked out one evening

As I walked out one evening,
Walking down Bristol Street,
The crowds upon the pavement
Were fields of harvest wheat.

And down by the brimming river   5
I heard a lover sing
Under an arch of the railway:
'Love has no ending.

'I'll love you, dear, I'll love you
Till China and Africa meet,   10
And the river jumps over the mountain   (an extract)
And the salmon sing in the street …   *W. H. Auden (1907–1973)*

GLOSSARY
harvest (l.4): ready to be cut
brimming (l.5): ready to overflow

i   Who is the narrator? Can you describe the context?

ii Does the metaphor in the third and fourth line help you 'see' the 'crowds'?
Is the word 'brimming' a good one in context? Why/Why not?
How does the eighth line contrast with the previous lines?
What is the effect of the exaggeration in the third stanza?
Is the ballad, as a whole, light? serious? funny?
How is this ballad different from the previous two ballads and the *Rime of the Ancient Mariner*?

9.8 Reading middle-English verse

9.8.1 *Geoffrey Chaucer's great poem* The Canterbury Tales *tells of a group of pilgrims who meet by chance at the Tabard Inn in Southwark (London) before setting off on horseback to go as pilgrims to the shrine of St. Thomas à Becket in Canterbury. The innkeeper, who offers to accompany them, suggests that to enliven the pilgrimage they each tell two stories on the outward journey and two on the way back: the person who's voted the best story-teller will then be entertained to supper by the others when they return to the Tabard.*

In the Prologue *to the Tales, Chaucer gives a lively description of some of the most important pilgrims, who are drawn from a wide variety of religious and secular backgrounds and whose later tales suit their personalities. Some are rogues but others are much gentler, more gracious folk.*

9.8.2 Listen to the following extracts. Don't worry if you don't understand everything. Simply try to match the characters with the following one line descriptions:

She had had five husbands	He loved freedom
She wept when she saw a mouse caught in a trap	He could break a door with his head
He said he had a piece of St. Peter's sail	He was a 'hot' lover

1) *The Knight*

A KNYGHT ther was, and that a worthy man,
That fro the tyme that he first bigan
To riden out, he loved chivalrie,
Trouthe and honour, fredom and curteisie.

2) *His son, the Squire*

With hym ther was his sone, a yong SQUIER,
A lovyere and a lusty bacheler,
With lokkes crulle as they were leyd in presse.
Of twenty yeer of age he was, I gesse.

......

Embrouded was he, as it were a meede   5
Al ful of fresshe floures, whyte and reede.
Syngynge he was, or floytynge, al the day;
He was as fressh as is the month of May.
Short was his gowne, with sleves longe and wyde.
Wel koude he sitte on hors and faire ryde.   10
He koude songes make and wel endite,
Juste and eek daunce, and weel purtreye and write.
So hoote he lovede that by nyghtertale
He sleep namoore than dooth a nyghtyngale.

3) *The Prioress*

Ther was also a Nonne, a PRIORESSE,

......

But, for to speken of hire conscience,
She was so charitable and so pitous
She wolde wepe, if that she saugh a mous
Kaught in a trappe, if it were deed or bledde.   5
Of smale houndes hadde she that she fedde
With rosted flessh, or milk and wastel-breed.
But soore wepte she if oon of hem were deed,
Or if men smoot it with a yerde smerte;
And al was conscience and tendre herte.   10

4) *The Wife of Bath*

A good WIF was ther of biside BATHE,
But she was somdel deef, and that was scathe.

......

Hir coverchiefs ful fyne weren of ground;
I dorste swere they weyeden ten pound
That on a Sonday weren upon hir heed.   5
Hir hosen weren of fyn scarlet reed,
Ful streite yteyd, and shoes ful moyste and newe.
Boold was hir face, and fair, and reed of hewe.
She was a worthy womman al hir lyve:
Housbondes at chirche dore she hadde fyve,   10
Withouten oother compaignye in youthe, –
But therof nedeth nat to speke as nowthe.

5) *The Miller*

The MILLERE was a stout carl for the nones;
Ful byg he was of brawn, and eek of bones.

That proved wel, for over al ther he cam,
At wrastlynge he wolde have alwey the ram.
He was short-sholdred, brood, a thikke knarre;   5
Ther was no dore that he nolde heve of harre,
Or breke it at a rennẏng with his heed.
His berd as any sowe or fox was reed,
And therto brood, as though it were a spade.

Upon the cop right of his nose he hade 10
A werte, and theron stood a toft of herys,
Reed as the brustles of a sowes erys;
His nosethirles blake were and wyde.
A swerd and bokeler bar he by his syde.
His mouth as greet was as a greet forneys. 15

6) *The Pardoner* – a person licensed to sell Indulgences for the forgiveness of sins

His walet lay biforn hym in his lappe,
Bretful of pardoun, comen from Rome al hoot.
... ...
He seyde he hadde a gobet of the seyl
That Seint Peter hadde, whan that he wente
Upon the see, til Jhesu Crist hym hente. 5
He hadde a croys of latoun ful of stones,
And in a glas he hadde pigges bones.
But with thise relikes, whan that he fond
A povre person dwellynge upon lond,
Upon a day he gat hym moore moneye 10
Than that the person gat in monthes tweye;
And thus, with feyned flaterye and japes,
He made the person and the peple his apes.

9.8.3 Read the following fairly literal, prose 'translation' into modern English of the description of the Pardoner:

His wallet lay in front of him on his lap, brimful of pardons, come all hot from Rome.
... ...
He said he had a small piece of the sail that Saint Peter had, when he walked upon the sea, until Jesus Christ caught hold of him. He had a cross of metal, set with stones, and in a glass he had some pigs' bones. But with these relics, when he found a poor parson living in the country, in one day he earned for himself more money than the parson earned in two months. And so, with false flattery and tricks, he made the parson and the people into his monkeys. 5

Do you think Chaucer likes this character? Do *you*? Do you prefer the original verse or the 'translation'? Why/Why not?

9.8.4 Read the following freer 'translations' of the descriptions of the Knight and the Miller. Notice that the translator (Nevill Coghill, Penguin Books 1951) has followed similar rhythms and rhyme-schemes to Chaucer but has tried to create more of an interesting poem in its own right than accurately 'translate' every single word.

242

The Knight

> There was a Knight, a most distinguished man,
> Who from the day on which he first began
> To ride abroad had followed chivalry,
> Truth, honour, generous thought and courtesy.

The Miller

> The Miller was a chap of sixteen stone
> A great stout fellow big in brawn and bone.
> He did well out of them, for he could go
> And win the ram at any wrestling show.
> Broad, knotty, short-shouldered, he would boast   5
> He could heave any door off hinge and post,
> Or take a run and break it with his head.
> His beard, like any sow or fox, was red
> And broad as well, as though it were a spade;
> And, at its tip, his nose displayed   10
> A wart on which there stood a tuft of hair
> Red as the bristles in an old sow's ear.
> His nostrils were as black as they were wide,
> He had a sword and buckler at his side,
> His mighty mouth was like a furnace door.   15

Obviously, Chaucer admires the Knight. How do you think he feels about the Miller?

Can you find any bits in the 'translation' that significantly differ from the original? (Make a close study.) Which do you prefer? Why?

9.8.5
Improving
understanding

Here is a glossary to assist you with your understanding of The Wife of Bath:

somdel (l.2): rather   *moyste (l.7):* fresh
scathe (l.2): a pity   *withouten (l.11):* besides
hosen (l.6): stockings   *as nowthe (l.12):* at present
streite yteyd (l.7): tightly fastened

Re-read the original Chaucer and try to complete the following 'translation' keeping the rhyme and rhythm working smoothly:

A worthy woman from beside _____ city
Was with us, somewhat _____, which was a _____.
Her kerchiefs were of finely woven ground;
I dared have sworn they _____ a good ten _____,
The ones she wore on _____, on her head.
Her hose were of the finest _____ red
And gartered tight, her _____ were _____ and _____

Bold was _____ _____, handsome, and _____ in hue.
A worthy woman all her life, what's more
She's had _____ _____, all at the church door,
Apart from other _____ in _____;
No need just now to _____ of that, forsooth.

What is Chaucer's attitude to the Wife of Bath?

9.8.6
Improving
understanding

Can you make verse or prose 'translations' of *either* The Prioress *or* The Squire, using the following glossaries to assist you?

The Squire

lokkes crulle (l.3): curly hair
leyd in presse (l.3): put in a press
meede (l.5): meadow
floytynge (l.7): playing the flute
endite (l.11): compose

juste (l.12): joust
eek (l.12): also
purtreye (l.12): draw
nyghtertale (l.13): night-time

The Prioress

wastel-breed (l.7): bread of the best quality
yerde (l.9): stick
smerte (adv) *(l.9):* smartly hard
conscience (l.10): kindliness

9.8.7
Do these extracts from the *Prologue* give you a vivid picture of medieval life? Would you like to have lived then? Why/Why not? Can you get hold of a copy of the *Prologue* and read some more?

9.8.8
Background

Listen to the tape to find out details of Chaucer's life and writings. Try to complete the chart below.

Geoffrey Chaucer	
APPROXIMATE DATE OF BIRTH:	
WIFE'S NAME:	
KINGS SERVED:	
COUNTRIES VISITED IN SERVICE ABROAD:	
ONE IMPORTANT OFFICE HELD:	
APPROXIMATE DATE OF DEATH:	
PLACE OF BURIAL:	
NAME OF THREE BOOKS WRITTEN BY HIM:	

The tapescript is printed in the Key in the back of the book.

9.9 Poetic drama and narrative

9.9.1
Anticipation

Tell each other all you know about the reign of Julius Caesar. (e.g. When was it? What was Caesar like? What were his victories? His losses?) If necessary, look in an encyclopaedia.

9.9.2
Following the main plot

Read the following short extracts from Acts I and II of *Julius Caesar* (1599–60) by Shakespeare. Summarise in your own words at the end of each scene what you imagine the plot to be. Some scenes have already been summarised.

ACT I
Scene 1. Rome. A street.
Enter FLAVIUS, MARULLUS *(two tribunes) and certain* COMMONERS.

SECOND COMMONER ... But, indeed, sir, we make holiday to see
Caesar and rejoice in his triumph.

MARULLUS

Wherefore rejoice? What conquest brings he home?
What tributaries follow him to Rome
To grace in captive bonds his chariot wheels?
You blocks, you stones, you worse than senseless things
O you hard hearts, you cruel men of Rome,
Knew you not Pompey?

wherefore: why
tributaries: one-time rulers that now acknowledge their submission
bonds: things used to tie up in order to restrain
Pompey: (the great Roman general 106–48 B.C.)

And do you now strew flowers in his way,
That comes in triumph over Pompey's blood?
Be gone!

strew: scatter

Exeunt: (i.e. they leave the stage)

(Exeunt all the commoners

FLAVIUS

... let no images
Be hung with Caesar's trophies. I'll about
And drive away the vulgar from the streets.

Summary:

245

Scene 2. The same. A public place.

Enter, in procession, with music, CAESAR; MARK ANTONY ...
CALPHURNIA *(Caesar's wife);* PORTIA *(Brutus' wife);* DECIUS; CICERO *(a
senator);* BRUTUS; CASSIUS *and* CASCA; *a great crowd following, among
them a* SOOTHSAYER.

Caesar and the Soothsayer

	CAESAR	What sayest thou to me now? Speak once again.
ides of March: 15th day of March	SOOTHSAYER	Beware the ides of March.
	CAESAR	He is a dreamer; let us leave him: pass.
		(Exeunt all but BRUTUS *and* CASSIUS

	BRUTUS	What means this shouting? I do fear the people
		Choose Caesar for their king.
	CASSIUS	Ay, do you fear it?
		Then must I think you would not have it so.
	BRUTUS	I would not, Cassius; yet I love him well.

Cassius and Brutus

CASSIUS	Brutus and Caesar: what should be in that 'Caesar'? Why should that name be sounded more than yours?

BRUTUS	What you have said I will consider ...

Re-enter CAESAR *and his* TRAIN.

<table>
<tr><td>CAESAR</td><td rowspan="2">Let me have men about me that are fat;
Sleek-headed men and such as sleep o' nights.
Yond Cassius has a lean and hungry look;
He thinks too much: such men are dangerous.
Fear him not, Caesar, he's not dangerous;
He is a noble Roman, and well given.</td></tr>
<tr><td>ANTONY</td></tr>
</table>

sleek-headed: with smooth and glossy hair
yond: over there

......	*(Exeunt* CAESAR *and his* TRAIN. CASCA *stays behind*

CASCA	... there was a crown offered him; and being offered him, he put it by with the back of his hand, thus; and then the people fell a-shouting.

CASSIUS	... who offered him the crown?
CASCA	Why, Antony.

	(Exit CASCA. *(Exit* BRUTUS.

CASSIUS	And after this let Caesar seat him sure; For we will shake him, or worse days endure.

Summary:

Scene 3

Summary:

During the night, thunder, lightning and other bad omens occur. Cicero, Casca and Cassius meet in the streets, and after Cicero has gone, Cassius wins Casca to the rising conspiracy.

ACT II
Scene 1
Enter BRUTUS

BRUTUS   I cannot, by the progress of the stars,
         Give guess how near to day.

spurn: show contempt
for the general: for the sake
   of all of us

It must be by his death: and, for my part,
I know no personal cause to spurn at him,
But for the general. He would be crown'd;
How that might change his nature, there's the
question.

Enter LUCIUS (his servant)

Is not tomorrow, boy, the ides of March?

Exit LUCIUS

whet: provoke

Since Cassius first did whet me against Caesar,
I have not slept.

*Enter the Conspirators, CASSIUS, CASCA, DECIUS, CINNA, METELLUS
CIMBER and TREBONIUS.*

CASSIUS   Let Antony and Caesar fall together.
BRUTUS   Our course will seem too bloody, Caius Cassius,
           To cut the head off and then hack the limbs
           Like wrath in death and envy afterwards;

hack: chop

For Antony is but a limb of Caesar.

CASSIUS	But it is doubtful yet
	Whether Caesar will come forth today or no;
	For he is superstitious grown of late.

Summary:

Scene 2

Summary

Strange portents in the night ('graves have yawn'd and yielded up their dead') have disturbed Calphurnia and she begs Caesar not to go to the Senate that day. At first, he yields to her persuasions, but he is won over by Decius and allows himself to be escorted there by the conspirators.

Scenes 3 and 4

Summary

Artemidorus, a Sophist, reads over a warning about Brutus and the others he wants to give to Caesar. Portia sends her servant to see how affairs are going in the Capitol.

ACT III
Scene 1
Rome. Before the Capitol, the Senate sitting above. A crowd of people; among them ARTEMIDORUS *and the* SOOTHSAYER. *Enter* CAESAR, BRUTUS, CASSIUS, CASCA, DECIUS, METELLUS, TREBONIUS, CINNA, ANTONY, LEPIDUS, POPILIUS, PUBLIUS *and others.*

CAESAR	*(to the* SOOTHSAYER*)* The ides of March are come.
SOOTHSAYER	Ay, Caesar, but not gone.
ARTEMIDORUS	Hail, Caesar! Read this schedule.
	......
CAESAR	What! is the fellow mad?

schedule: written document on a roll of paper

	CASSIUS	Pardon, Caesar; Caesar, pardon;
		As low as to thy foot doth Cassius fall,
		To beg enfranchisement for Publius Cimber.
pardon: forgive	CAESAR	I could be well mov'd if I were as you;
enfranchisement: liberty		If I could pray to move, prayers would move me;
resting: permanent		But I am constant as the northern star,
fellow: one similar		Of whose true-fix'd and resting quality
firmament: sky		There is no fellow in the firmament.

	CAESAR	Doth not Brutus bootless kneel?
	CASCA	Speak, hands, for me!
		(*They stab* CAESAR)
	CAESAR	Et tu, Brute? Then fall, Caesar!
		(*Dies*)
bootless: uselessly	CINNA	Liberty, Freedom, Tyranny is dead!
hence: from here		Run hence, proclaim, cry it about the streets.

	CASSIUS	Where's Antony?
	TREBONIUS	Fled to his house amaz'd.
		Men, wives and children stare, cry out and run
doomsday: the Day of		As it were doomsday.
Judgement		

Enter a servant.		
	BRUTUS	Soft! Who comes here? A friend of Antony's.
	SERVANT	Thus, Brutus, did my master bid me kneel;
		Thus did Mark Antony bid me fall down;
		And being prostrate, thus he bade me say:
		Brutus is noble, wise, valiant, and honest;
		Caesar was mighty, bold, royal and loving
Soft!: quiet		Say I love Brutus, and I honour him;
bid: order		Say I fear'd Caesar, honour'd him, and lov'd him.
prostrate: face down		

Re-enter ANTONY.		
	BRUTUS	But here comes Antony. Welcome, Mark Antony.
	ANTONY	O mighty Caesar! dost thou lie so low?
spoils: profits from war		Are all thy conquests, glories, triumphs, spoils,
measure: amount		Shrunk to this little measure? Fare thee well.

250

CASSIUS ...

Aside to Brutus You know not what you do; do not consent
That Antony speak in his funeral;
Know you how much the people may be mov'd
By that which he will utter?

(Exeunt all but Antony

ANTONY O! pardon me, thou bleeding piece of earth,
That I am meek and gentle with these butchers.

Summary:

9.9.3 By concentrating on the main plot we leave behind a lot of other things
Beneath the surface which happen, a lot of subtlety, a lot of detail in the build-up of character
and a lot of fine poetry.

*In Scene III Brutus unemotionally explains to the citizens in the Forum the reasons that
made Caesar's death necessary. Shakespeare, probably to highlight Brutus' inability to
inspire and control, writes in prose.*

Here is an extract:

BRUTUS Romans, countrymen, and lovers! hear me for my
cause; and be silent, that you may hear: believe
me for mine honour, and have respect to mine
honour, that you may believe: censure me in your
wisdom, and awake your senses, that you may the   5
better judge. If there be any in this assembly, any
dear friend of Caesar's, to him I say that Brutus'
love to Caesar was no less than his.

GLOSSARY
censure (l.4): condemn

*Antony, by contrast, wishes to stir up the crowd, which he does in fine oratorical poetry,
echoing Brutus' words and making them seem weak.*

i Listen:

🔲 ANTONY	Friends, Romans, countrymen, lend me your ears;
	I come to bury Caesar, not to praise him.
	The evil that men do lives after them,
	The good is oft interred with their bones;
	So let it be with Caesar. The noble Brutus 5
	Hath told you Caesar was ambitious;
	If it were so, it was a grievous fault,
	And grievously hath Caesar answer'd it.
	Here, under leave of Brutus and the rest, –
	For Brutus is an honourable man; 10
	So are they all, all honourable men, –
	Come I to speak in Caesar's funeral.
	He was my friend, faithful and just to me:
	But Brutus says he was ambitious;
	And Brutus is an honourable man. 15
	He hath brought many captives home to Rome,
	Whose ransoms did the general coffers fill:
	Did this in Caesar seem ambitious?
	When that the poor have cried, Caesar hath wept;
	Ambition should be made of sterner stuff: 20
	Yet Brutus says he was ambitious;
	And Brutus is an honourable man.
	You all did see that on the Lupercal
	I thrice presented him a kingly crown,
	Which he did thrice refuse: was this ambition? 25
	Yet Brutus says he was ambitious.
	And, sure, he is an honourable man.
	I speak not to disprove what Brutus spoke,
	But here I am to speak what I do know.
	You all did love him once, not without cause: 30
	What cause withholds you then to mourn for him?
	O judgment! thou art fled to brutish beasts,
	And men have lost their reason. Bear with me;
	My heart is in the coffin there with Caesar,
	And I must pause till it come back to me. 35
FIRST CITIZEN	Methinks there is much reason in his sayings.

GLOSSARY

interred (l.4): buried

grievous̆ (l.7): serious

under leave of (l.9): with the permission of

ransoms (l.17): captured valuables

general coffers (l.17): public treasury

sterner (l.20): more severe

Lupercal (l.23): Roman festival on the 15th February to ensure fertility for the people

brutish (l.32): unfeeling

Improving awareness

ii What is Antony's argument? Can you re-tell it in your own words?

iii Can you find at least one example of the following:

– Antony saying he is not going to do what in fact he does do
– a phrase repeated

– Antony saying the opposite of what he means
– a part of the speech that has echoes in another part of the speech
– a phrase which echoes Brutus' words
– balance (e.g. two opposites put side by side)
– a phrase which is meant to sound impressive and echo in your ears?

What is the overall effect?

    iv Where does Antony change theme? Can you divide the speech into sections?

    v What is the effect of the rhetorical questions? What is the answer meant to be in each case?

    vi How does the opening of Antony's speech differ from Brutus'?

    vii In what ways does Antony show his contempt for the conspirators?

    viii In what ways are sound and rhythm more important than *what* he has to say? What effect do they have?

    ix Which of the following do you agree with most?

'Antony cheapens the truth, he flatters, he persuades, he deceives, he mocks and he manipulates the sentiments of the crowd.'

'Antony genuinely feels what he is saying and he knows what the crowd is really feeling.'

Is it possible for both statements to be true?

9.9.4 How do you think the play continues? Can you find out?

9.9.5
Discussion It is often said that power corrupts the person who has it. Do you agree? Can you think of examples where this has been true in history? Can you think of examples where it is true today? Can you think of examples of power having a beneficial effect on the person who has it? Is power generally used for the public good?

9.10 Conclusion

9.10.1 Discuss the Unit in pairs.

UNIT 10

Working with language

10.1 Before reading a text

10.1.1
Language work   **i Ways of seeing**
Match the verbs with the definitions:

glimpse	look very carefully or searchingly (as if not able to see very well)
glance	have a passing view of
peep	look for a long time with eyes fixed and open
peer	look secretly
watch	give a rapid look
stare	be a spectator of

Use a dictionary to help you if necessary. Can all the verbs be used as nouns? Which prepositions (if any) follow them?

Complete the following sentences with one of the verbs in its correct form.

1 He _____ the match with great interest.

2 It was a most extraordinary sight! She just _____ and _____.

3 _____ over the wall, he could see what the neighbours were up to.

4 She quickly _____ at her watch.

In which can more than one verb be used?

ii Ways of taking hold
The words in the left-hand column have a very similar meaning. Put a tick in the boxes to indicate the attributes the words usually have. (One has been done for you; the ticks in brackets indicate attributes the word could have in certain contexts.) If necessary, add other words/ phrases in the 'other' column to help indicate the meaning. Use a dictionary if you wish .

	arms	hands	motion	suddenness	tightness	force	other
grasp							
grip							
grab							
embrace	✓	(✓)	(✓)	(✓)	(✓)	(✓)	closely with affection (usually a person)
seize							
clutch							
clench							
clasp							

Which prepositions (if any) follow them?

In the columns 'tightness' and 'force' add an extra tick for any verb that has greater intensity than the others.

Complete the following sentences with one of the verbs.

1 The two lovers _____.

2 Terrified, he _____ the sides of the chair, not daring to move.

3 The pickpocket _____ her bag and ran off.

4 The police _____ a large quantity of heroin.

In which can more than one verb be used?

10.1.2
Context *In the mistaken belief that she is an important heiress, Catherine Morland has been invited to an isolated and mysterious country manor by the family of the young man she wishes to marry. A reader of fashionable Gothic horror novels, she imagines the place to be like one of the places she has read about, inhabited by ghosts and full of other mysterious terrors. It turns out that what she really needs to fear is not these fancies but the greed of her future father-in-law. This is a scene where her 'romantic' imaginings about the house are at their height.*

10.1.3 Read the following passage once quickly without the glossary. Read again *with* the glossary (if necessary).

GLOSSARY
shutters (l.3): wooden outer covers for the window

She looked round the room. The window curtains seemed in motion. It could be nothing but the violence of the wind penetrating through the divisions of the shutters; and she stepped boldly forward, care-lessly humming a tune, to assure herself of its being so, peeped courageously behind each curtain, saw nothing on either low window   5
seat to scare her, and on placing a hand against the shutter, felt the strongest conviction of the wind's force. A glance at the old chest, as

she turned away from this examination, was not without its use; she scorned the causeless fears of an idle fancy, and began with a most happy indifference to prepare herself for bed. 'She should take her time; she should not hurry herself; she did not care if she were the last person up in the house. But she would not make up her fire; *that* would seem cowardly, as if she wished for the protection of light after she were in bed.' The fire therefore died away, and Catherine, having spent the best part of an hour in her arrangements, was beginning to think of stepping into bed, when, on giving a parting glance round the room, she was struck by the appearance of a high, old-fashioned black cabinet, which, though in a situation conspicuous enough, had never caught her notice before …

She took her candle and looked closely at the cabinet. It was not absolutely ebony and gold; but it was japan, black and yellow japan of the handsomest kind; and as she held her candle, the yellow had very much the effect of gold. The key was in the door, and she had a strange fancy to look into it; not, however, with the smallest expectation of finding anything, but it was so very odd … In short, she could not sleep till she had examined it. So, placing the candle with great caution on a chair, she seized the key with a very tremulous hand and tried to turn it; but it resisted her utmost strength. Alarmed, but not discouraged, she tried it another way; a bolt flew, and she believed herself successful; but how strangely mysterious! The door was still immovable. She paused a moment in breathless wonder. The wind roared down the chimney, the rain beat in torrents against the windows, and everything seemed to speak the awfulness of her situation. To retire to bed, however, unsatisfied on such a point, would be vain, since sleep must be impossible with the consciousness of a cabinet so mysteriously closed in her immediate vicinity. Again, therefore, she applied herself to the key, and after moving it in every possible way for some instants with the determined celerity of hope's last effort, the door suddenly yielded to her hand: her heart leaped with exultation at such a victory, and having thrown open each folding door, the second being secured only by bolts of less wonderful construction than the lock, though in that her eye could not discern anything unusual, a double range of small drawers appeared in view, with some larger drawers above and below them; and in the centre, a small door, closed also with a lock and key, secured in all probability a cavity of importance.

Catherine's heart beat quick, but her courage did not fail her. With a cheek flushed by hope, and an eye straining with curiosity, her fingers grasped the handle of a drawer and drew it forth. It was entirely empty. With less alarm and greater eagerness she seized a second, a third, a fourth; each was equally empty. Not one was left

ebony (l.21): made of a kind of hard, dark wood

japan (l.21): covered in hard varnish

tremulous (l.28): trembling

in torrents (l.32): violent floods

celerity (l.39): speed

discern (l.43): detect

unsearched, and in not one was anything found. Well read in the art of concealing a treasure, the possibility of false linings to the drawers did not escape her, and she felt round each with anxious acuteness in vain. The place in the middle alone remained now unexplored; and though she had 'never from the first had the smallest idea of finding anything in any part of the cabinet, and was not in the least disappointed at her ill success thus far, it would be foolish not to examine it thoroughly while she was about it.' It was some time however before she could unfasten the door, the same difficulty occurring in the management of this inner lock as of the outer; but at length it did open; and not vain, as hitherto, was her search; her quick eyes directly fell on a roll of paper pushed back into the further part of the cavity, apparently for concealment, and her feelings at that moment were indescribable. Her heart fluttered, her knees trembled, and her cheeks grew pale. She seized, with an unsteady hand, the precious manuscript, for half a glance sufficed to ascertain written characters and … resolved instantly to peruse every line before she attempted to rest.

The dimness of the light her candle emitted made her turn to it with alarm; but there was no danger of its sudden extinction; it had yet some hours to burn; and that she might not have any greater difficulty in distinguishing the writing than what its ancient date might occasion, she hastily snuffed it. Alas! It was snuffed and extinguished in one. A lamp could not have expired with more awful effect. Catherine, for a few moments, was motionless with horror. It was done completely; not a remnant of light in the wick could give hope to the rekindling breath. Darkness impenetrable and immovable filled the room. A violent gust of wind, rising with sudden fury, added fresh horror to the moment. Catherine trembled from head to foot. In the pause which succeeded, a sound like receding footsteps and the closing of a distant door struck on her affrighted ear. Human nature could support no more. A cold sweat stood on her forehead, the manuscript fell from her hand, and groping her way to bed, she jumped hastily in, and sought some suspension of agony by creeping far underneath the clothes …

The manuscript so wonderfully found, so wonderfully accomplishing the morning's prediction, how was it to be accounted for? What could it contain? To whom could it relate? By what means could it have been so long concealed? And how singularly strange that it should fall to her lot to discover it! …

The housemaid's folding back her window-shutters at eight o'clock the next day was the sound which first roused Catherine; and she opened her eyes, wondering that they could ever have been closed,

linings (l.53): material used to cover an inner space

sufficed (l.67): was sufficient

snuffed (l.74): trimmed the burnt part of the cord (the wick) in the candle

on objects of cheerfulness; her fire was already burning, and a bright morning had succeeded the tempest of the night. Instantaneously, with the consciousness of existence, returned her recollection of the manuscript; and springing from the bed in the very moment of the maid's going away, she eagerly collected every scattered sheet which had burst from the roll on its falling to the ground, and flew back to enjoy the luxury of their perusal on her pillow …

95

100

Her greedy eye glanced rapidly over a page. She started at its import. Could it be possible, or did not her senses play her false? An inventory of linen, in coarse and modern characters, seemed all that was before her! If the evidence of sight might be trusted, she held a washing-bill in her hand. She seized another sheet, and saw the same articles with little variation; a third, a fourth, and a fifth presented nothing new. Shirts, stockings, cravats, and waistcoats faced her in each. Two others, penned by the same hand, marked an expenditure scarcely more interesting, in letters, hair-powder, shoe-string, and breeches-ball. And the larger sheet, which had enclosed the rest, seemed by its first cramp line, 'To poultice chestnut mare' – a farrier's bill! Such was the collection of papers (left perhaps, as she could then suppose, by the negligence of a servant in the place whence she had taken them) which had filled her with expectation and alarm and robbed her of half her night's rest! She felt humbled to the dust…

105

110

115

- started (l.102): jumped with surprise
- import (l.103): meaning
- inventory (l.104): list of particular items
- characters (l.104): letters of the alphabet
- cravats (l.108): broad loosely-knotted neckties
- breeches-ball (l.111): a ball made of special cleaning material for the cleaning of breeches (garments buttoned below the knee worn for horse-riding)
- cramp (l.112): written in a small space with the letters close together
- poultice (l.112): apply a heated soft mass to the skin to reduce inflammation
- mare (l.112): female horse
- farrier's (l.112): horse-doctor's

Nothing could now be clearer than the absurdity of her recent fancies. To suppose that manuscript of many generations back could have remained undiscovered in a room such as that, so modern, so habitable! – or that she should be the first to possess the skill of unlocking a cabinet, the key of which was open to all!

120

10.1.4 What is your first reaction to reading the story?

10.1.5 Improving understanding and awareness

i Try to answer the following questions in pairs.

What caused the curtains to move?
What do you think Catherine imagined caused them to move?
Was she right to be afraid?
How did she react to her fear?
Why does she look in the cabinet?
Why wouldn't she be able to sleep without looking in?
What did she find inside?
Why did her 'heart flutter' and her knees tremble?
How did the candle go out?
What had she wanted to do?
Why did a cold sweat stand on her forehead?
What was her reaction to finding the roll of paper?

How was the house 'different' in the morning?

Why was she 'humbled to the dust'?

What was her mood at the end of the extract?

ii Find two examples of Catherine's rather unconvincing determination not to be afraid.

What do the sentences in speech marks show?

What was the cabinet like, both inside and outside?

How did Catherine open it? (Describe the actions in your own words.)

How does the writer show us that Catherine is nervous?

What sort of events do you imagine occur in the horror novels Catherine reads? Which to Catherine seem parallelled in her night in the Abbey?

What part does the weather play in this passage?

Do you find Catherine silly or just innocent? How would you describe her character?

10.1.6
Language

i **Vocabulary**

a) Find examples of some of the words you explored in 10.1.1.

How are they used? Do they mean in context what you thought they meant? What prepositions follow the verbs? What other words occur in the passage (either verbs or nouns) that relate to ways of seeing?

b) What are the following:

– the past tense of 'step'
– a noun related to the verb 'arrange'
– the opposite of 'encourage'
– a noun related to the adjective 'dim'
– an adjective that describes 'sweat' when you are frightened
– another word for 'storm'
– a preposition which can follow 'yield'

Answers can be found in the passage.

ii **Structure**

The first and second sentences of the extract are short, the third long. Examine carefully how they are constructed (e.g. the use of conjunctions, punctuation, the position of the subject). What does the construction help the writer to suggest?

iii **Style**

a) Can you indicate some of the structural features in the passage (e.g. verb forms) which show the writer is telling a story?

b) What words/phrases are used to describe the weather? Why do you think the writer chooses to use cliches?

c) What do you think the writer's attitude to Catherine is? How is it conveyed? Does she tell us explicitly?

10.1.7
Discussion
Do you read romantic novels or go to see romantic films? Why/Why not? Can you describe an occasion when your imagination led you into romantic ideas that later proved false?

10.1.8
Notes
The previous extract is from Northanger Abbey *by Jane Austen. It was written in her early twenties but not published until after her death in 1817 at the age of 42. Her other novels include* Sense and Sensibility *(1811),* Pride and Prejudice *(1813),* Mansfield Park *(1814) and* Emma *(1815). She did not achieve fame until after her death. In what year was she born?*

10.2 After reading a text

10.2.1
Anticipation
Discuss one of the following statements:

 a) Man's view of God differs from country to country.
 b) Nowadays, religion is in decline.

10.2.2
Listen to the following poem as many times as you like. Try to answer the questions:

Who are the main 'characters' in the poem?
What is the situation?
Where does the dialogue begin?

 Love

Love bade me welcome; yet my soul drew back,
Guilty of dust and sin.
But quick-eyed Love, observing me grow slack
From my first entrance in,
Drew nearer to me, sweetly questioning,   5
If I lack'd any thing.

A Guest, I answer'd worthy to be here:
Love said, You shall be he.
I the unkind, ungrateful? Ah, my dear,
I cannot look on thee.   10
Love took my hand, and smiling did reply,
Who made the eyes but I?

Truth, Lord, but I have marr'd them: let my shame
Go where it doth deserve.
And know you not, says Love, who bore the blame?   15
My dear, then I will serve.
You must sit down, says Love, and taste my meat:
So I did sit and eat.

GLOSSARY
bade me welcome (l.1): welcomed me
slack (l.3): inactive and limp
ungrateful (l.9): showing no gratitude
marr'd (l.13): spoilt

i Improving understanding

Which of these comments would you accept as being a fair interpretation of the poem?
Change any you don't agree with.
Add others if you wish.

The poet describes an encounter between love and the poet's soul.

Love and the poet's soul are metaphors for God and Man.

The offering of a meal – a traditional expression of friendship – is a sign of God's hospitality.

The poet's humility and guilt at his sin contrast with God's generous and gentle nobility.

The meal represents the communion table at the altar.

God is both patient and humane.

'Who bore the blame?' refers to Jesus on the Cross.

ii Style

Love is personified throughout the poem. Can you find three or four different kinds of words which show that 'he' acts/speaks or looks like a real person?

Can you pick out some words to illustrate how the poet shows his sense of unworthiness to be a guest at Love's feast?

The poem is based on a complicated rhyme scheme.
Try to identify it.

There are contrasts in the poem between
– the host and the guest
– questions and answers in the dialogue
– servant and guest

Can you find words that build up these contrasts?

Can you find a pun in the poem? What effect does it have?

The words and images have a homely vividness. Which words/phrases in particular give the poem concreteness and strength?

What is the effect of the last two lines?

There is a contrast in the poem between short and long sentences. What effect does it have?

10.2.3 Listen to the following poem as many times as you like.

Drowning is not so pitiful
As the attempt to rise.
Three times, 'tis said, a sinking man
Comes up to face the skies,
And then declines forever   5
To that abhorred abode,
Where hope and he part company –
For he is grasped of God.
The Maker's cordial visage,
However good to see,   10
Is shunned, we must admit it,
Like an adversity.

GLOSSARY
abhorred (l.6): hateful
abode (l.6): dwelling-place
cordial (l.9): friendly
shunned (l.11): avoided

i Improving understanding

Which of these comments would you accept as being a fair
interpretation of the meaning of the poem? Change any you don't
agree with. Add others if you wish.

The poem expresses Man's unwillingness to meet God in death.
In trying to avoid death we are trying to avoid God, even though God
   is a friend.
Man's clinging on to life is worthy of contempt.

ii Style

What rhyme scheme does the poem have?
Is there any regularity in the rhythm?
What is the 'abhorred abode'? Is it an effective phrase? Why/why not?

Pick out words which describe

   – Man

   – God

   – Man's attitude to God

What contrasts are there in the poem?

iii How is this poem different from the previous one?

**10.2.4
Language**

i Find an example in the first poem of 'reported speech'.

ii What tense is the second poem in? Find two examples of the passive
voice.

**10.2.5
Notes**

*The first poem is by George Herbert (1593–1633). He had an aristocratic background and
was a favourite at the Court of James I. He was a friend of John Donne's and like Donne,
turned away from secular advancement to enter the Church. He did not seek any preferment
but instead remained a country parson in a small Wiltshire village until his death.*

*The second poem is by Emily Dickinson, the American poetess (1830–1886). A recluse for
most of her life, she wrote nearly 2000 poems, only six of which were published in her
lifetime. Her strange, passionate poems have a distinctive, epigrammatic style.*

262

10.3 Focus on language work

If you wish to improve your English you may like to take note of such things as the vocabulary and the grammar of what you read. Of course a lot of grammar in literature is used creatively and is not common in everyday use. Many words, too, are now out-of-date and no longer useful for you. But this is not true for a large part of the literature chosen for this book. Much you can take note of and remember. Where difficult words are probably *not* useful they have been put in the glossaries. (Nevertheless, some you might find useful!) The more useful ones have sometimes been put in exercises. You can extend this work if you wish by doing such things as checking on the pronunciation of the words, classifying them (e.g. abode – noun) and finding in a dictionary other words that relate to them (e.g. abide – verb; abiding – adjective, etc.). Grammar is worked on when it is thought to be helpful for you. Overall, though, probably the best way to improve your English is to simply read the literature as best you can and talk or write about it in English!

10.4 Irony

10.4.1 Irony is a form of subtle mockery. In its purest form it is a way of speaking or writing in which words are made to mean the opposite of their normal or their apparent meaning.

Read this extract:

GLOSSARY
lodging (l.2): accommodation in someone else's house
queer (l.3): strange
cordial (l.5): reviving drink
haranguing (l.6): loudly criticising
rattling (l.6): lively

This was the sort of discourse that went on between them every day now. The landlord of the lodging, who had heard that they were a queer couple, had doubted if they were married at all, especially as he had seen Arabella kiss Jude one evening when she had taken a little cordial; and he was about to give them notice to quit, till by chance overhearing her one night haranguing Jude in rattling terms, and ultimately flinging a shoe at his head, he recognised the note of genuine wedlock; and concluding that they must be respectable, said no more.

5

from *Jude the Obscure (1895)* by *Thomas Hardy*

What details are represented ironically? How do you know they are ironic?

Jane Austen is often thought of as an ironic writer. Can you find examples of irony in the extract at the beginning of this Unit?

Can you find any other examples in previous Units?

10.5 Reading without assistance

In the first Unit, there were poems and passages about the very young. In this, the last Unit, we have a poem about a baby. What does he mean to the writer?

Ecce Homo

Suddenly, in the middle of the floor,
Without holding on to anything,
There you are, standing up!
Startled, we all cheer and clap round you: 'clever!'

You stare at us as if we were mad,   5
Gingerly bend your knees, then brace them:
Just my natural human posture, your face says.
But then you catch on, and clap your hands too,
Sit down with a bump, too hard, and cry a little.

So, you make the great transition: 10
You are an upright man.
Just for a moment this time:
Soon it will seem primitive to you to crawl.

Imagine the tall noisy individuals you call 'Man!'
Going on all fours down the street!   15
Such nonchalant pride to join us,
You with your pale hair and face clear as an angel's.
Bare puppy buttocks quivering with pride!

We'll try not to let you down.

Eventually we shall need to lead you to the discovery   20
How it is possible to be both upright and abject:
Or like you, wavering at first stance,
But without an audience to cheer:
The inward primitive, shakily taking to the attitude of the body,
Hardly daring to explore the perspective around it,   25
As the slow-learning psyche joins the body, so much of a life-time after
This first elevation to the two-legged assertion.

David Holbrook (born 1923)

Do you like babies? What do they suggest to you? Innocence? The future? New life? Or just plain, hard work!?

264

10.6 Different kinds of reading

10.6.1   **i Anticipation**
What are these people doing? What are they using? What is their occupation? Can you describe the process?

ii Context
Silas Marner, a weaver, used to live in 'Lantern Yard' in the town where he was a member of a 'narrow religious sect'. Fifteen years ago he moved into the country having been falsely accused of stealing church money and having lost his fiancee. He settled in Raveloe, 'a village where many of the old echoes lingered, undrowned by new voices' which lies 'in the rich central plain of what we are pleased to call Merry England'. In those days it was unusual to move from town to country – the move was mainly the other way – and Silas was regarded with fear and suspicion.

iii Scanning (Reading to pick out details)
Read the following quickly and underline the features which distinguished Raveloe from Lantern Yard (e.g. 'orchards looking lazy').

GLOSSARY
lounging (l.3): standing lazily
service-time (l.4): the time when the regular ceremonies at the church took place
the Rainbow (l.5): (the name of the pub)

And what could be more unlike that Lantern Yard world than the world in Raveloe? – orchards looking lazy with neglected plenty; the large church in the wide churchyard, which men gazed at lounging at their own doors in service-time; the purple-faced farmers jogging along the lanes or turning in at the Rainbow; homesteads, where men supped heavily and slept in the light of the evening hearth, and where women seemed to be laying up a stock of linen for the life to come.

5

iv Beneath the surface

What do the following words tell you about Raveloe and its inhabitants?

lazy	wide	purple-faced
neglected	gazed	jogging
large	lounging	heavily

What does the last phrase from 'and where women ...' imply? What do you think the author's attitude to the women is?

v Skimming (Reading to get the general idea)

Read the rest of the paragraph quickly and summarise the essential points in a single sentence.

GLOSSARY
benumbed (l.2): dulled
groves (l.6): small woods
sullenness (l.9): ill-humour
unpropitious (l.10): not benevolent

There were no lips in Raveloe from which a word could fall that would stir Silas Marner's benumbed faith to a sense of pain. In the early ages of the world, we know, it was believed that each territory was inhabited and ruled by its own divinities, so that a man could cross the bordering heights and be out of the reach of his native gods, whose presence was confined to the streams and the groves and the hills among which he had lived from his birth. And poor Silas was vaguely conscious of something not unlike the feeling of primitive men, when they fled thus, in fear or in sullenness, from the face of an unpropitious deity. It seemed to him that the Power he had vainly trusted in among the streets and at the prayer-meetings, was very far away from this land in which he had taken refuge, where men lived in careless abundance, knowing and needing nothing of that trust, which, for him, had been turned to bitterness.

5

10

---

vi Beneath the surface

a) What do we learn about:

– Silas' feelings
– the effect of Raveloe on Silas
– the difference between Lantern Yard and Raveloe

b) What do the following words refer to?

'faith' 'the Power' 'that trust'

**10.6.2
Intensive reading**
(Reading to try to understand everything)

i Read the following passage carefully as many times as you like. Which words/phrases *tell* us explicitly about Silas' present personal state and which *suggest* it implicitly?

His first movement after the shock had been to work in his loom; and he went on with this unremittingly, never asking himself why, now he was come to Raveloe, he worked far on into the night to finish the tale of Mrs Osgood's table-linen sooner than she expected – without contemplating beforehand the money she would put into his hands for the work. He seemed to weave, like the spider, from pure impulse, without reflection. Every man's work, pursued steadily, tends in this way to become an end in itself, and so to bridge over the loveless chasms of his life. Silas's hand satisfied itself with throwing the shuttle, and his eye with seeing the little squares in the cloth complete themselves under his effort. Then there were the calls of hunger; and Silas, in his solitude, had to provide his own breakfast, dinner, and supper, to fetch his own water from the well, and put his own kettle on the fire; and all these immediate promptings helped, along with the weaving, to reduce his life to the unquestioning activity of a spinning insect. He hated the thought of the past; there was nothing that called out his love and fellowship toward the strangers he had come amongst; and the future was all dark, for there was no Unseen Love that cared for him. Thought was arrested by utter bewilderment, now its old narrow pathway was closed, and affection seemed to have died under the bruise that had fallen on its keenest nerves.

GLOSSARY
unremittingly (l.2): without stopping
chasms (l.9): huge gaps
promptings (l.14): things which moved him to action
bewilderment (l.20): uncertainty
keenest (l.21): most sensitive

5
10
15
20

ii   Are there any phrases that suggest Silas' feelings before he came to Raveloe?

iii   What are the changes that have taken place in Silas? (Summarise them in your own words.)

10.6.3   *Mrs Osgood paid Silas in gold – five bright guineas. In one way the guineas were nothing to a man who 'saw no vista beyond countless days of weaving'. However, they were 'another element of life' and he was pleased 'to feel them in his palm'.*

i   Intensive reading
Read carefully and note how Silas' attitude to money subtly changes.

He had seemed to love it little in the years when every penny had its purpose for him; for he loved the *purpose* then. But now, when all the purpose was gone, that habit of looking towards the money and grasping it with a sense of fulfilled effort made a loam that was deep enough for the seeds of desire; and as Silas walked homeward across the fields in the twilight, he drew out the money and thought it was brighter in the gathering gloom.

GLOSSARY
loam (l.4): good earth for growing plants in

5

Extensive reading (Reading for pleasure)
Read the following extract quickly. At this stage don't worry about any
words you don't understand. See if you find satisfaction in the way the
writer helps you to understand the change in Silas.

Gradually the guineas, the crowns, and the half-crowns, grew to a
heap, and Marner drew less and less for his own wants, trying to
solve the problem of keeping himself strong enough to work sixteen
hours a day on as small an outlay as possible …

… the love of accumulating money grows an absorbing passion in   5
men whose imaginations, even in the very beginning of their hoard,
showed them no purpose beyond it. Marner wanted the heaps of ten
to grow into a square, and then into a larger square; and every added
guinea, while it was itself a satisfaction, bred a new desire. In this
strange world, made a hopeless riddle to him, he might, if he had a   10
less intense nature, have sat weaving, weaving – looking towards the
end of his pattern, or towards the end of his web, till he forgot the
riddle, and everything else but his immediate sensations; but the
money had come to mark off his weaving into periods, and the
money not only grew, but it remained with him. He began to think it   15
was conscious of him, as his loom was, and he would on no account
have exchanged those coins, which had become his familiars, for
other coins with unknown faces. He handled them, he counted them,
till their form and colour were like the satisfaction of a thirst to him;
but it was only in the night, when his work was done, that he drew   20
them out to enjoy their companionship. He had taken up some bricks
in his floor underneath his loom, and here he had made a hole in
which he set the iron pot that contained his guineas and silver coins,
covering the bricks with sand whenever he replaced them …

So, year after year, Silas Marner had lived in this solitude, his guineas 25
rising in the iron pot, and his life narrowing and hardening itself more
and more into a mere pulsation of desire and satisfaction that had no
relation to any other being. His life had reduced itself to the functions
of weaving and hoarding, without any contemplation of an end
towards which the functions tended. The same sort of process has   30
perhaps been undergone by wiser men, when they have been cut off
from faith and love – only, instead of a loom and a heap of guineas,
they have had some erudite research, some ingenious project, or
some well-knit theory. Strangely Marner's face and figure shrank and
bent themselves into a constant mechanical relation to the objects of   35
his life, so that he produced the same sort of impression as a handle
or a crooked tube, which has no meaning standing apart. The
prominent eyes that used to look trusting and dreamy, now looked as
if they had been made to see only one kind of thing that was very

small, like tiny grain, for which they hunted everywhere: and he was 40
so withered and yellow, that, though he was not yet forty, the children
always called him 'Old Master Marner'...

... at night he closed his shutters, and made fast his doors, and drew
forth his gold. Long ago the heap of coins had become too large for
the iron pot to hold them, and he had made for them two thick leather 45
bags, which wasted no room in their resting place, but lent
themselves flexibly to every corner. How the guineas shone as they
came pouring out of the dark leather mouths! ...

He loved the guineas best, but he would not change the silver – the
crowns and half-crowns that were his own earnings, begotten by his 50
labour; he loved them all. He spread them out in heaps and bathed
his hands in them; then he counted them and set them up in regular
piles, and felt their rounded outlines between his thumb and fingers,
and thought fondly of the guineas that were only half-earned by the
work in his loom, as if they had been unborn children – thought of the 55
guineas that were coming slowly through the coming years, through
all his life, which spread far away before him, the end quite hidden
by countless days of weaving...

iii   What feelings does the extract arouse in you? What do you think about
      Silas and his life?

iv   **Looking more closely**
      Re-read the passage. Look up in a dictionary – or ask another person in
      your class – any words you would like to know the meaning of.

      What extra details do you now know about Silas (e.g. his age, his
      appearance, the length of his working day etc.)? How has he changed?

      His coins are described as his 'familiars', his 'companions', his
      'children'. What do these images tell you about his feelings for his
      money?

      Why does he take up 'some bricks in the floor'?

      Can you find some phrases that show Silas' pleasure in actually
      handling his money?

      What is the 'riddle'?

      The 'weaving' becomes a metaphor. What is it made to suggest?

v   **Making comparisons**
      Look back at the extract from Volpone (Unit 8). Compare Silas' and
      Volpone's attitude to money. Which do you have most sympathy
      with? Why?

vi   **Follow-up work**
      Tell the story of a time when you felt guilty about spending some money.

10.6.4
Language

i The *past perfect* tense indicates a time further in the past as seen from a definite viewpoint in the past.

e.g. 'He *had seemed* (past perfect) to love it little in the years when every penny *had* (past simple) its purpose for him.' *Had seemed* refers to a point further in the past than *had*.

Look back over the extracts from *Silas Marner* and find other examples. Select *one* example. What does it show?

ii Comment on the use of punctuation in the first extract in 10.6.1.

10.6.5
Notes

Mary Ann Evans (1819–1880) wrote the novel Silas Marner *in 1861 under the male pseudonym George Eliot by which she is now known. She lived with the writer George Henry Lewes and never married him. Her novels deal with social problems of the day, not least the role of the poor and underprivileged. Her best-known novel is probably* Middlemarch. *Why do you think she chose to write under a male pseudonym?*

10.7 Conclusion

i Go back to 1.1.2. and 1.1.3. Make as many changes to your original notes as you wish.

ii Write answers to the following questions:

What did you find most difficult in the book?
What did you find easy?
What do you need more help on?
What did you like?
What did you dislike?
What other English literature did you read when studying this book?

Discuss your answers with a partner and then with the whole class.

A short history of British and American literature

The first major work in English still read today – though generally read in a modern English translation – is the Anglo-Saxon epic poem, *Beowulf*. The story has no known author and while elements of it may have been passed down in oral tradition between 300 and 600 A.D., it probably was not composed until the eighth century. The first great writer read in the original is Geoffrey Chaucer (?1343–1400) author of *The Canterbury Tales*. Other long poems of the fourteenth century, written in the alliterative verse style characteristic of early English poetry, are *Sir Gawain and The Green Knight* (?1375) written in the dialect of North-West England and *Piers Plowman* by William Langland (?1330–?1386). The medieval *Mystery* and *Miracle Plays* based on Christian stories and performed first in churches and then in the street at festival times are still important and popular, as is Sir Thomas Malory's *Morte D'Arthur*, a prose version of the legends of King Arthur.

Poetry The cultivated Renaissance man of the sixteenth century was expected to be skilled in the arts of music and poetry and it is not surprising that two major poets of this period were courtiers of Henry VIII: Sir Thomas Wyatt (1503–1542), who introduced the sonnet form to England, and the Earl of Surrey (?1517–1547), who established the blank verse form used by later poets. Other than William Shakespeare (1564–1616), the two most significant poets of the second half of the century were Sir Philip Sidney (1554–1586), often referred to as the perfect Elizabethan courtier, and Edmund Spenser (1552–1599), whose dream-like, yet morally earnest, *Faerie Queen* recreated the world of King Arthur. Shakespeare's best poetry – vivid and inspired – is to be found in his plays. Nevertheless, his *Sonnets* and even his long early poems, like *Venus and Adonis*, still appeal today. His near-contemporaries include John Donne (1572–1631), the most dazzling of the so-called 'metaphysical' poets, whose poems on love and religion were enlivened by colloquial language and by images drawn from secular learning; the clergyman George Herbert (1593–1633) and the stylistically more classical Ben Jonson (?1573–1637).

The confusion of the Civil War (1642–1652), where the country roughly divided into Royalists on the one hand and Puritans and Parliamentarians on the other, were reflected in the 'metaphysical' verse of Andrew Marvell (1621–1678), both a Puritan and, later, a favourite of King Charles II. The Cavalier poets (followers of King Charles I), much influenced by Ben Jonson, included Robert Herrick (1591–1674) and Thomas Carew (?1595–?1640). A committed Puritan was the unique, but nowadays rather unfashionable, John Milton (1608–1674). His epic poem *Paradise Lost* attempted to 'justify the ways of God to man' and was written in very latinized English.

After the Restoration of the monarchy (1660), poets such as John Dryden (1631–1700) and later, so-called 'Augustans' like Alexander Pope (1688–1744) were – in common with other artists of their day – much more 'social' and satirical in tone. Late eighteenth- and early nineteenth-century writers include the Scot, Robert Burns (1759–1796), the extraordinary and highly individual William Blake (1757–1827) and George Crabbe (1754–1832), a skilled narrator in verse.

Looking back, the individuality of Blake seems to announce the beginning of the Romantic movement, which emphasised the importance of the human imagination and the central position of the individual in Nature. It stood up against the spirit of science and the effects of industrialisation. The poems of William Wordsworth (1770–1850) set out to describe 'incidents and situations from common life' in 'language really used by men', while those of his friend Samuel Coleridge (1772–1834) concentrate on 'persons and characters supernatural'. The egocentric Percy Shelley (1792–1822) and the young genius John Keats (1795–1821) both survived their disillusionment with Revolutionary France to write some inspired poetry. The glamorous Lord Byron (1788–1821), also sometimes thought of as a

271

Romantic, was both more humorous and more socially satirical in his verse.

During the reign of Queen Victoria (1837–1901) the novel was the major literary achievement. By comparison, poetry was self-consciously public and artificial. The most characteristic poetry, perhaps, was the melancholic verse written by the enormously successful Alfred Lord Tennyson (1809–1892), the impressive-sounding verse of Matthew Arnold (1822–1888) and the energetic but odd *Dramatic Monologues* of Robert Browning (1812–1889). American poetry was noted for the Transcendentalist verse of Walt Whitman (1819–1892), in particular his autobiographical *Leaves of Grass*, and the unique contributions of Emily Dickinson (1830–1886). The Georgian poets (1911–1922) were essentially minor poets although some – for example, Isaac Rosenberg (1890–1918) and Wilfred Owen (1893–1918) – wrote some extraordinary poetry about their experience as soldiers in the First World War.

Later, two American expatriates T. S. Eliot (1888–1965) and Ezra Pound (1885–1972) changed the direction of English poetry and gave it an essentially twentieth-century voice in the face of a disintegrating civilization. W. B. Yeats (1865–1939), the great Irish poet, was both more directly political and more consciously symbolic. The other poets of the thirties and forties either displayed their social conscience, like W. H. Auden (1907–1973), or their gifts with language, like Dylan Thomas (1914–1953). Noted American poets of recent years have been William Carlos Williams (1883–1963), Robert Frost (1874–1963) and Robert Lowell (1917–1977). Two well-known contemporary poets in England are the low-key Philip Larkin (1922–1985) and the, at times, intensely bleak Ted Hughes (1930–   ), who is now the Poet Laureate.

Prose   In Tudor times (1485–1603), there were many fine preachers, critics, historians and translators, although some educated writers of the early part of the period, like the humanist Sir Thomas More (1478–1535), wrote their best work in Latin. The Authorized Version of the Bible, which has since had an enormous influence on English Literature, was translated in 1611. John Donne preached at St. Pauls from 1621 to 1631. His sermons were witty and inspired. However, it was John Bunyan (1628–1680), whose *Pilgrim's Progress* was at one time the most widely read book in England next to the Bible, who was the Authorized Version's natural successor.

Even during Donne's lifetime Jacobean prose was becoming more utilitarian and plain. Later, under the influence of Francis Bacon (1561–1626), the Royal Society was founded (1662) and prose sought for the first time to become scientific in tone: precise, analytical and practical. However, other styles still existed. Milton's pamphlets like the *Areopagitica* (1644) were rhetorical, Samuel Pepys (1633–1703) in his *Diary* was gossipy and domestic and Jonathan Swift (1667–1745) was both polemical and ironic.

Modern journalism was born out of the *Spectator* and *Tatler* in the early eighteenth century through the enormous influence of the coffee-houses. These periodicals aimed to 'cultivate and polish human life by promoting virtue and knowledge'. The light of reason was spread over a wide range of subjects. The greatest prose writer of this century was Dr. Samuel Johnson (1709–1784), a conformist as well as a sensitive, powerful individual. Edward Gibbon (1737–1794) wrote his account of the *History of the Decline and Fall of the Roman Empire* (1776–1778).

From the middle of the eighteenth century the greatest prose is probably to be found in the novel but *The Confessions of an English Opium Eater* (1822) by Thomas de Quincey (1785–1859) is still read today. Other prose traditions can be found in William Cobbett (1763–1835), who wrote about both politics and farming and protested against the effects of industrialisation, William Hazlitt (1778–1830), the literary and social critic, and Charles Lamb (1775–1834), more of a literary propagandist.

Victorian prose outside the novel is distinguished by the essays of Arnold, Thomas Carlyle (1795–1881), John Ruskin (1819–1900) and J. S. Mill (1806–1873), all great commentators on Victorian industrial and commercial society. Charles Darwin (1809–1882), in *The Origin of the Species* (1859) represents the scientific tradition. In

America, notable writers were Henry Thoreau (1817–1862), who wrote *Walden* (1854) celebrating American individualism, and his mentor the Transcendentalist Ralph Emerson (1803–1882).

Twentieth-century prose is best represented in the essays and letters of D. H. Lawrence (1885–1930), the essays of T. S. Eliot and the invigorating literary criticism of F. R. Leavis (1895–1978), although at their best all three ran counter to the mass of academic and scientific prose of their day.

The Novel The novel as we know it began in the early eighteenth century, although it has roots in earlier forms of story-telling. The first major novels are *Robinson Crusoe* (1719), by the journalist Daniel Defoe (?1660–1731), a realistic novel portraying a practical man coping on a desert island; *Pamela* (1740–1741) by Samuel Richardson (1689–1761), a rather unpleasant but highly dramatic novel made up of fictional letters; *Tom Jones* (1749) by Henry Fielding (1707–1754), a picaresque novel giving a panoramic view of eighteenth-century society and *The Life and Opinions of Tristram Shandy* (1760) by Laurence Sterne (1713–1768), a unique collection of comic portraits.

At the beginning of the nineteenth century, in America, James Fenimore Cooper (1789–1851) wrote a series of novels celebrating the fontiersman, Edgar Allen Poe (1809–1849) wrote Gothic tales of horror and Nathaniel Hawthorne (1804–1864) wrote about Puritan New England in novels like *The Scarlet Letter* (1850). In England, Jane Austen (1775–1817) wrote delicately ironic novels satirising the polite society of her day. W. M. Thackeray (1811–1863) wrote less incisive novels with a good narrative drive on the same theme (*Vanity Fair* being the best known) and Anthony Trollope (1815–1882) wrote popular fiction about the political and social scene of his day. The most widely-read novels of the day in England, however, were the historical novels of the Scot, Sir Walter Scott (1771–1832).

Although *Jane Eyre* by Charlotte Bronte (1816–1855) and *Wuthering Heights* by her sister Emily (1818–1848) were published in the same year (1847), Charlotte's book was immediately successful whereas Emily's was not properly appreciated until the twentieth century. At the same time Charlotte's friend and biographer Elizabeth Gaskell (1810–1865) was writing what is sometimes called 'social-conscience' fiction.

Other great novelists of the period are the great and prolific Charles Dickens (1812–1870), still deservedly popular today, and George Eliot (1819–1880) whose novels like *Middlemarch* are noted for their deep character analysis. From America, there are the sometimes portentous novels of Herman Melville (1819–1891), the comic novels of Mark Twain (1835–1910) and the more self-consciously civilized novels of Henry James (1843–1916). Late in the century, Thomas Hardy (1840–1928) wrote popular love novels rooted in agricultural England. In the early twentieth century the novel is dominated by the highly individual and still very widely read D. H. Lawrence, although there are also the extraordinary stories of Joseph Conrad (1857–1924) and the stylistic experiments of both James Joyce (1882–1941) and Virginia Woolf (1882–1941). Later, there are the 'social-conscience' novels of George Orwell (1903–1950).

American fiction of recent years is noted for the 'manly' novels of Ernest Hemingway (1899–1961), the high-society novels of F. Scott Fitzgerald (1896–1940) and the 'realism' of John Steinbeck (1902–1968).

Living novelists include Grahame Greene (1904–   ), William Golding (1911–   ), Doris Lessing (1919–   ) and, in America, Joseph Heller (1923–   ).

A widely-read novelist from Nigeria is Chinua Achebe (1930–   ).

The Theatre In the literary renaissance of the Elizabethan era (1558–1603) drama was the chief art form. In part, it developed out of earlier communal festivals and pageants, including the Mystery plays and Morality plays (like *Everyman* – ?1509–1519). It was also influenced by street ballads and sermons. One of the early plays of the period, *Gorboduc* (1561) by Thomas Norton (1532–1584) and Thomas Sackville (1536–1608), was written with its roots in the more legendary past of British history. Elizabethan dramatists, however, brought eloquent individual expression to the stage. The majority of plays were written for the communal theatres, whose repertory the Court shared. The dramatists were not only educated humanists, influenced in part by classical tragedy, they also set out to appeal to popular taste.

The first permanent theatre was built in 1576. Christopher Marlowe (1564–1593), known in particular for *Doctor Faustus*, first brought Renaissance humanism to the theatre. Bloody revenge tragedies such as *The Spanish Tragedy* (1592) by Thomas Kyd (1558–1594) were also popular.

However, it is Shakespeare's plays, ranging from history plays (e.g. *Henry V* – 1599) to comedies (e.g. *A Midsummer Night's Dream* – 1600) to tragedies (e.g. *Macbeth* – 1606) to tragi-comedies (e.g. *The Tempest* – 1611), that are the greatest of all and still widely loved today.

In the reign of James 1 (1603–1625), drama began to move away from popular taste and go into the Court. The masques, where spectacular drama was mixed with song, dance and disguise, were a new genre. However, there were still the vigorous satirical comedies of Ben Jonson and powerful 'revenge' plays like *The Duchess of Malfi* (1612–1613) by John Webster (?1578–1632) and *The Revenger's Tragedy* (1606–1607) by Cyril Tourneur (?1575–1626).

On the outbreak of the Civil War (1642), the theatres were closed and did not re-open until after the Restoration of Charles II in 1660. After that, a new kind of play came into being, performed indoors, and with female as well as male actors. There were then very few theatres and they were dominated by a small aristocratic clique. The most elegant and witty of the new dramatists was William Congreve (1670–1729). John Dryden made a notable break from the currently fashionable 'heroic couplet' in his plays and returned to the blank verse of the Elizabethan and Jacobean playrights. With the exception of Oliver Goldsmith (?1730–1774) in, for example, *She Stoops to Conquer* (1773), a farcical comedy, and the Restoration-like comedies of Richard Sheridan (1751–1816) the eighteenth century was poor in original drama.

In fact there was no significant revival in the theatre until the end of the nineteenth century with the social wit of Oscar Wilde (1854–1900) and, at the beginning of the twentieth century, the social-cum-philosophical plays of George Bernard Shaw (1856–1950). T. S. Eliot wrote four plays including the religious drama *Murder in the Cathedral* (1935) and in America Eugene O'Neill (1888–1953) wrote some Greek-influenced tragedies. O'Neill's successors are Tennessee Williams (1911–1982) and Arthur Miller (1915–   ).

A turning point for the English theatre came in 1956 with *Look Back in Anger* by John Osborne (1929–   ) when plays became much more realistic and less socially elitist. The modern theatre, with Harold Pinter (1930–   ), the most well-known of the dramatists, has become highly experimental. Other notable playwrights are Samuel Becket (1906–   ) and David Storey (1933–   ).

Key

1.11.2 *The Thought Fox*

I imagine this midnight moment's forest;
Something else is alive
Beside the clock's loneliness
And this blank page where my fingers move.

Through the window I see no star;
Something more near
Though deeper within darkness
Is entering the loneliness;

Across clearings, an eye,
A widening deepening greenness,
Brilliantly, concentratedly,
Coming about its own business

Sets neat prints into the snow
Between trees, and warily a lame
Shadow lags by stump and in hollow
Of a body that is bold to come

Cold, delicately as the dark snow,
A fox's nose touches twig, leaf;
Two eyes serve a movement, that now
And again now, and now, and now

Till, with a sudden sharp stink of fox
It enters the dark hole of the head.
The window is starless still; the clock ticks,
The page is printed.

2.7.3 1 monotonous
2 square
3 hard set
4 dictatorial
5 crust
6 stubborn

2.9.3 lacking energy
left behind
bored
tired
cut off from all that is good and positive
passionless
lacking inspiration
needing to restore order
feeling of monotony in her work
unable to articulate what she feels

4.3.2 *to shoot him*
a long distance on either side
was going to be shot
I was momentarily worth watching
could shoot the elephant after all
expected it of me

5.1.1 Battle of Trafalgar 1805
Napoleon's retreat from Moscow 1812
The Greek Revolt 1821
The Crimean War 1854–1856
The French Revolution 1789
The Unification of Italy 1861
The Congress of Vienna 1814–15
American War of Independence 1775–1781
Accession of Queen Victoria 1837

5.4.2 Earth has not anything to show more fair:
Dull would he be of soul who could pass by
A sight so touching in its majesty:
This City now doth, like a garment, wear
The beauty of the morning; silent, bare,
Ships, towers, domes, theatre, and temples lie
Open unto the fields, and to the sky;
All bright and glittering in the smokeless air.
Never did sun more beautifully steep
In his first splendour, valley, rock, or hill
Ne'er saw I, never felt, a calm so deep!
The river glideth at his own sweet will:
Dear God! the very houses seem asleep!
And all that mighty heart is lying still!

5.4.5 My mistress' eyes are nothing like the sun;
Coral is far more red than her lips' red:
If snow be white, why then her breasts are dun,
If hairs be wires, black wires grow on her head.
I have seen roses damask'd, red and white,
But no such roses see I in her cheeks;
And in some perfumes is there more delight
Than in the breath that from my mistress reeks.
I love to hear her speak, yet well I know
That music hath a far more pleasing sound:
I grant I never saw a goddess go, –
My mistress, when she walks, treads on the ground:
And yet, by heaven, I think my love as rare
As any she belied with false compare.

TAPESCRIPT

6.1.6 *Gerard Manley Hopkins*

Gerard Manley Hopkins was born in 1844. At school he won a prize for poetry and in 1863 went to study Classics at Balliol College, Oxford, where he was an outstanding scholar. In 1868 he entered the Jesuit novitiate and burned his early poems, determined to write no more. However, until 1875 he kept a journal to record his philosophical responses to nature. In the journal he stressed the individuality of everyday, natural things. In 1874 he began to write poetry again and in 1875 wrote a long poem called the *Wreck of the Deutschland* inspired by the tragic death at sea of a group of Franciscan nuns. However, his poems were only read in manuscript by his friends since he refused to have them published. In 1877 he was ordained to the priesthood and served as both a missionary and parish priest. In 1884 he became Professor of Greek Literature at University College, Dublin, but he was not happy in Ireland, where he wrote what became known as the 'terrible sonnets' and which expressed a great sense of despair. In 1889, he died of glandular fever. His poems, however, were not published until 1918 and did not achieve fame until the second edition in 1930. Since then he has influenced many modern poets including T. S. Eliot. As a man he was thought to be both generous and brilliant, with a rare integrity of mind and purpose.

As a poet, Hopkins was a remarkable technical innovator and at times used language as creatively as Shakespeare. His poems, written to be read aloud, were intensely religious whether he was expressing his observations of nature or his troubled relationship with God. His early poems were lively and buoyant, though the later poems, the 'terrible sonnets', were rather more austere in style.

6.3.5 Byron's pictures looking from left to right: 3.4.1.2.5.

8.3.1 Writers discussed

1 Charlotte Bronte
2 Alexander Pope
3 W. B. Yeats: Nor dread, nor hope
4 Byron

TAPESCRIPT

9.8.8 *Geoffrey Chaucer*

We don't really know the date of Chaucer's birth: it was sometime between 1339 and 1346 and a lot of people now think that 1343 is the most likely year. He was the son of John Chaucer, a London wine-merchant, who also had connections with the court. Young Geoffrey served as a page in the household of the Duke of Clarence, and later he joined the king's army and fought in France. He was taken prisoner, and King Edward III paid a ransom for his release.

He married, perhaps in 1366, one Philippa, whose family was related by marriage to that of John of Gaunt, the Duke of Lancaster; throughout his life Chaucer held a number of positions at court and in the service of three kings: Edward III and then Richard II and Henry IV. He travelled abroad in Europe on many diplomatic missions: we know that he visited Genoa and Florence in 1372–73 and he could perhaps have met Boccaccio and Petrarch there. He went again to France, too.

In 1374 he was appointed Controller of Customs in the Port of London, and lived quite grandly in a house in Aldgate in the City of London. Later he moved into the country where he was made Knight of the Shire of Kent. For most of his life he received some allowances and pensions from the court in return for his services at home and abroad; and although there were some periods when civil wars and quarrels deprived him of his income, he was buried, on his death, perhaps in 1400, in Westminster Abbey and a monument was erected to him in 1555. If you visit Westminster Abbey in London you can see this memorial to him in Poets' Corner.

It's also difficult to date his writings. But some of the most famous fall into perhaps three periods; the earliest ones show quite a lot of influence from the French and they include a translation of *The Romance of the Rose*, and *The Book of the Duchess*, perhaps about 1370. The middle period, with *The House of Fame*, *Troilus and Criseyde*, about 1385, have more of an Italian influence. Later ones include *The Parlement of Fowles*, *The Legend of Good Women* and the very famous, and perhaps most English, *The Canterbury Tales*.

Index

Authors

Verse forms

Literary devices